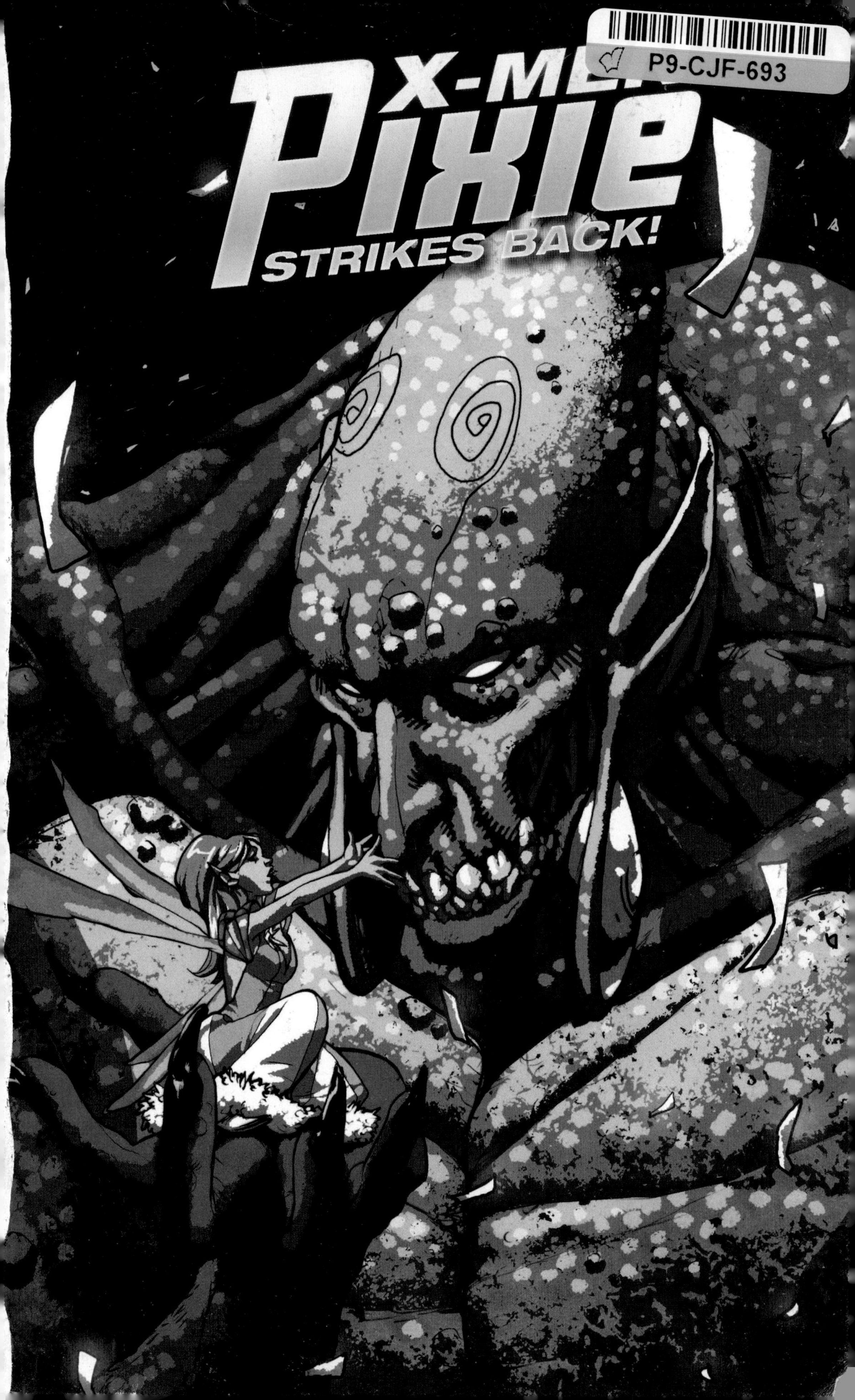
X-ME
Pixie
STRIKES BACK!

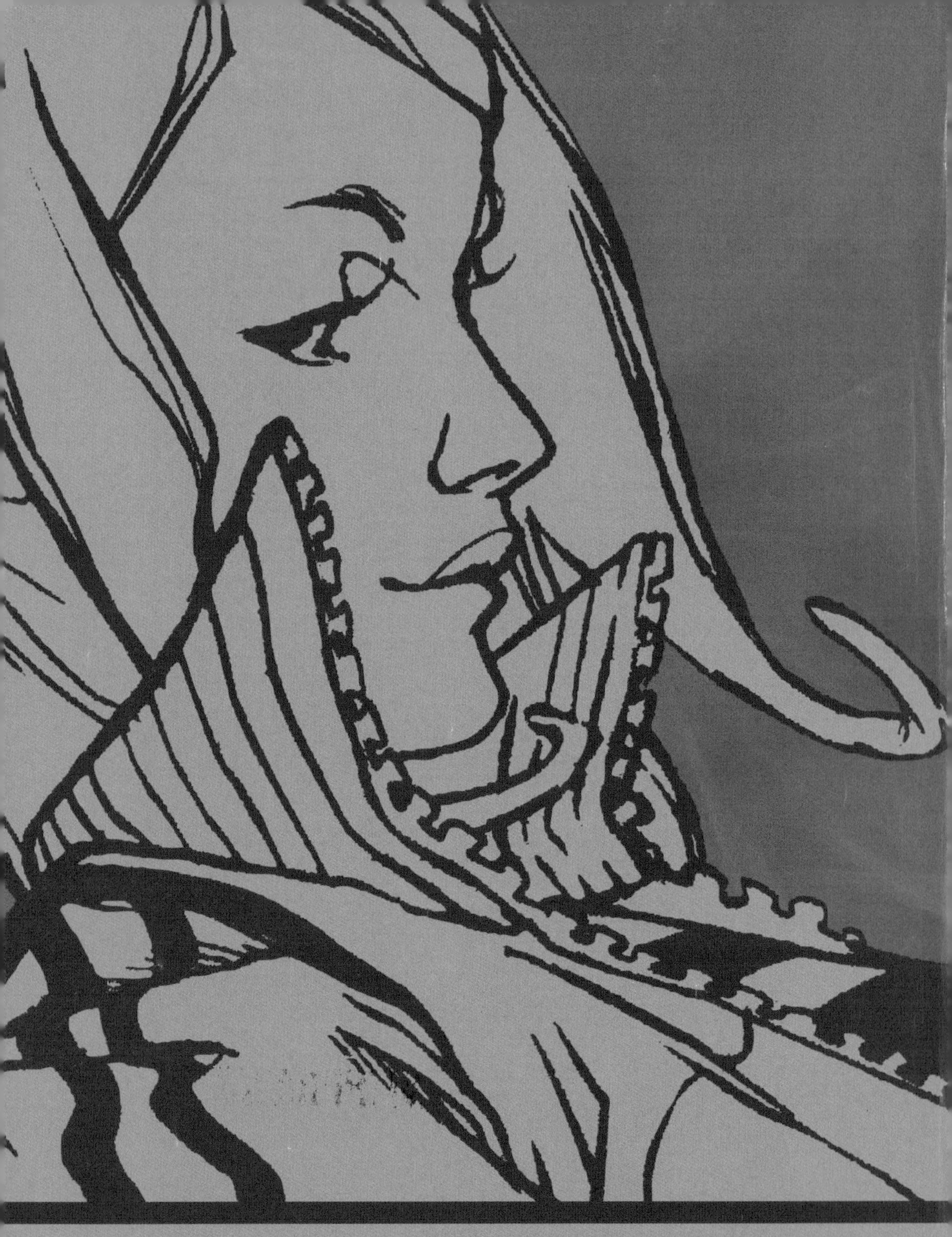


COLLECTION EDITOR
JENNIFER GRÜNWALD

ASSISTANT EDITOR
ALEX STARBUCK

ASSOCIATE EDITOR
JOHN DENNING

EDITOR, SPECIAL PROJECTS
MARK D. BEAZLEY

SENIOR EDITOR, SPECIAL PROJECTS
JEFF YOUNGQUIST

SENIOR VICE PRESIDENT OF SALES
DAVID GABRIEL

BOOK DESIGN
JEFF POWELL

EDITOR IN CHIEF
JOE QUESADA

PUBLISHER
DAN BUCKLEY

EXECUTIVE PRODUCER
ALAN FINE

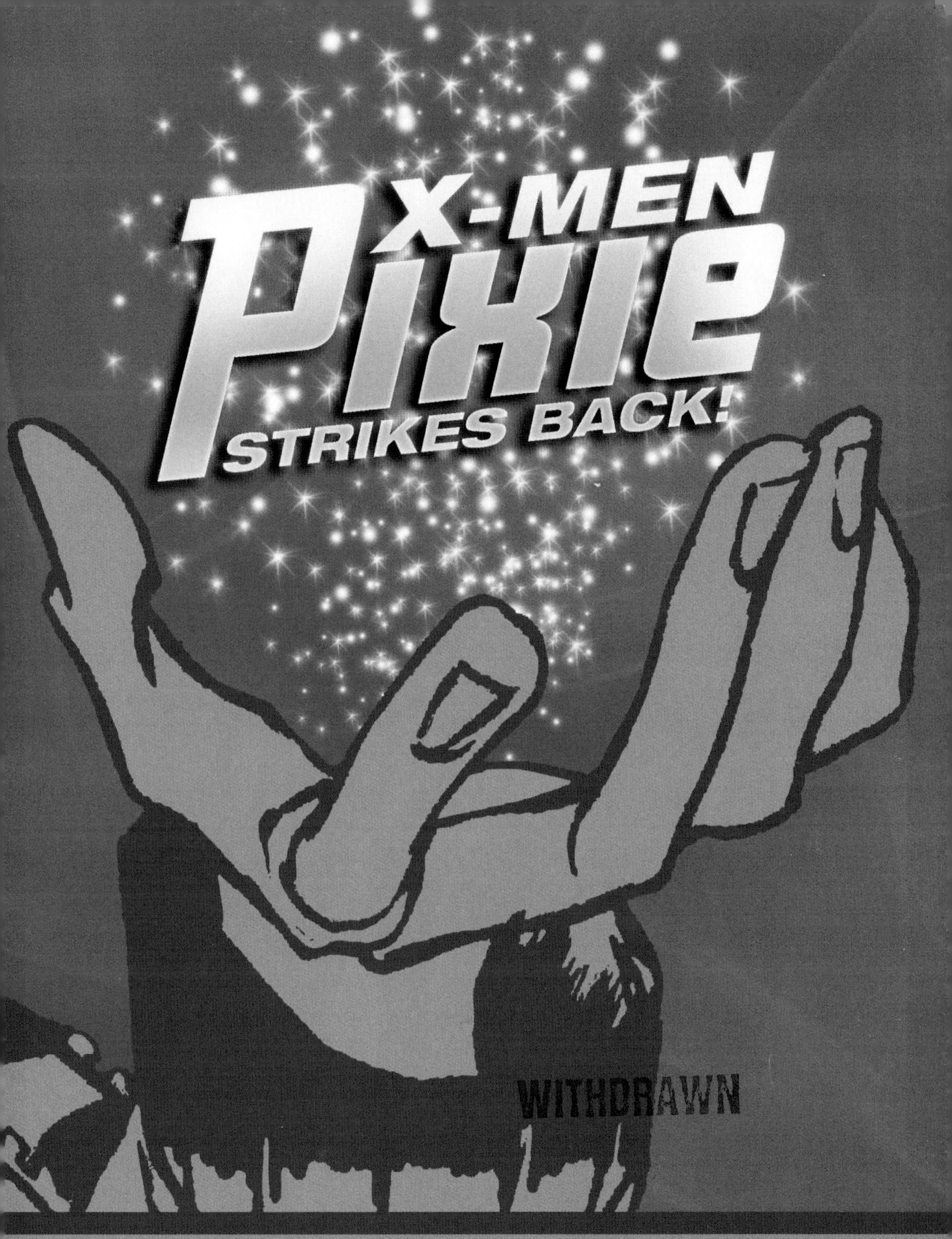
X-MEN
Pixie
STRIKES BACK!
WITHDRAWN

WRITER
**KATHRYN IMMONEN**

ARTIST
**SARA PICHELLI**

COLORS
CHRISTINA STRAIN

LETTERS
DAVE SHARPE

COVER ARTIST
STUART IMMONEN
WITH JUSTIN PONSOR (ISSUE #4)

ASSOCIATE EDITOR
DANIEL KETCHUM

EDITOR
NICK LOWE

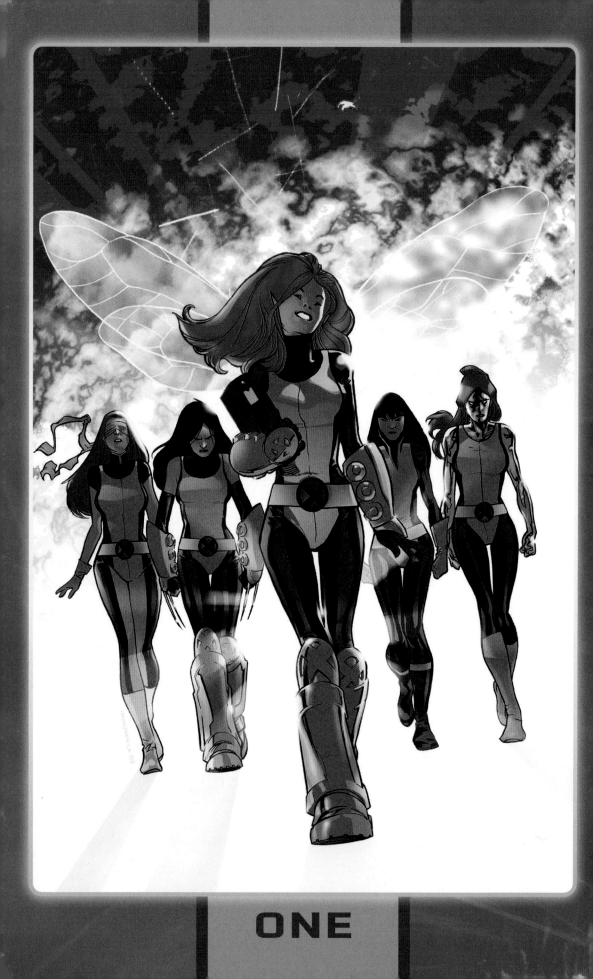

ONE

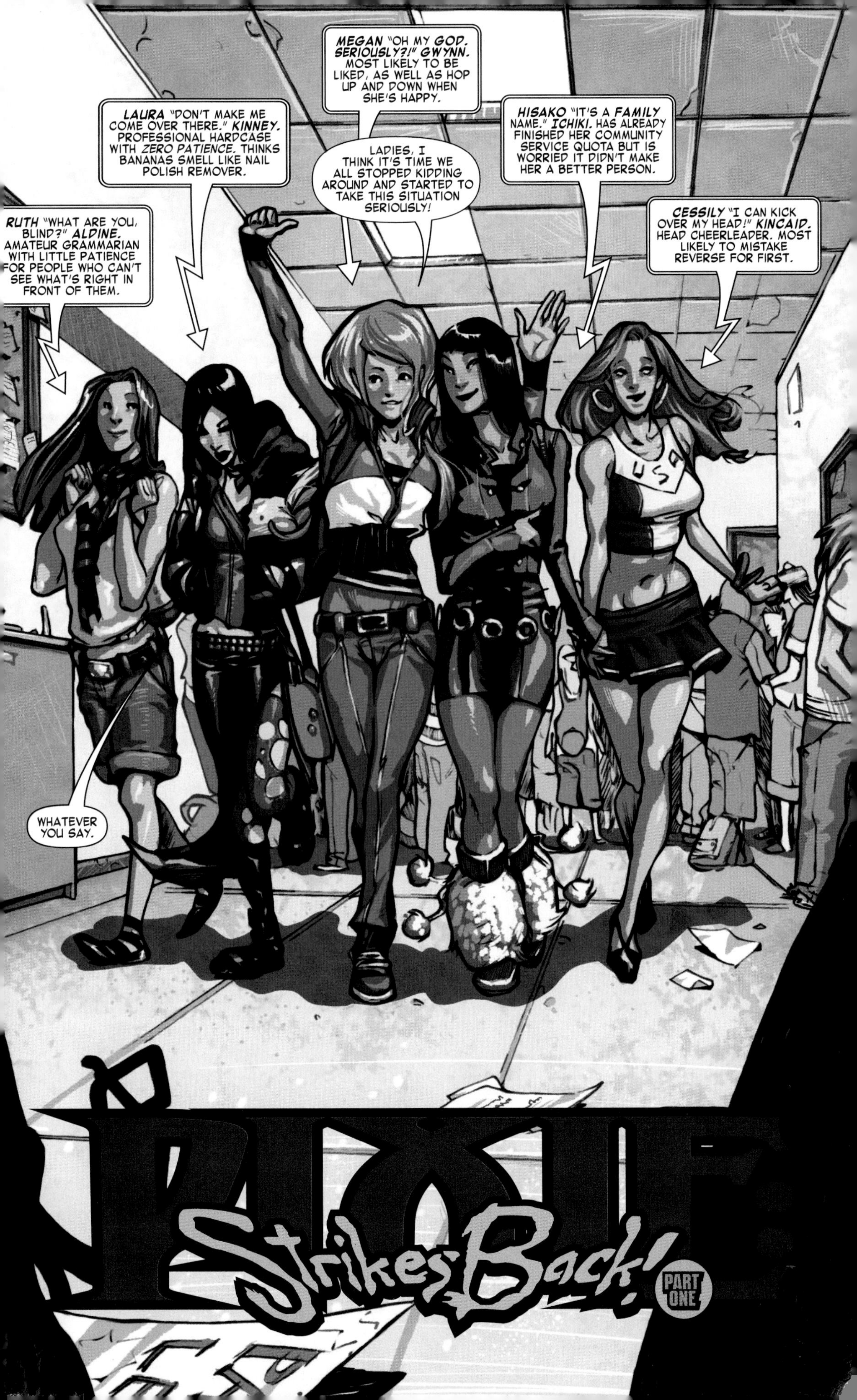
RUTH "WHAT ARE YOU, BLIND?" ALDINE. AMATEUR GRAMMARIAN WITH LITTLE PATIENCE FOR PEOPLE WHO CAN'T SEE WHAT'S RIGHT IN FRONT OF THEM.
LAURA "DON'T MAKE ME COME OVER THERE." KINNEY. PROFESSIONAL HARDCASE WITH ZERO PATIENCE. THINKS BANANAS SMELL LIKE NAIL POLISH REMOVER.
MEGAN "OH MY GOD. SERIOUSLY?!" GWYNN. MOST LIKELY TO BE LIKED, AS WELL AS HOP UP AND DOWN WHEN SHE'S HAPPY.
LADIES, I THINK IT'S TIME WE ALL STOPPED KIDDING AROUND AND STARTED TO TAKE THIS SITUATION SERIOUSLY!
HISAKO "IT'S A FAMILY NAME." ICHIKI. HAS ALREADY FINISHED HER COMMUNITY SERVICE QUOTA BUT IS WORRIED IT DIDN'T MAKE HER A BETTER PERSON.
CESSILY "I CAN KICK OVER MY HEAD!" KINCAID. HEAD CHEERLEADER. MOST LIKELY TO MISTAKE REVERSE FOR FIRST.
WHATEVER YOU SAY.
USA
Strikes Back!
PART ONE

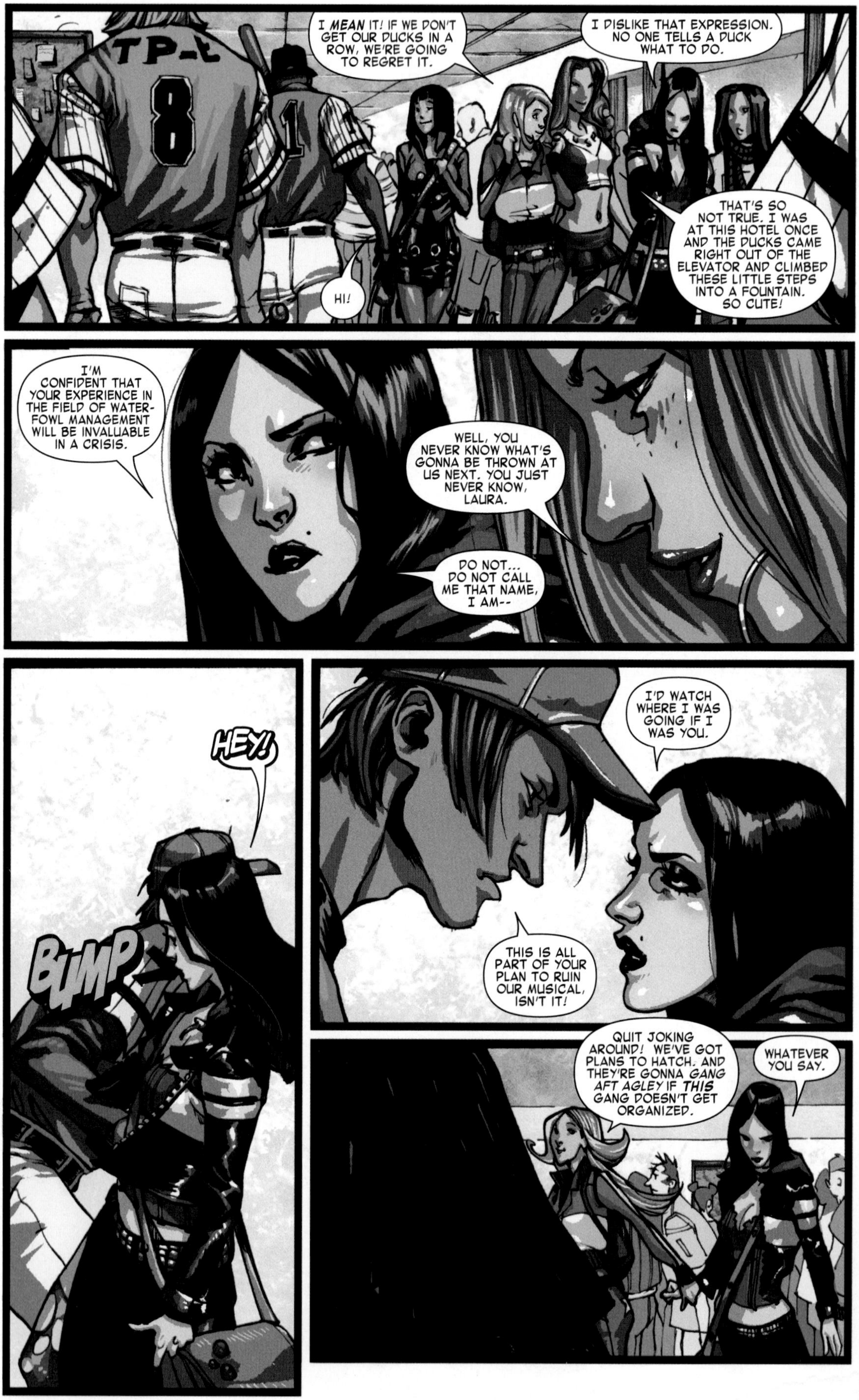
I MEAN IT! IF WE DON'T GET OUR DUCKS IN A ROW, WE'RE GOING TO REGRET IT.
I DISLIKE THAT EXPRESSION. NO ONE TELLS A DUCK WHAT TO DO.
HI!
THAT'S SO NOT TRUE. I WAS AT THIS HOTEL ONCE AND THE DUCKS CAME RIGHT OUT OF THE ELEVATOR AND CLIMBED THESE LITTLE STEPS INTO A FOUNTAIN. SO CUTE!
I'M CONFIDENT THAT YOUR EXPERIENCE IN THE FIELD OF WATER-FOWL MANAGEMENT WILL BE INVALUABLE IN A CRISIS.
WELL, YOU NEVER KNOW WHAT'S GONNA BE THROWN AT US NEXT. YOU JUST NEVER KNOW, LAURA.
DO NOT... DO NOT CALL ME THAT NAME, I AM--
HEY!
BUMP
I'D WATCH WHERE I WAS GOING IF I WAS YOU.
THIS IS ALL PART OF YOUR PLAN TO RUIN OUR MUSICAL, ISN'T IT!
QUIT JOKING AROUND! WE'VE GOT PLANS TO HATCH. AND THEY'RE GONNA GANG AFT AGLEY IF THIS GANG DOESN'T GET ORGANIZED.
WHATEVER YOU SAY.

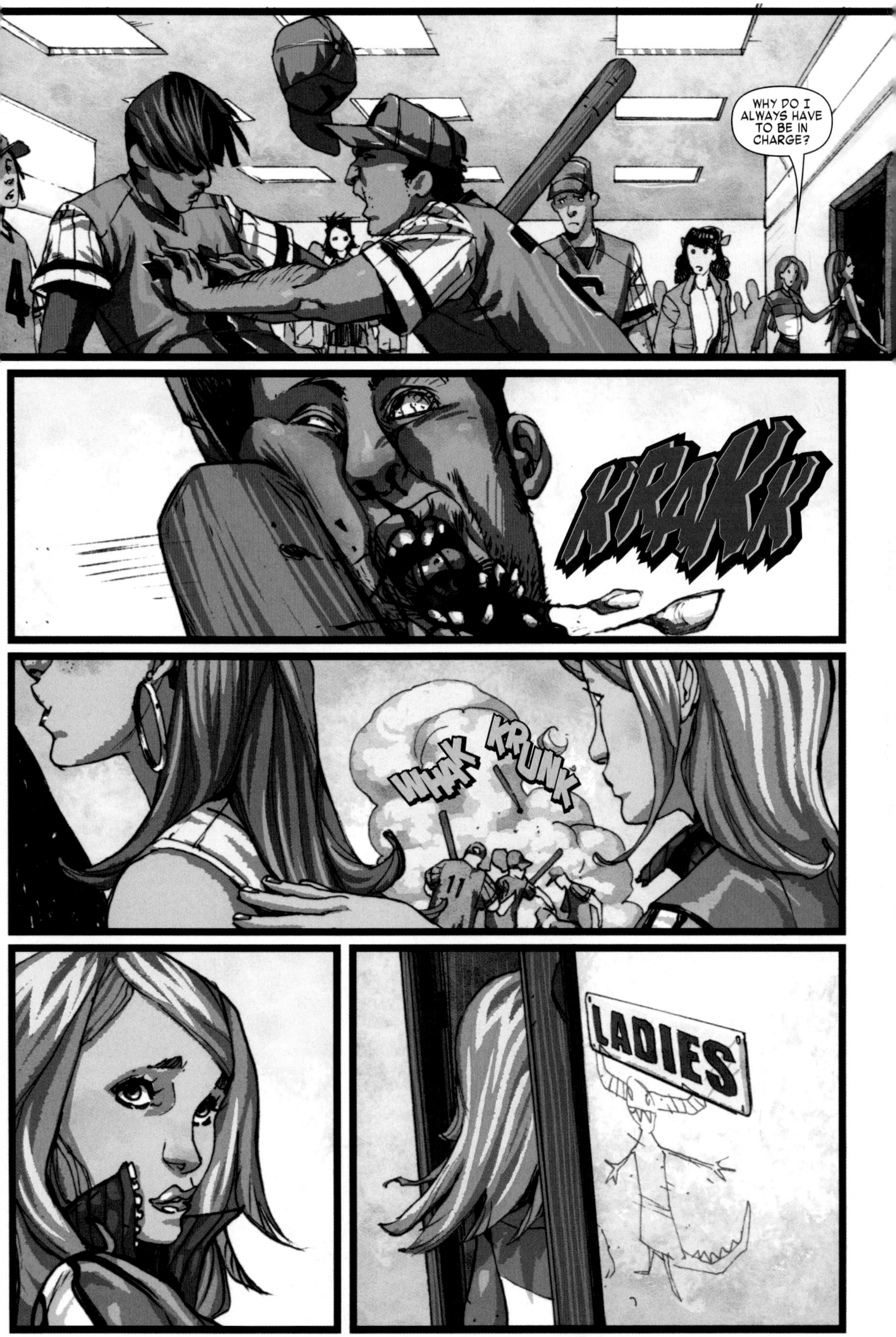
WHY DO I ALWAYS HAVE TO BE IN CHARGE?
KRAKK
WHAK
KRUNK
LADIES

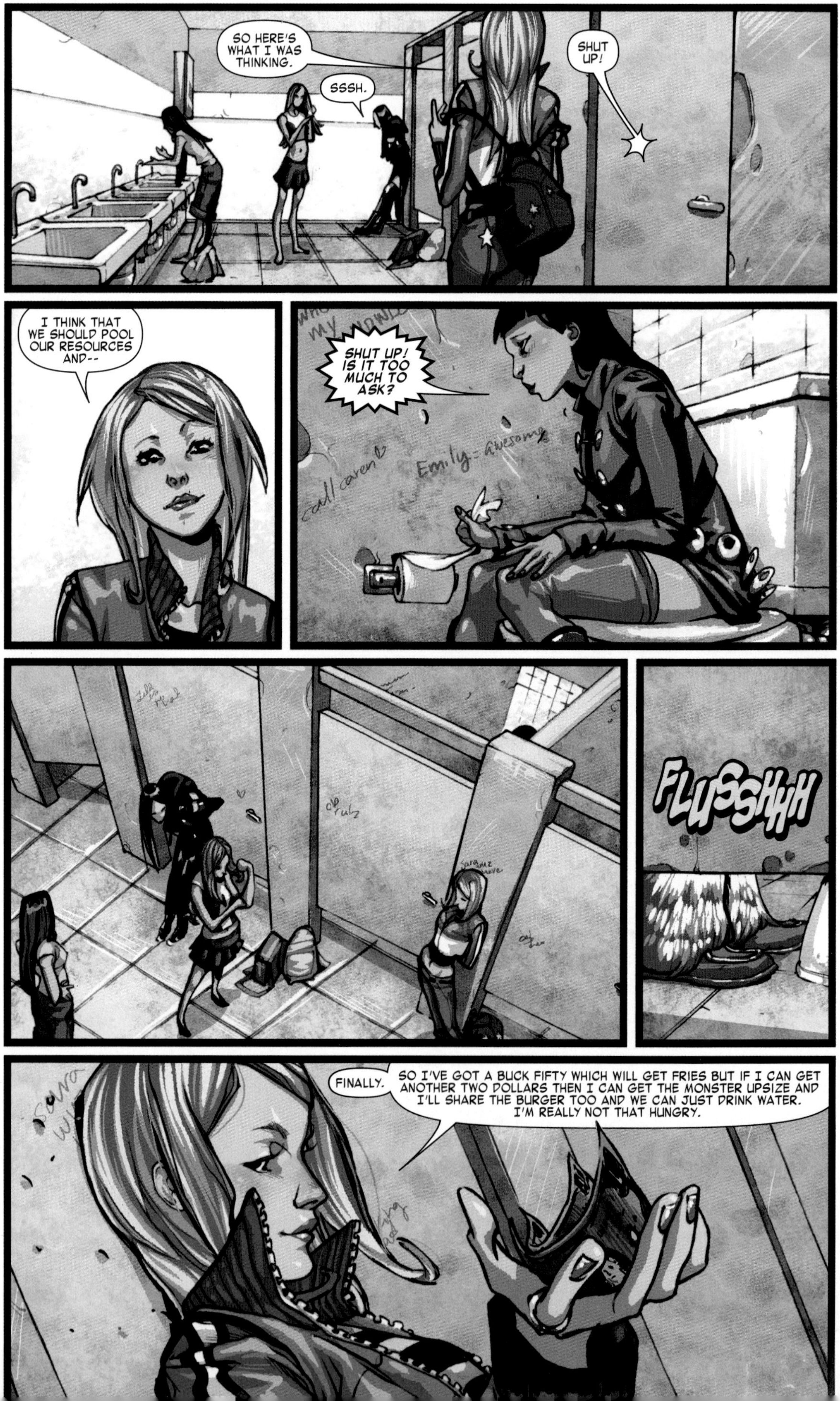
SO HERE'S WHAT I WAS THINKING.
SSSH.
SHUT UP!
I THINK THAT WE SHOULD POOL OUR RESOURCES AND--
SHUT UP! IS IT TOO MUCH TO ASK?
Emily = awesome
call caren
FLUSSHHH
FINALLY.
SO I'VE GOT A BUCK FIFTY WHICH WILL GET FRIES BUT IF I CAN GET ANOTHER TWO DOLLARS THEN I CAN GET THE MONSTER UPSIZE AND I'LL SHARE THE BURGER TOO AND WE CAN JUST DRINK WATER. I'M REALLY NOT THAT HUNGRY.

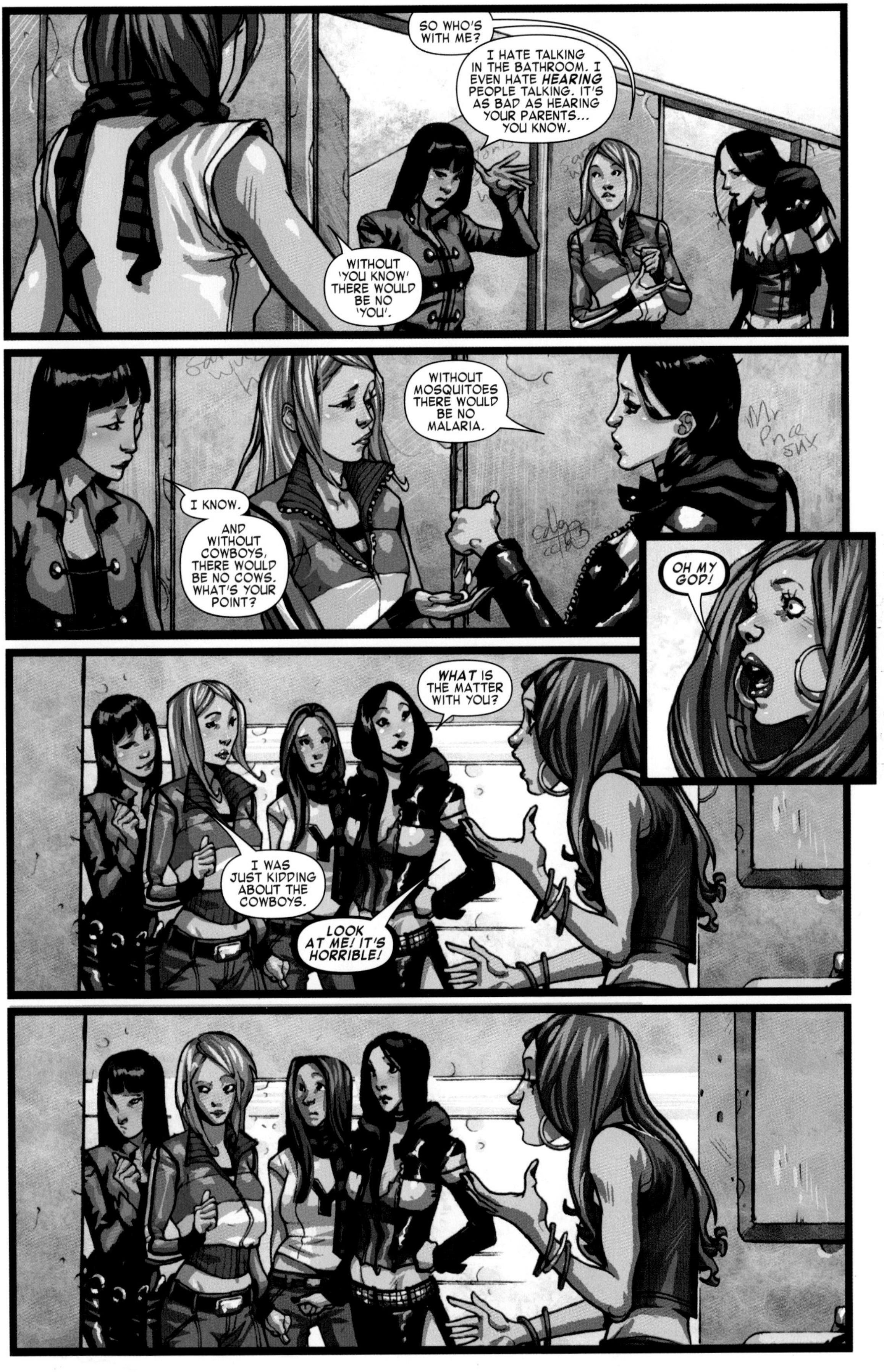

SO WHO'S WITH ME?
I HATE TALKING IN THE BATHROOM. I EVEN HATE HEARING PEOPLE TALKING. IT'S AS BAD AS HEARING YOUR PARENTS... YOU KNOW.
WITHOUT 'YOU KNOW' THERE WOULD BE NO 'YOU'.
WITHOUT MOSQUITOES THERE WOULD BE NO MALARIA.
I KNOW.
AND WITHOUT COWBOYS, THERE WOULD BE NO COWS. WHAT'S YOUR POINT?
OH MY GOD!
WHAT IS THE MATTER WITH YOU?
I WAS JUST KIDDING ABOUT THE COWBOYS.
LOOK AT ME! IT'S HORRIBLE!

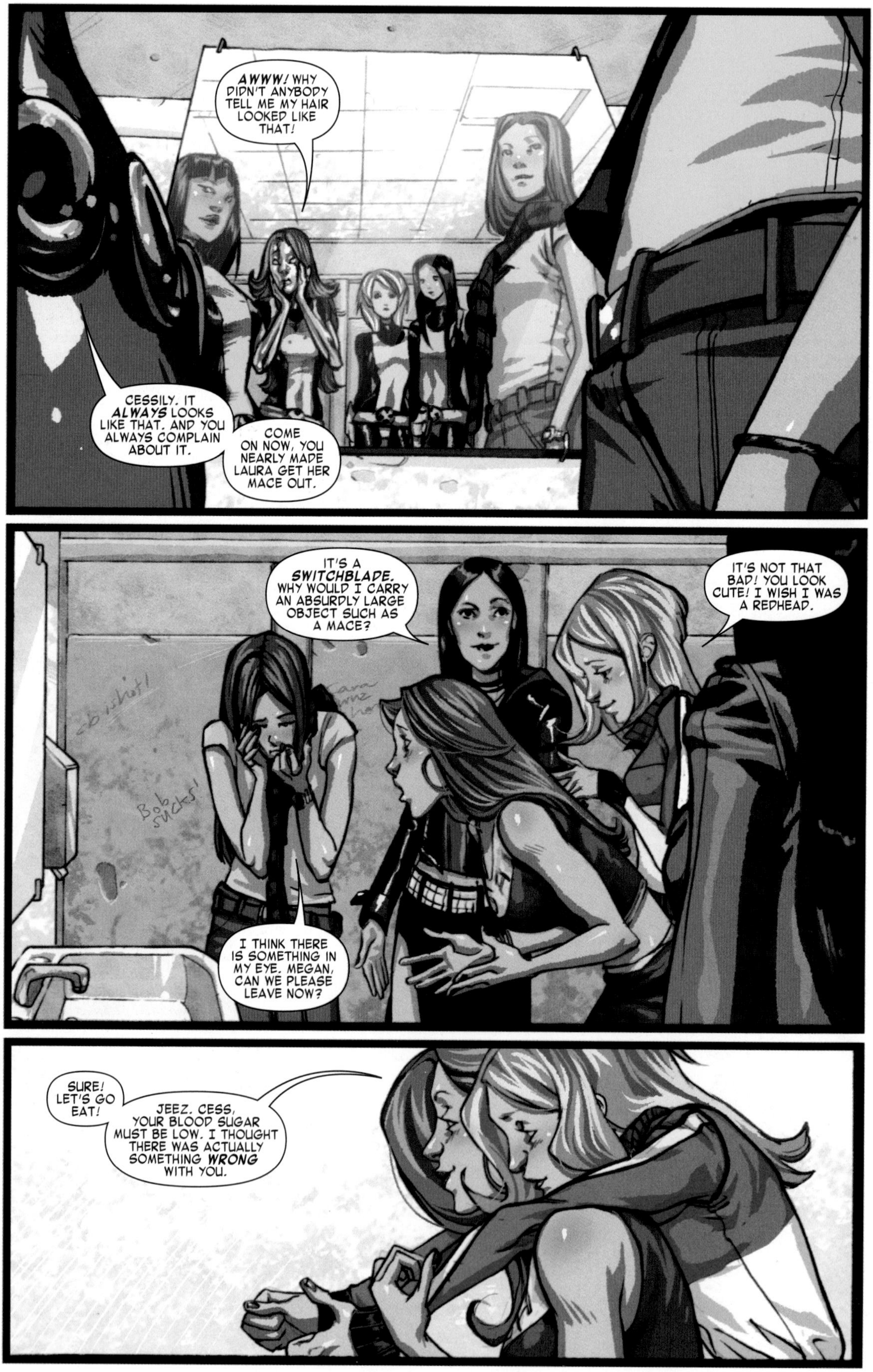
AWWW! WHY DIDN'T ANYBODY TELL ME MY HAIR LOOKED LIKE THAT!
CESSILY. IT ALWAYS LOOKS LIKE THAT. AND YOU ALWAYS COMPLAIN ABOUT IT.
COME ON NOW, YOU NEARLY MADE LAURA GET HER MACE OUT.
IT'S A SWITCHBLADE. WHY WOULD I CARRY AN ABSURDLY LARGE OBJECT SUCH AS A MACE?
IT'S NOT THAT BAD! YOU LOOK CUTE! I WISH I WAS A REDHEAD.
Bob sucks!
I THINK THERE IS SOMETHING IN MY EYE. MEGAN, CAN WE PLEASE LEAVE NOW?
SURE! LET'S GO EAT!
JEEZ. CESS, YOUR BLOOD SUGAR MUST BE LOW. I THOUGHT THERE WAS ACTUALLY SOMETHING WRONG WITH YOU.

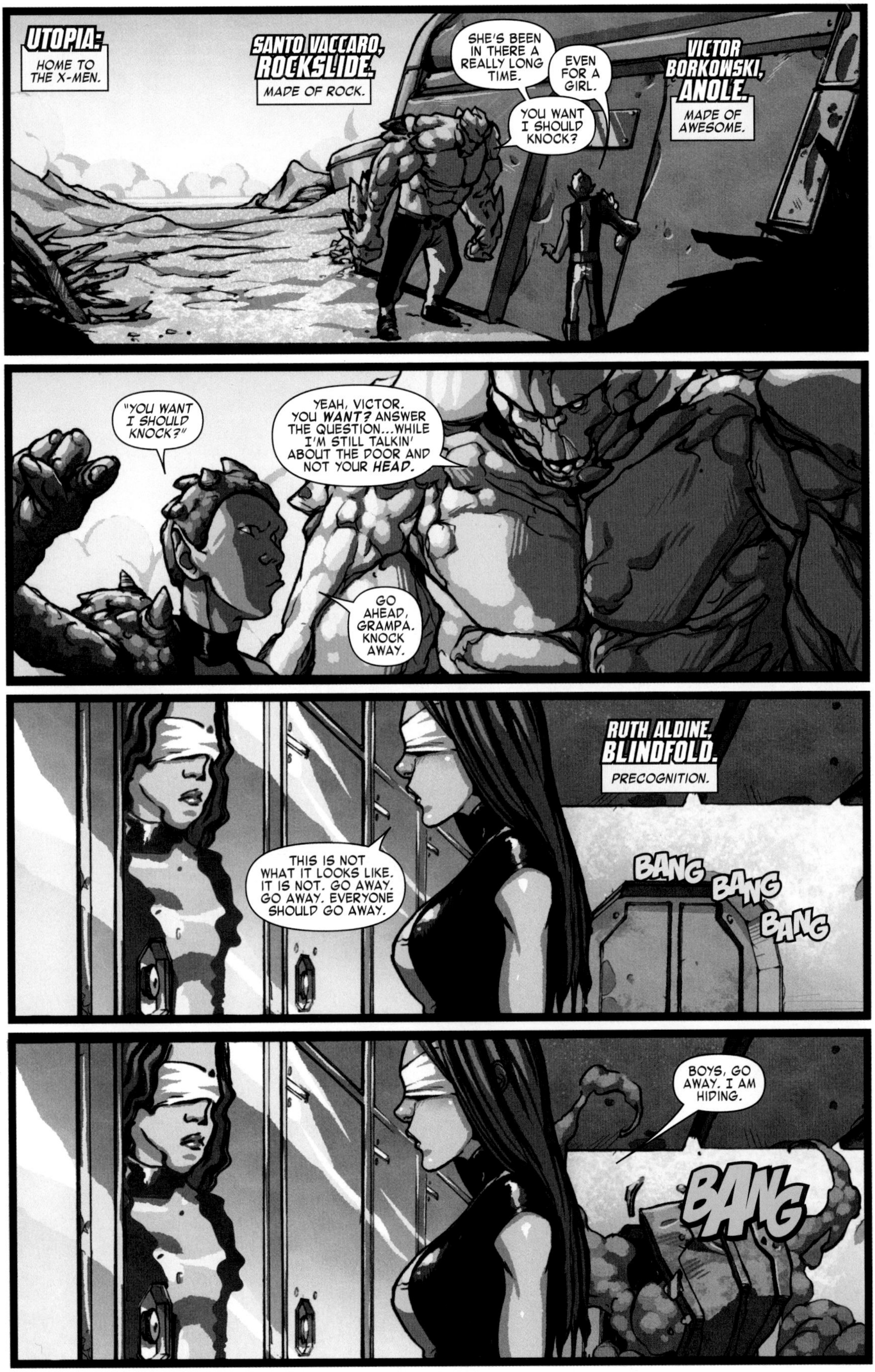
UTOPIA:
HOME TO THE X-MEN.
SANTO VACCARO, ROCKSLIDE.
MADE OF ROCK.
SHE'S BEEN IN THERE A REALLY LONG TIME.
EVEN FOR A GIRL.
YOU WANT I SHOULD KNOCK?
VICTOR BORKOWSKI, ANOLE.
MADE OF AWESOME.
"YOU WANT I SHOULD KNOCK?"
YEAH, VICTOR. YOU WANT? ANSWER THE QUESTION...WHILE I'M STILL TALKIN' ABOUT THE DOOR AND NOT YOUR HEAD.
GO AHEAD, GRAMPA. KNOCK AWAY.
RUTH ALDINE, BLINDFOLD.
PRECOGNITION.
THIS IS NOT WHAT IT LOOKS LIKE. IT IS NOT. GO AWAY. GO AWAY. EVERYONE SHOULD GO AWAY.
BANG BANG BANG
BOYS, GO AWAY. I AM HIDING.
BANG

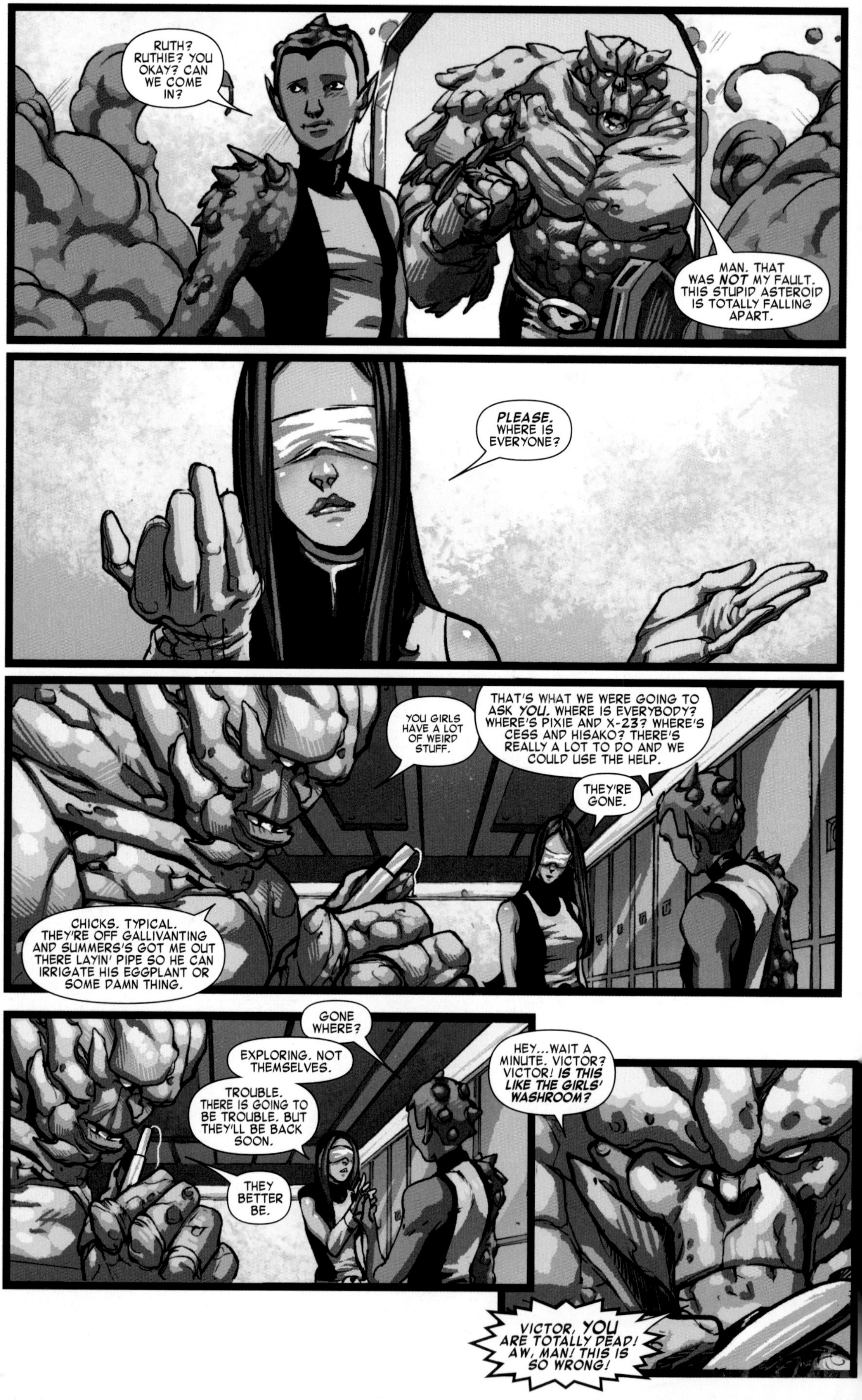
RUTH? RUTHIE? YOU OKAY? CAN WE COME IN?
MAN. THAT WAS NOT MY FAULT. THIS STUPID ASTEROID IS TOTALLY FALLING APART.
PLEASE. WHERE IS EVERYONE?
YOU GIRLS HAVE A LOT OF WEIRD STUFF.
THAT'S WHAT WE WERE GOING TO ASK YOU. WHERE IS EVERYBODY? WHERE'S PIXIE AND X-23? WHERE'S CESS AND HISAKO? THERE'S REALLY A LOT TO DO AND WE COULD USE THE HELP.
THEY'RE GONE.
CHICKS. TYPICAL. THEY'RE OFF GALLIVANTING AND SUMMERS'S GOT ME OUT THERE LAYIN' PIPE SO HE CAN IRRIGATE HIS EGGPLANT OR SOME DAMN THING.
GONE WHERE?
EXPLORING. NOT THEMSELVES.
TROUBLE. THERE IS GOING TO BE TROUBLE. BUT THEY'LL BE BACK SOON.
THEY BETTER BE.
HEY...WAIT A MINUTE. VICTOR? VICTOR! IS THIS LIKE THE GIRLS' WASHROOM?
VICTOR, YOU ARE TOTALLY DEAD! AW, MAN! THIS IS SO WRONG!

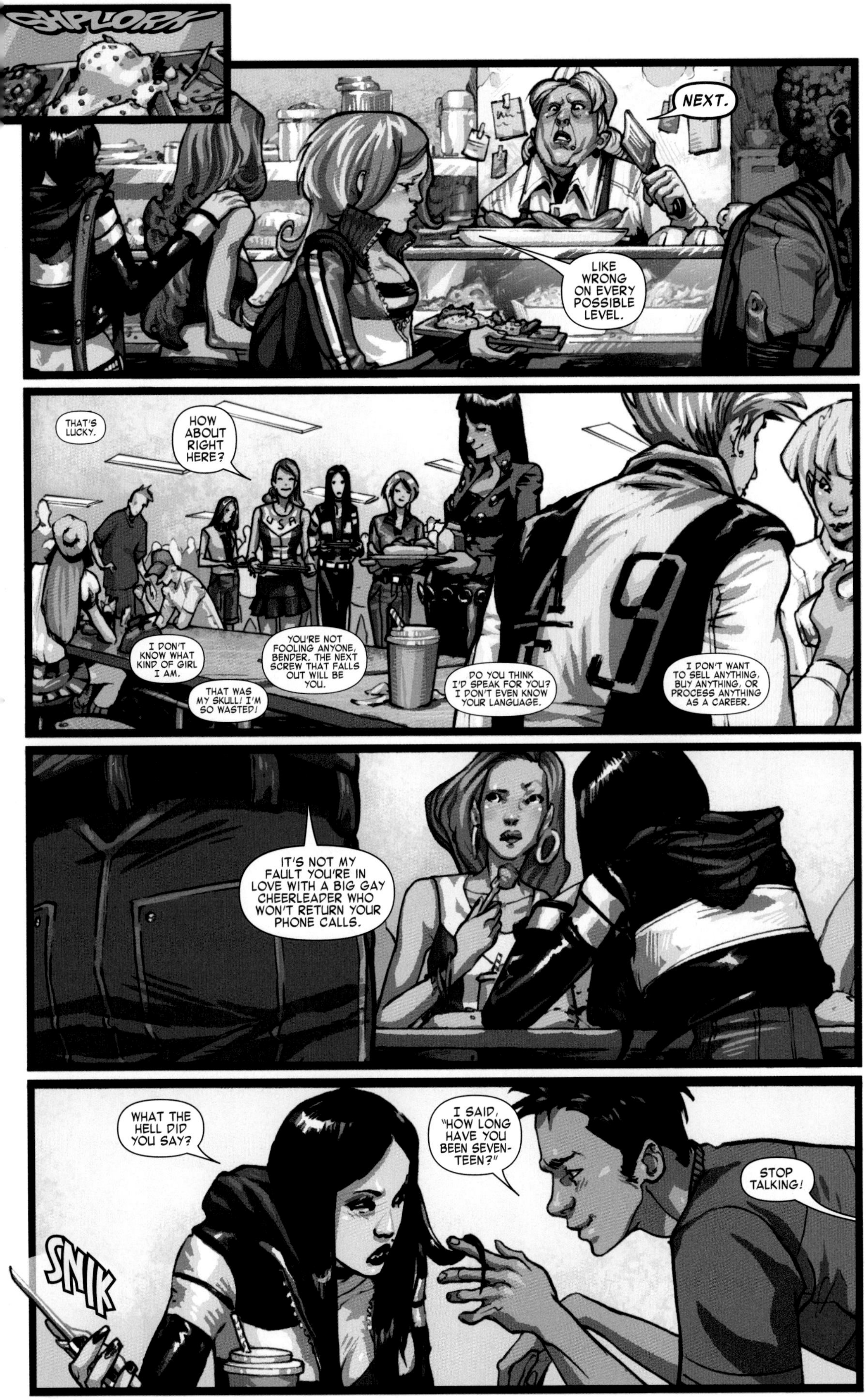
SHPLORK
NEXT.
LIKE WRONG ON EVERY POSSIBLE LEVEL.
THAT'S LUCKY.
HOW ABOUT RIGHT HERE?
I DON'T KNOW WHAT KIND OF GIRL I AM.
THAT WAS MY SKULL! I'M SO WASTED!
YOU'RE NOT FOOLING ANYONE, BENDER. THE NEXT SCREW THAT FALLS OUT WILL BE YOU.
DO YOU THINK I'D SPEAK FOR YOU? I DON'T EVEN KNOW YOUR LANGUAGE.
I DON'T WANT TO SELL ANYTHING, BUY ANYTHING, OR PROCESS ANYTHING AS A CAREER.
IT'S NOT MY FAULT YOU'RE IN LOVE WITH A BIG GAY CHEERLEADER WHO WON'T RETURN YOUR PHONE CALLS.
WHAT THE HELL DID YOU SAY?
I SAID, "HOW LONG HAVE YOU BEEN SEVEN-TEEN?"
STOP TALKING!
SNIK

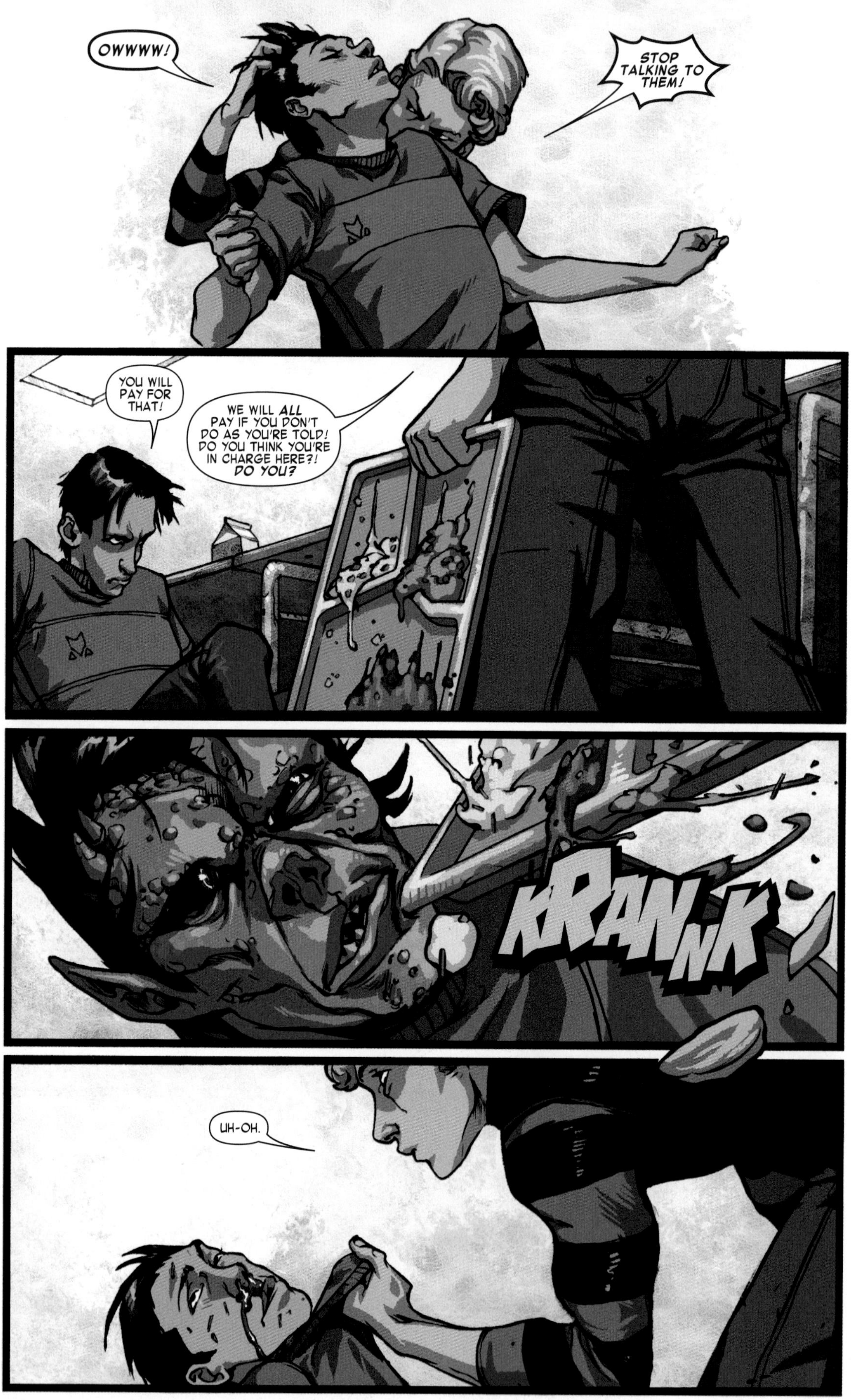
OWWWW!
STOP TALKING TO THEM!
YOU WILL PAY FOR THAT!
WE WILL ALL PAY IF YOU DON'T DO AS YOU'RE TOLD! DO YOU THINK YOU'RE IN CHARGE HERE?! DO YOU?
KRANNK
UH-OH.

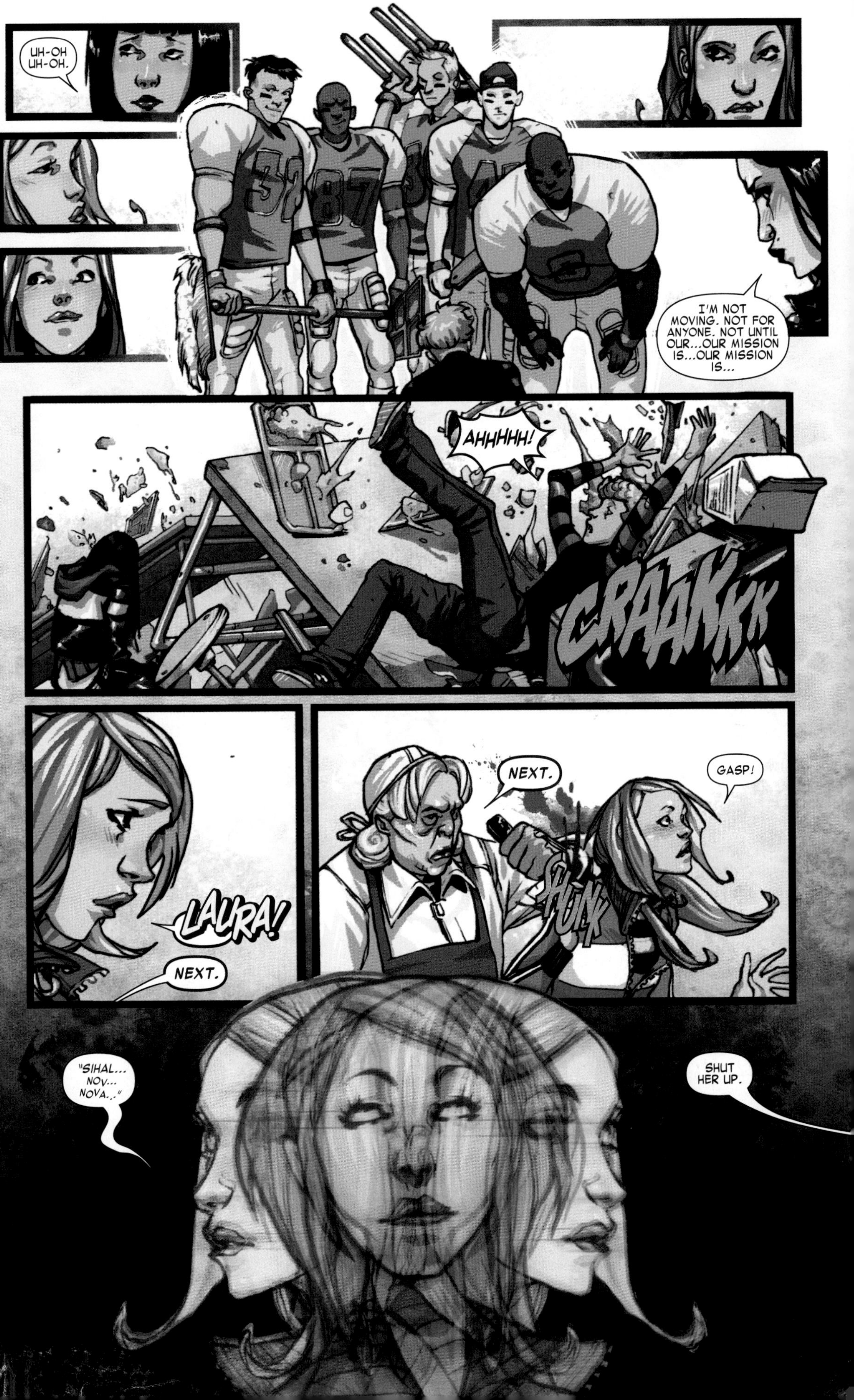

UH-OH UH-OH.
I'M NOT MOVING. NOT FOR ANYONE. NOT UNTIL OUR...OUR MISSION IS...OUR MISSION IS...
AHHHHH!
CRAAKKK
LAURA!
NEXT.
NEXT.
SHUNK
GASP!
"SIHAL... NOV... NOVA..."
SHUT HER UP.

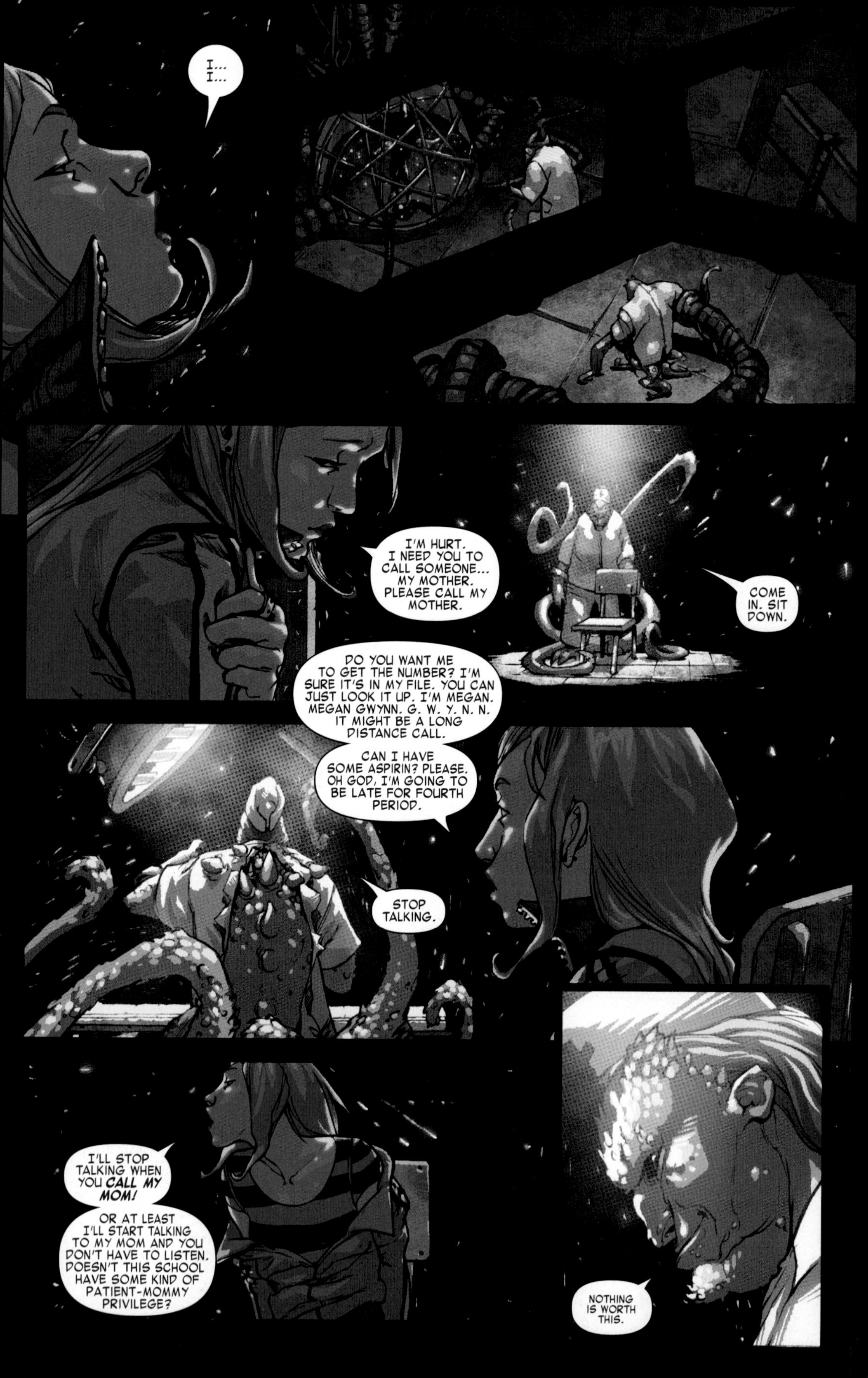
I...
I...
I'M HURT. I NEED YOU TO CALL SOMEONE... MY MOTHER. PLEASE CALL MY MOTHER.
COME IN. SIT DOWN.
DO YOU WANT ME TO GET THE NUMBER? I'M SURE IT'S IN MY FILE. YOU CAN JUST LOOK IT UP. I'M MEGAN. MEGAN GWYNN. G. W. Y. N. N. IT MIGHT BE A LONG DISTANCE CALL.
CAN I HAVE SOME ASPIRIN? PLEASE. OH GOD, I'M GOING TO BE LATE FOR FOURTH PERIOD.
STOP TALKING.
I'LL STOP TALKING WHEN YOU CALL MY MOM!
OR AT LEAST I'LL START TALKING TO MY MOM AND YOU DON'T HAVE TO LISTEN. DOESN'T THIS SCHOOL HAVE SOME KIND OF PATIENT-MOMMY PRIVILEGE?
NOTHING IS WORTH THIS.

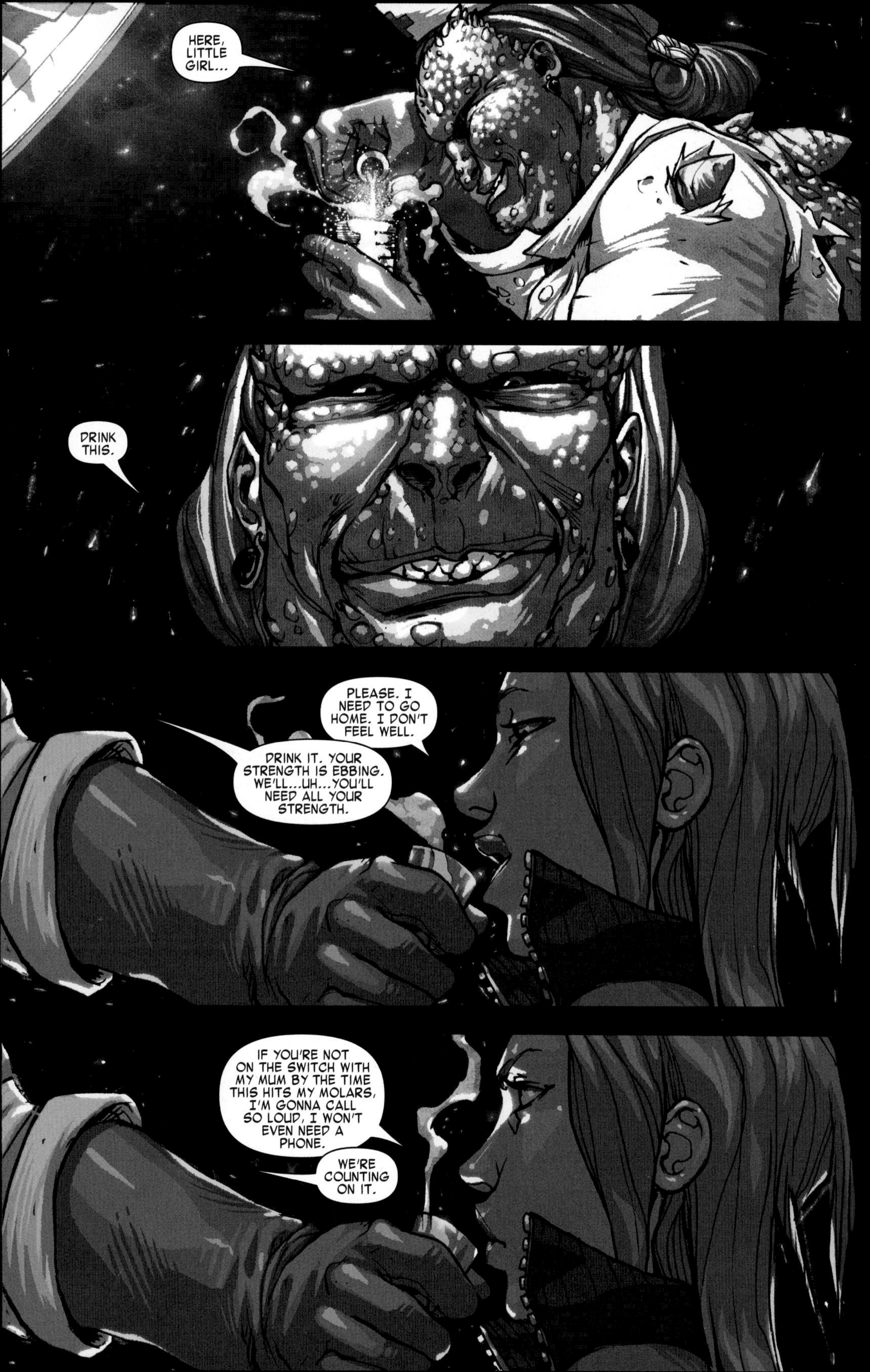
HERE, LITTLE GIRL...
DRINK THIS.
PLEASE. I NEED TO GO HOME. I DON'T FEEL WELL.
DRINK IT. YOUR STRENGTH IS EBBING. WE'LL...UH...YOU'LL NEED ALL YOUR STRENGTH.
IF YOU'RE NOT ON THE SWITCH WITH MY MUM BY THE TIME THIS HITS MY MOLARS, I'M GONNA CALL SO LOUD, I WON'T EVEN NEED A PHONE.
WE'RE COUNTING ON IT.

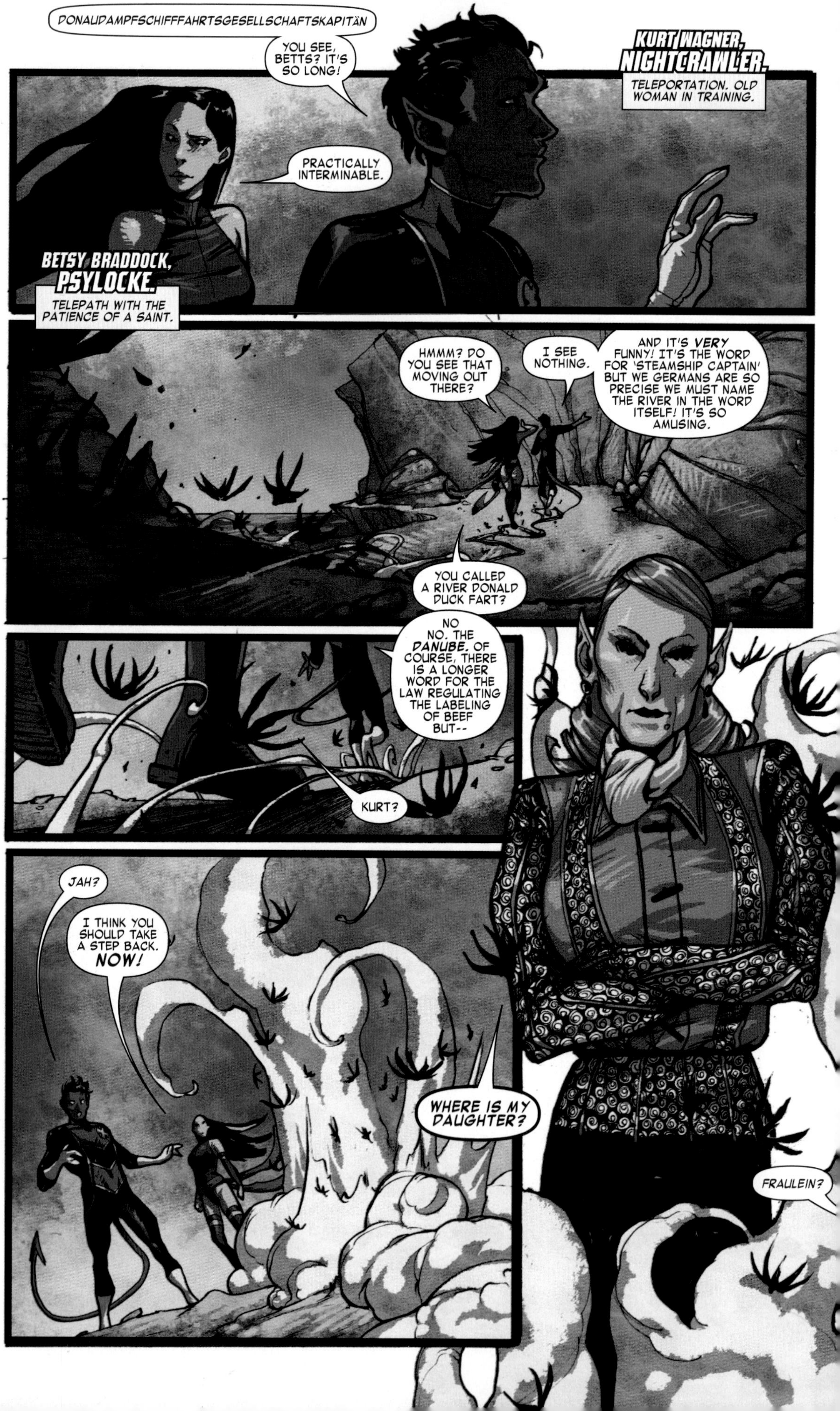

DONAUDAMPFSCHIFFFAHRTSGESELLSCHAFTSKAPITÄN
YOU SEE, BETTS? IT'S SO LONG!
KURT WAGNER, NIGHTCRAWLER.
TELEPORTATION. OLD WOMAN IN TRAINING.
PRACTICALLY INTERMINABLE.
BETSY BRADDOCK, PSYLOCKE.
TELEPATH WITH THE PATIENCE OF A SAINT.
HMMM? DO YOU SEE THAT MOVING OUT THERE?
I SEE NOTHING.
AND IT'S VERY FUNNY! IT'S THE WORD FOR 'STEAMSHIP CAPTAIN' BUT WE GERMANS ARE SO PRECISE WE MUST NAME THE RIVER IN THE WORD ITSELF! IT'S SO AMUSING.
YOU CALLED A RIVER DONALD DUCK FART?
NO NO. THE DANUBE. OF COURSE, THERE IS A LONGER WORD FOR THE LAW REGULATING THE LABELING OF BEEF BUT--
KURT?
JAH?
I THINK YOU SHOULD TAKE A STEP BACK. NOW!
WHERE IS MY DAUGHTER?
FRAULEIN?

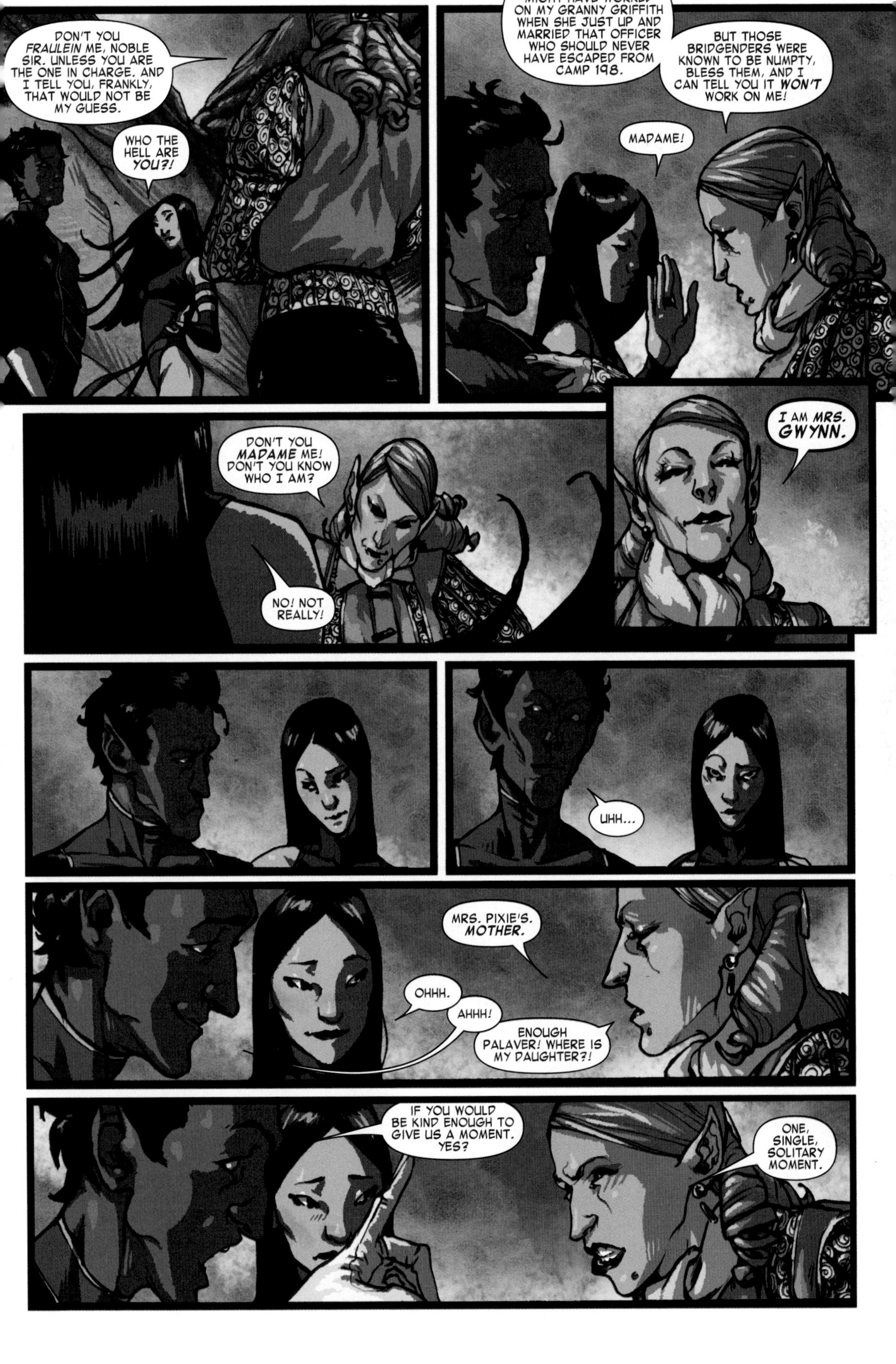
DON'T YOU FRAULEIN ME, NOBLE SIR. UNLESS YOU ARE THE ONE IN CHARGE. AND I TELL YOU, FRANKLY, THAT WOULD NOT BE MY GUESS.
WHO THE HELL ARE YOU?!
YOUR KIND OF TEUTONIC CHARM MIGHT HAVE WORKED ON MY GRANNY GRIFFITH WHEN SHE JUST UP AND MARRIED THAT OFFICER WHO SHOULD NEVER HAVE ESCAPED FROM CAMP 198.
BUT THOSE BRIDGENDERS WERE KNOWN TO BE NUMPTY, BLESS THEM, AND I CAN TELL YOU IT WON'T WORK ON ME!
MADAME!
DON'T YOU MADAME ME! DON'T YOU KNOW WHO I AM?
NO! NOT REALLY!
I AM MRS. GWYNN.
UHH...
MRS. PIXIE'S. MOTHER.
OHHH.
AHHH!
ENOUGH PALAVER! WHERE IS MY DAUGHTER?!
IF YOU WOULD BE KIND ENOUGH TO GIVE US A MOMENT. YES?
ONE, SINGLE, SOLITARY MOMENT.

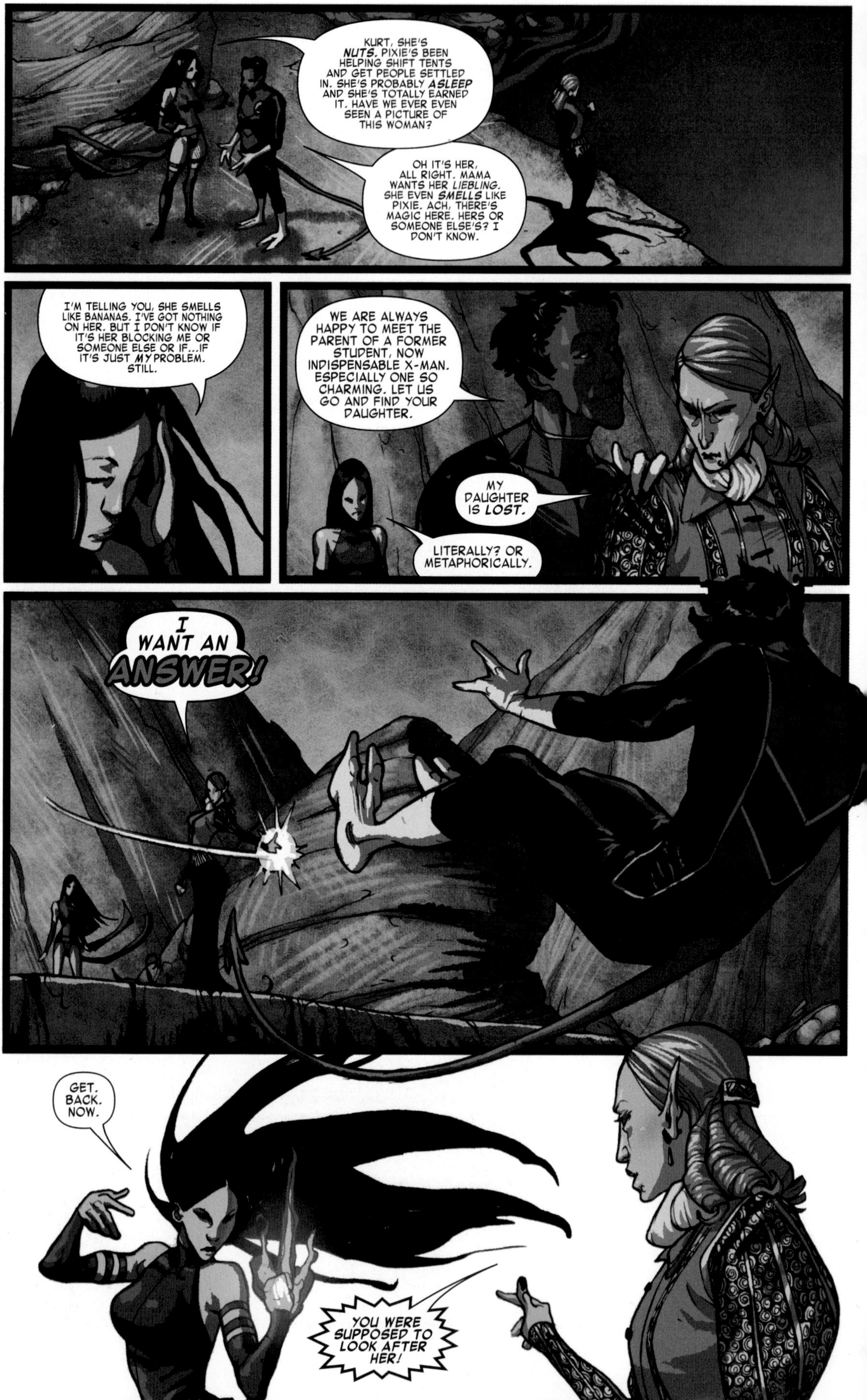

KURT, SHE'S NUTS. PIXIE'S BEEN HELPING SHIFT TENTS AND GET PEOPLE SETTLED IN. SHE'S PROBABLY ASLEEP AND SHE'S TOTALLY EARNED IT. HAVE WE EVER EVEN SEEN A PICTURE OF THIS WOMAN?
OH IT'S HER, ALL RIGHT. MAMA WANTS HER LIEBLING. SHE EVEN SMELLS LIKE PIXIE. ACH, THERE'S MAGIC HERE. HERS OR SOMEONE ELSE'S? I DON'T KNOW.
I'M TELLING YOU, SHE SMELLS LIKE BANANAS. I'VE GOT NOTHING ON HER. BUT I DON'T KNOW IF IT'S HER BLOCKING ME OR SOMEONE ELSE OR IF...IF IT'S JUST MY PROBLEM. STILL.
WE ARE ALWAYS HAPPY TO MEET THE PARENT OF A FORMER STUDENT, NOW INDISPENSABLE X-MAN. ESPECIALLY ONE SO CHARMING. LET US GO AND FIND YOUR DAUGHTER.
MY DAUGHTER IS LOST.
LITERALLY? OR METAPHORICALLY.
I WANT AN ANSWER!
GET. BACK. NOW.
YOU WERE SUPPOSED TO LOOK AFTER HER!

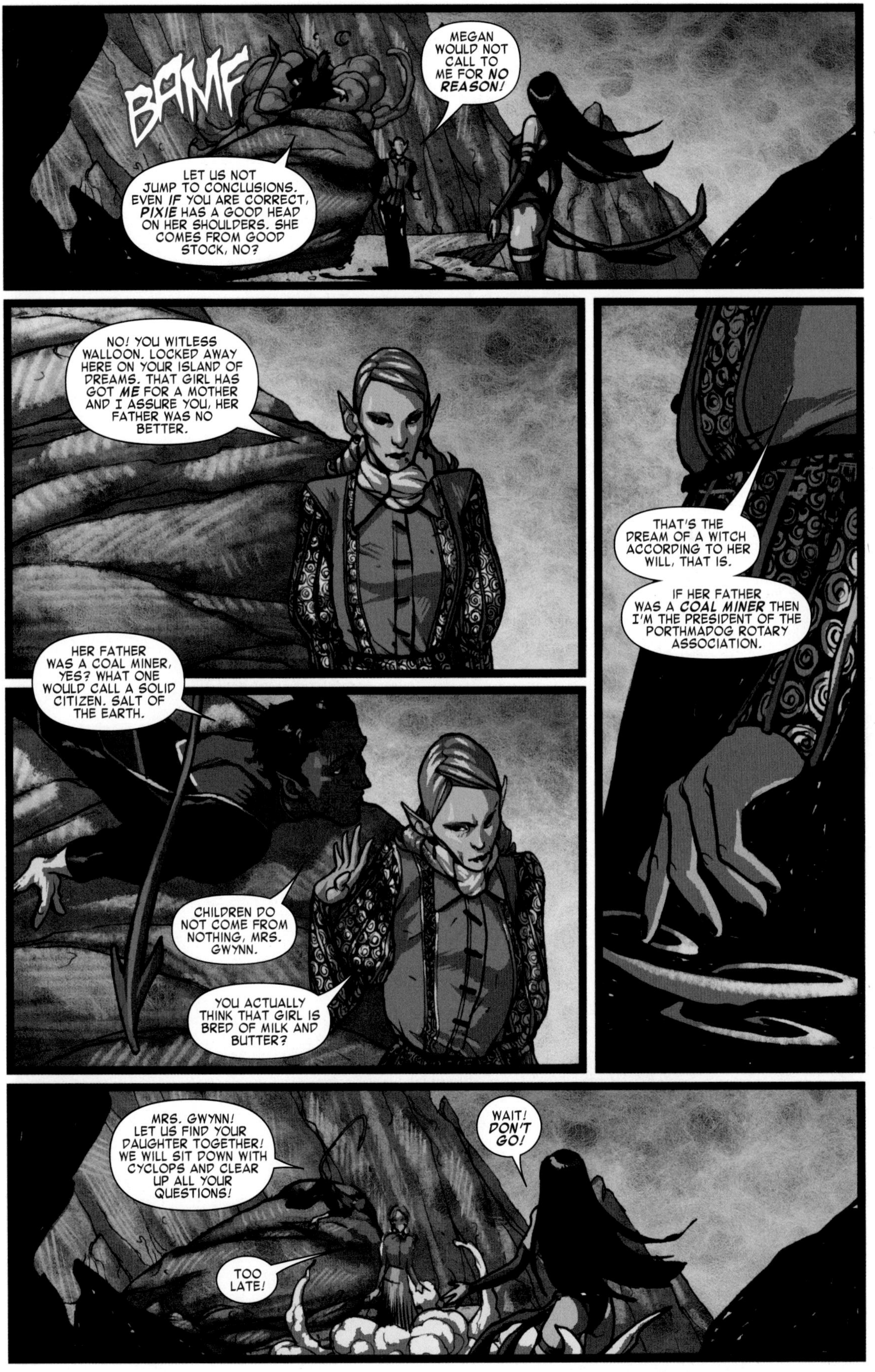
BAMF
MEGAN WOULD NOT CALL TO ME FOR NO REASON!
LET US NOT JUMP TO CONCLUSIONS. EVEN IF YOU ARE CORRECT, PIXIE HAS A GOOD HEAD ON HER SHOULDERS. SHE COMES FROM GOOD STOCK, NO?
NO! YOU WITLESS WALLOON. LOCKED AWAY HERE ON YOUR ISLAND OF DREAMS. THAT GIRL HAS GOT ME FOR A MOTHER AND I ASSURE YOU, HER FATHER WAS NO BETTER.
THAT'S THE DREAM OF A WITCH ACCORDING TO HER WILL, THAT IS.
IF HER FATHER WAS A COAL MINER THEN I'M THE PRESIDENT OF THE PORTHMADOG ROTARY ASSOCIATION.
HER FATHER WAS A COAL MINER, YES? WHAT ONE WOULD CALL A SOLID CITIZEN. SALT OF THE EARTH.
CHILDREN DO NOT COME FROM NOTHING, MRS. GWYNN.
YOU ACTUALLY THINK THAT GIRL IS BRED OF MILK AND BUTTER?
MRS. GWYNN! LET US FIND YOUR DAUGHTER TOGETHER! WE WILL SIT DOWN WITH CYCLOPS AND CLEAR UP ALL YOUR QUESTIONS!
WAIT! DON'T GO!
TOO LATE!

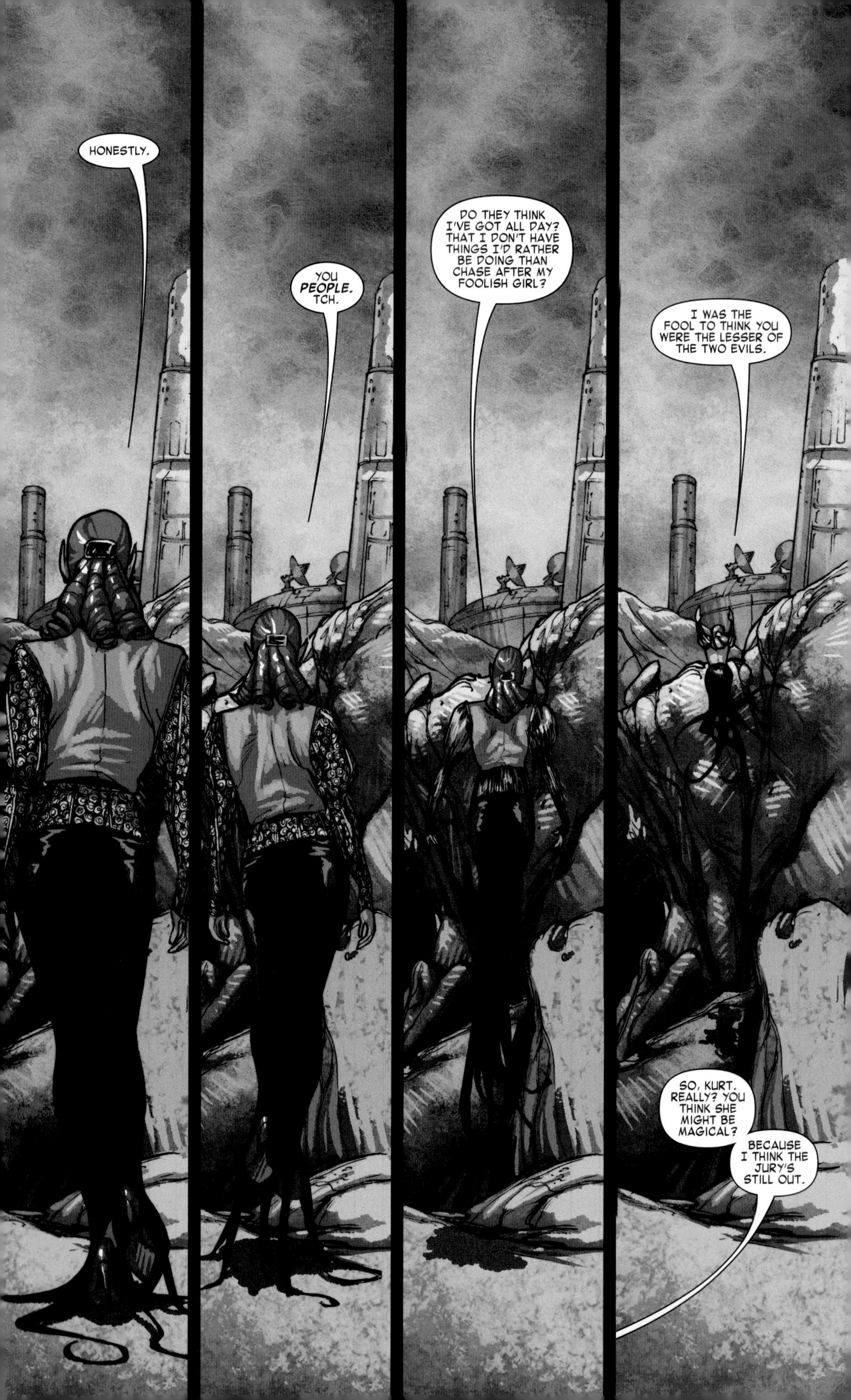
HONESTLY.
YOU *PEOPLE.* TCH.
DO THEY THINK I'VE GOT ALL DAY? THAT I DON'T HAVE THINGS I'D RATHER BE DOING THAN CHASE AFTER MY FOOLISH GIRL?
I WAS THE FOOL TO THINK YOU WERE THE LESSER OF THE TWO EVILS.
SO, KURT. REALLY? YOU THINK SHE MIGHT BE MAGICAL?
BECAUSE I THINK THE JURY'S STILL OUT.

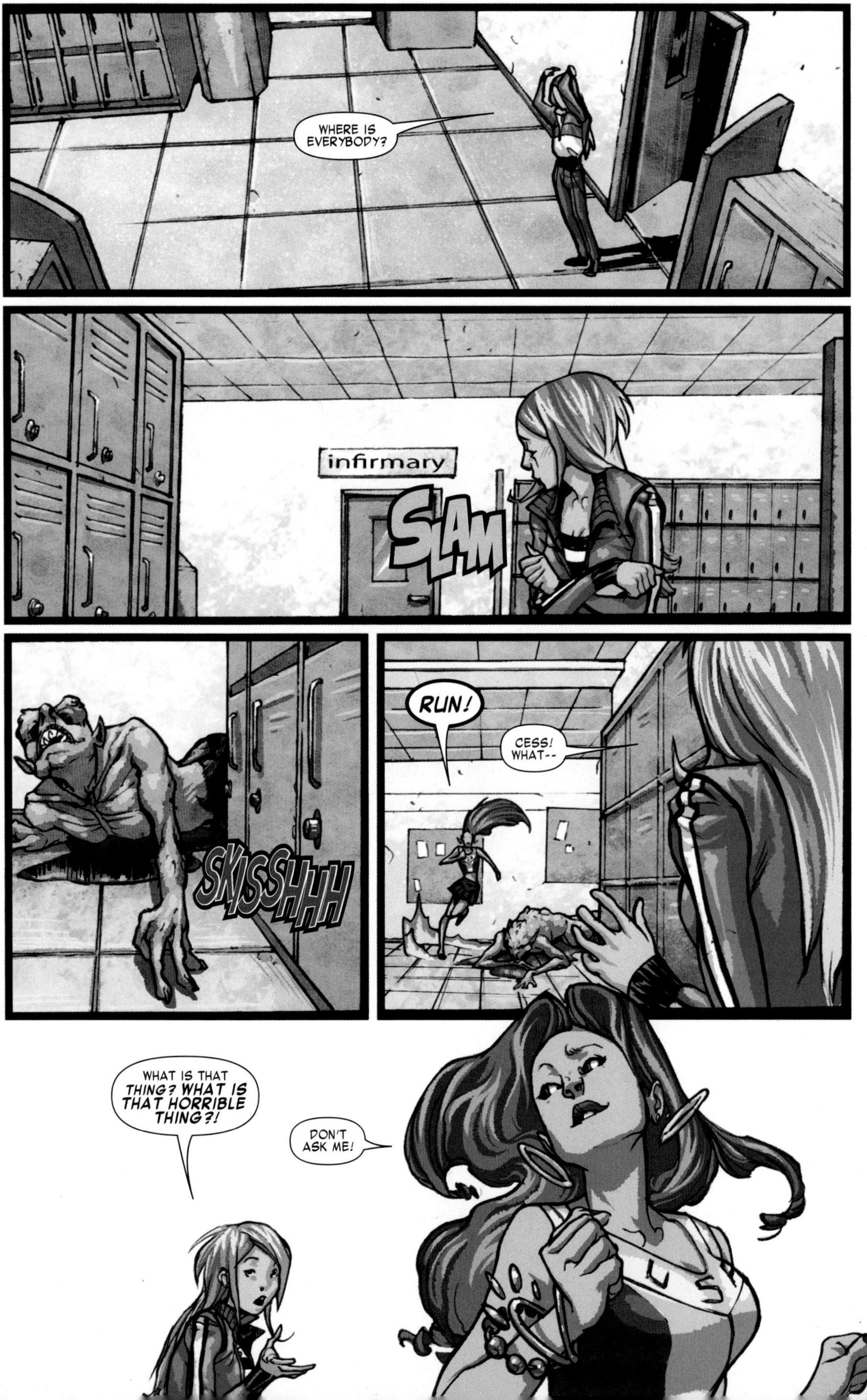
WHERE IS EVERYBODY?
infirmary
SLAM
SKISSHHH
RUN!
CESS! WHAT--
WHAT IS THAT THING? WHAT IS THAT HORRIBLE THING?!
DON'T ASK ME!

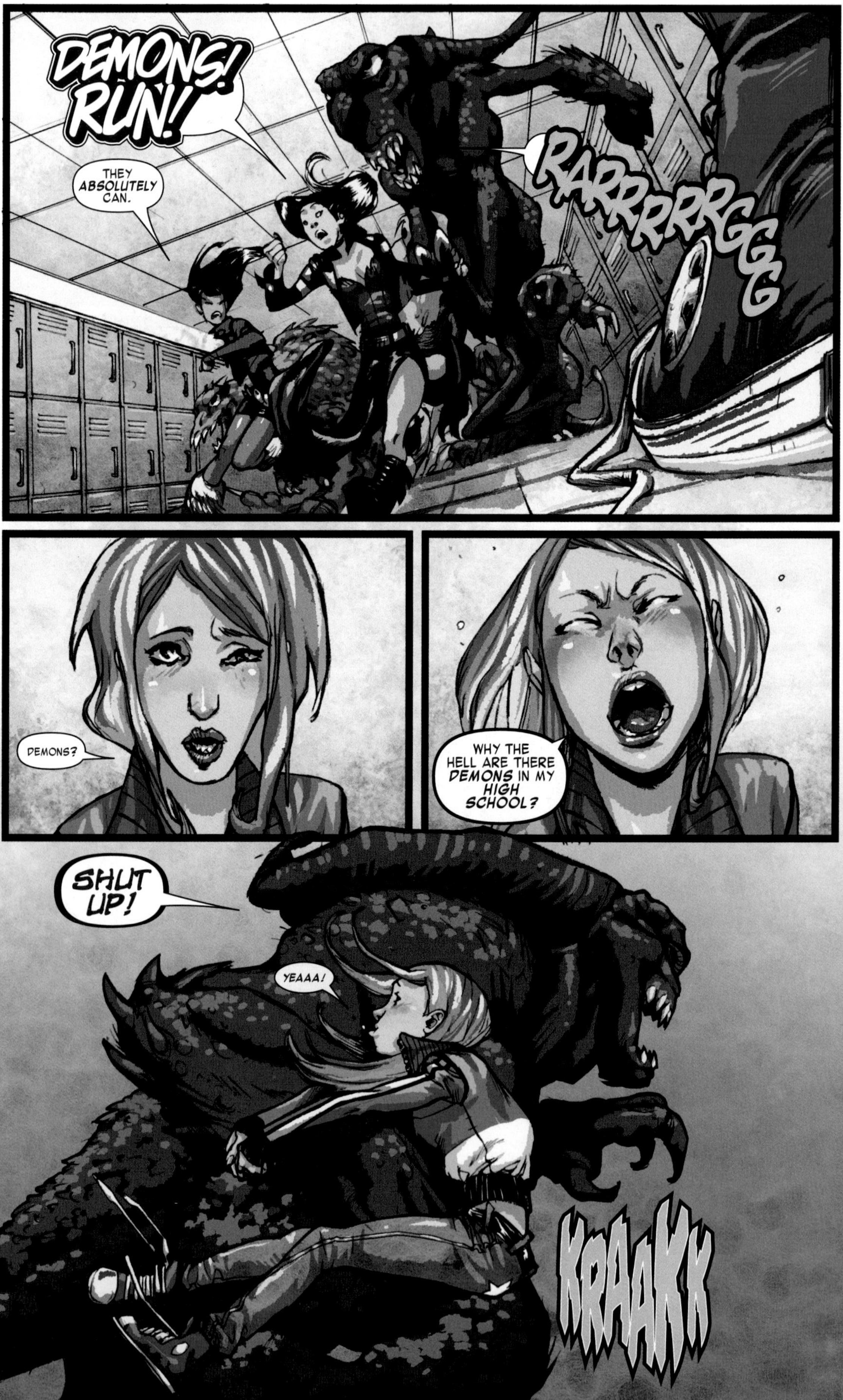
DEMONS! RUN!
THEY ABSOLUTELY CAN.
RARRRRRRGGG
DEMONS?
WHY THE HELL ARE THERE DEMONS IN MY HIGH SCHOOL?
SHUT UP!
YEAAA!
KRAAKK

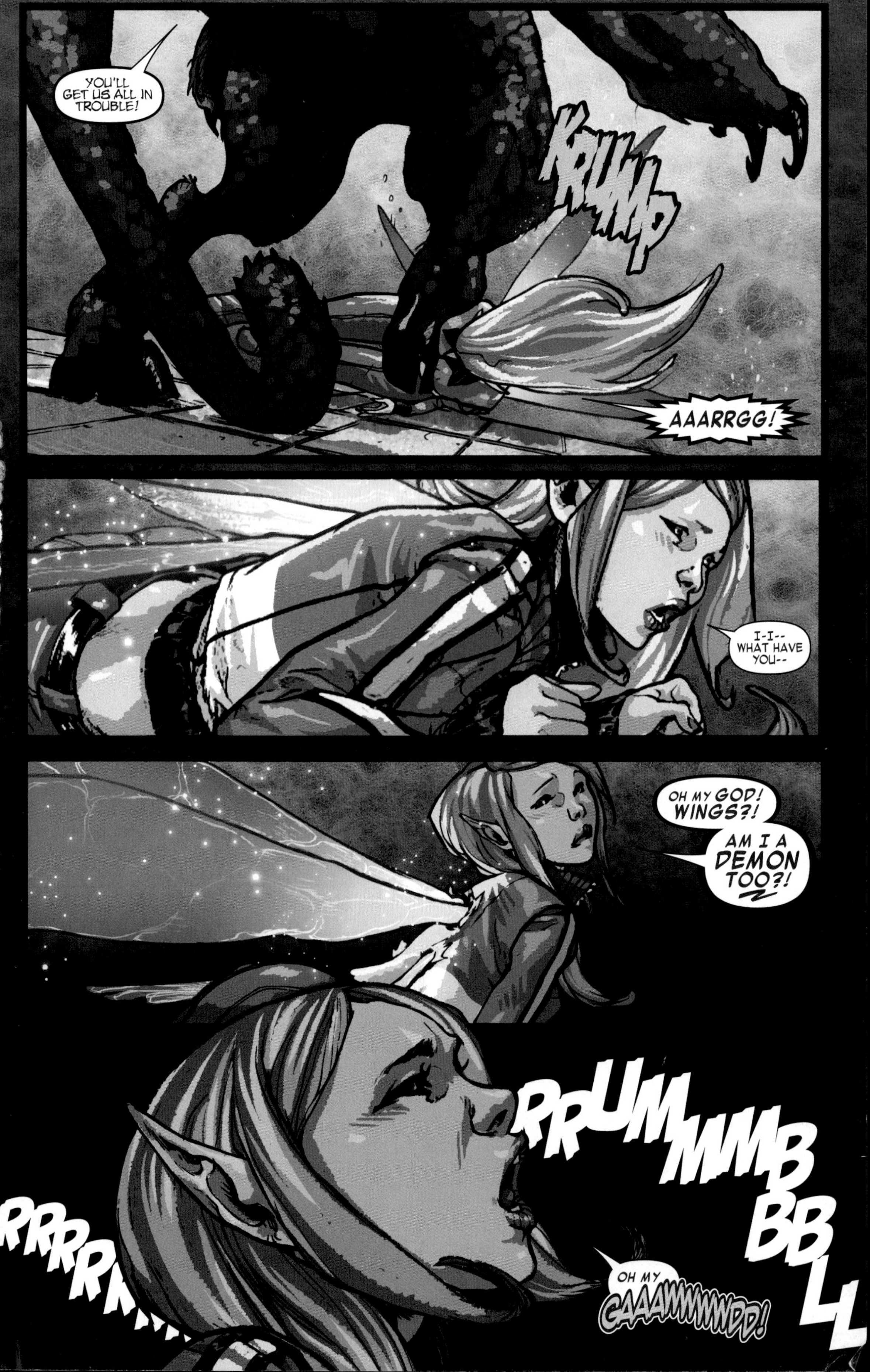
YOU'LL GET US ALL IN TROUBLE!
KRUMP
AAARRGG!
I-I-- WHAT HAVE YOU--
OH MY GOD! WINGS?!
AM I A DEMON TOO?!
RRUMMMBBLL
RRRR
OH MY GAAAWWWWDD!

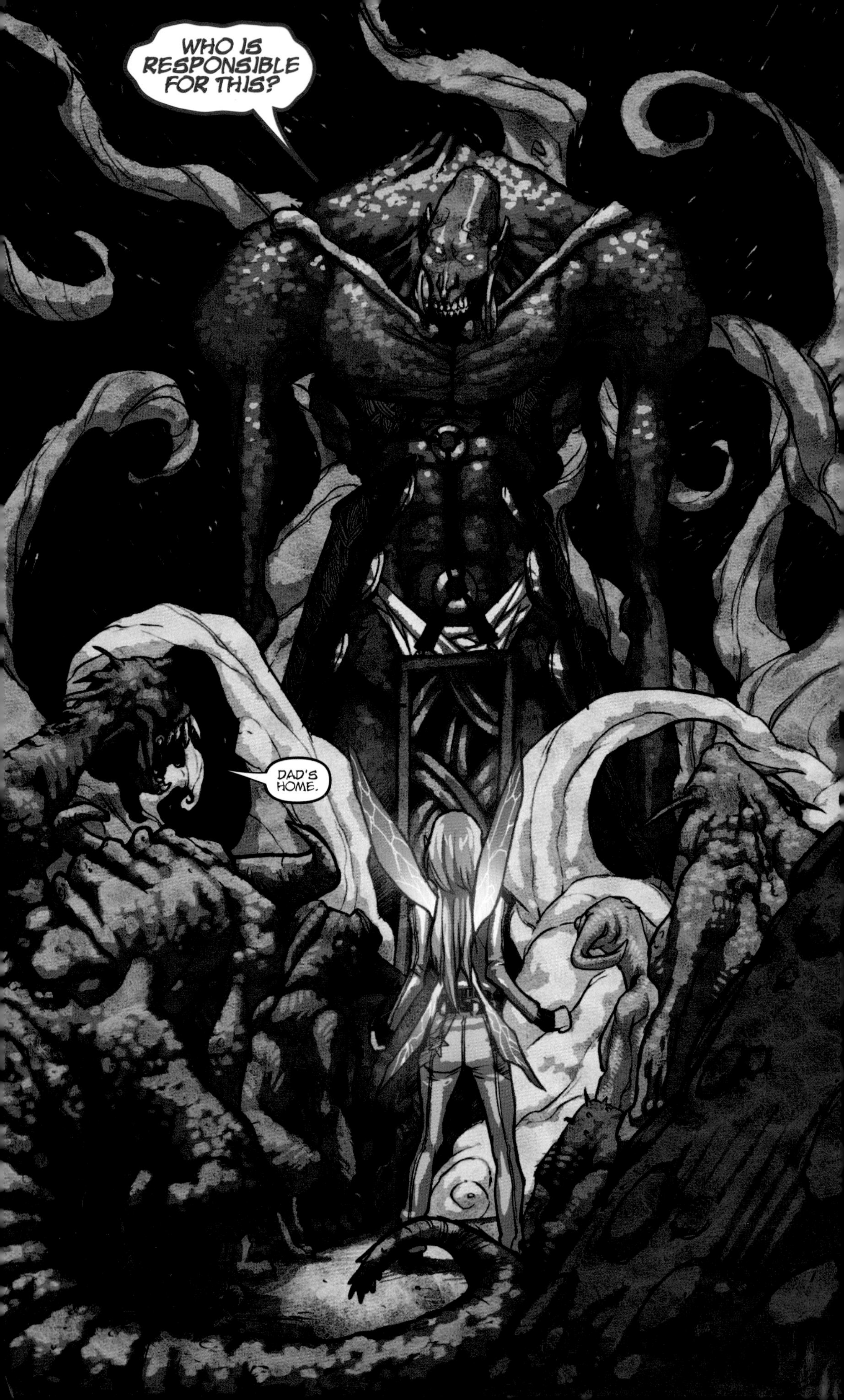
WHO IS RESPONSIBLE FOR THIS?
DAD'S HOME.

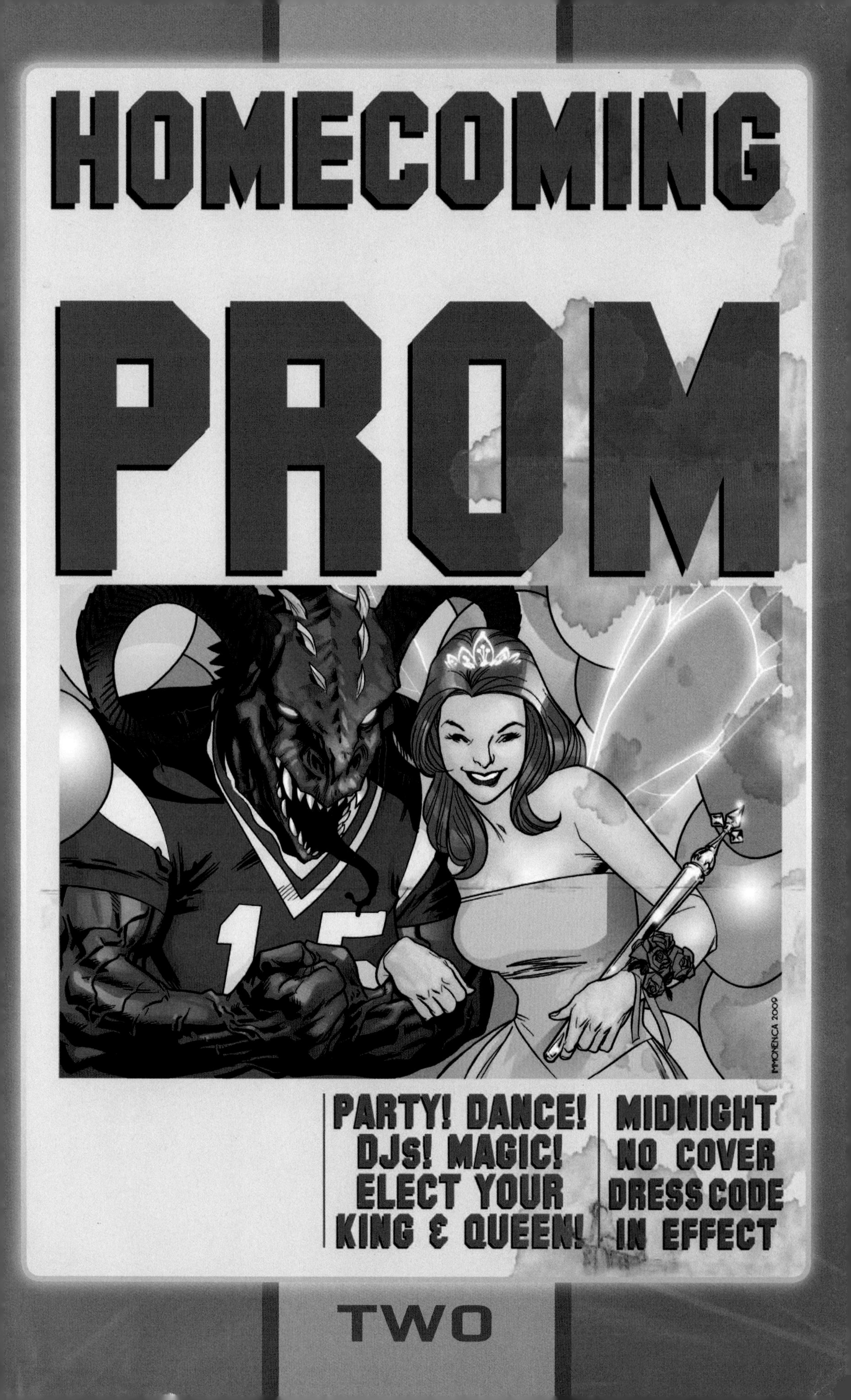
HOMECOMING
PROM
1
PARTY! DANCE!
DJs! MAGIC!
ELECT YOUR
KING & QUEEN!
MIDNIGHT
NO COVER
DRESS CODE
IN EFFECT
TWO

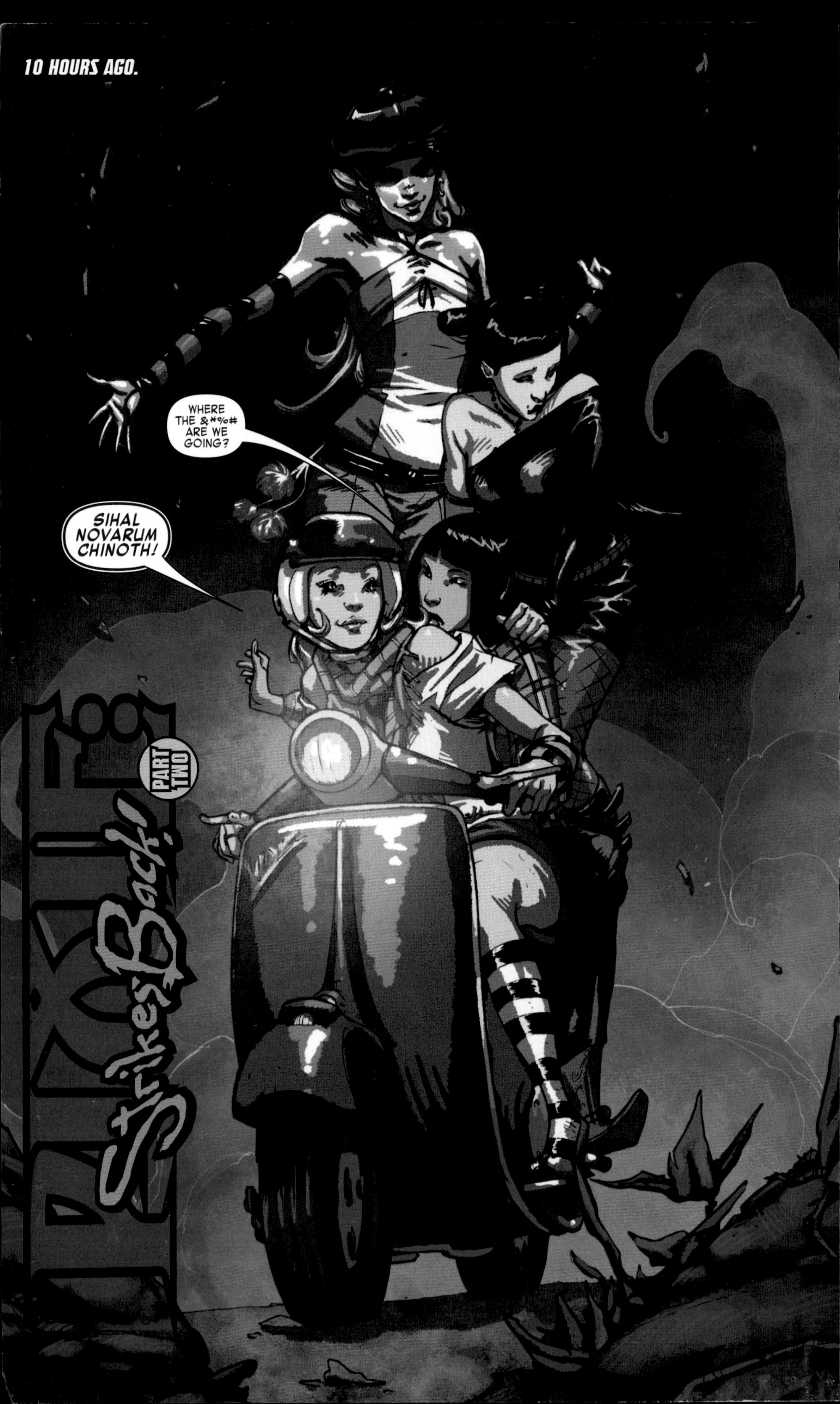
10 HOURS AGO.
WHERE THE &*%# ARE WE GOING?
SIHAL NOVARUM CHINOTH!
Strikes Back!
PART TWO

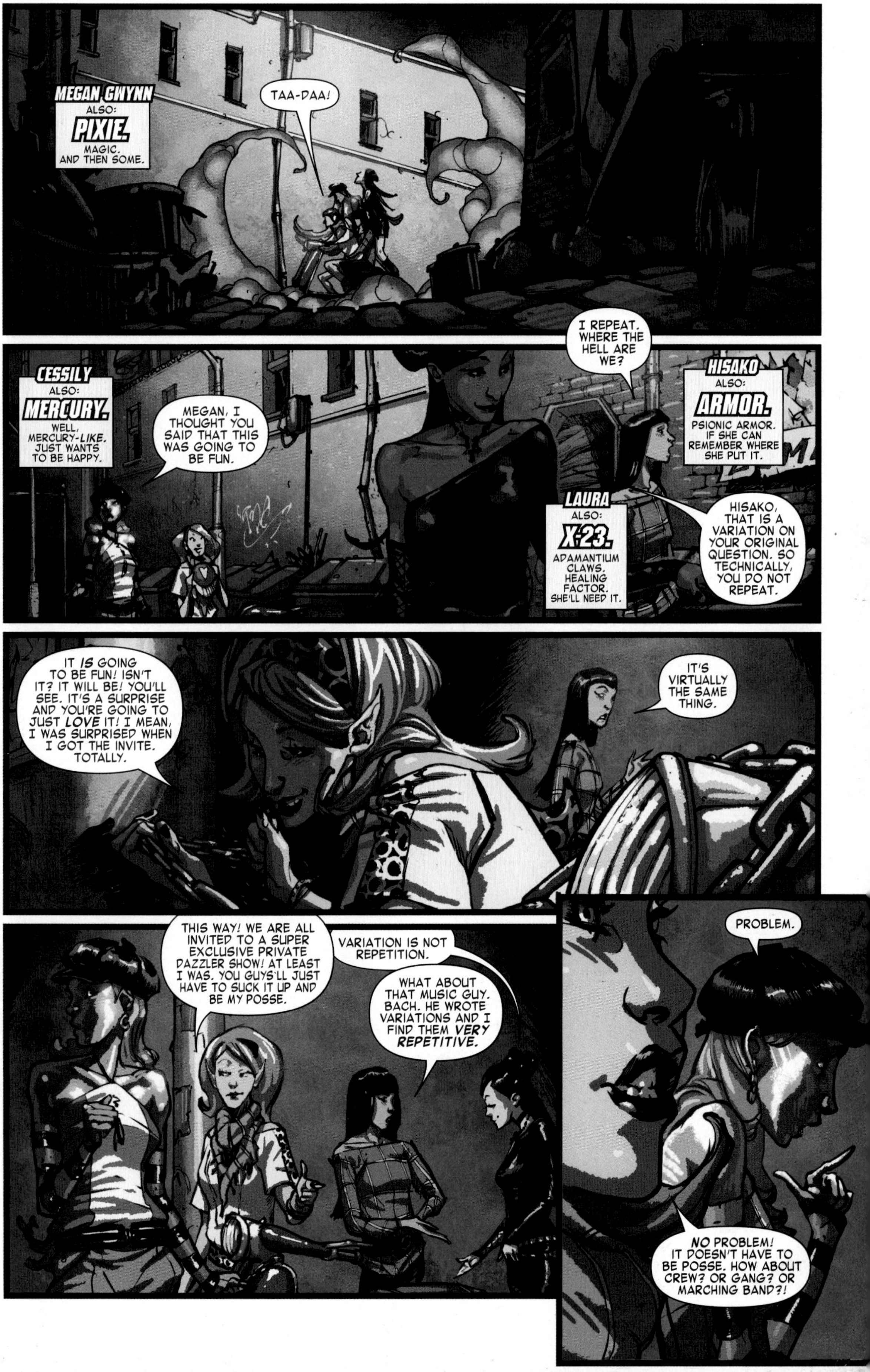
MEGAN GWYNN
ALSO:
PIXIE.
MAGIC. AND THEN SOME.
TAA-DAA!
CESSILY
ALSO:
MERCURY.
WELL, MERCURY-LIKE. JUST WANTS TO BE HAPPY.
MEGAN, I THOUGHT YOU SAID THAT THIS WAS GOING TO BE FUN.
I REPEAT. WHERE THE HELL ARE WE?
HISAKO
ALSO:
ARMOR.
PSIONIC ARMOR. IF SHE CAN REMEMBER WHERE SHE PUT IT.
LAURA
ALSO:
X-23.
ADAMANTIUM CLAWS. HEALING FACTOR. SHE'LL NEED IT.
HISAKO, THAT IS A VARIATION ON YOUR ORIGINAL QUESTION. SO TECHNICALLY, YOU DO NOT REPEAT.
IT IS GOING TO BE FUN! ISN'T IT? IT WILL BE! YOU'LL SEE. IT'S A SURPRISE AND YOU'RE GOING TO JUST LOVE IT! I MEAN, I WAS SURPRISED WHEN I GOT THE INVITE. TOTALLY.
IT'S VIRTUALLY THE SAME THING.
THIS WAY! WE ARE ALL INVITED TO A SUPER EXCLUSIVE PRIVATE DAZZLER SHOW! AT LEAST I WAS. YOU GUYS'LL JUST HAVE TO SUCK IT UP AND BE MY POSSE.
VARIATION IS NOT REPETITION.
WHAT ABOUT THAT MUSIC GUY. BACH. HE WROTE VARIATIONS AND I FIND THEM VERY REPETITIVE.
PROBLEM.
NO PROBLEM! IT DOESN'T HAVE TO BE POSSE. HOW ABOUT CREW? OR GANG? OR MARCHING BAND?!

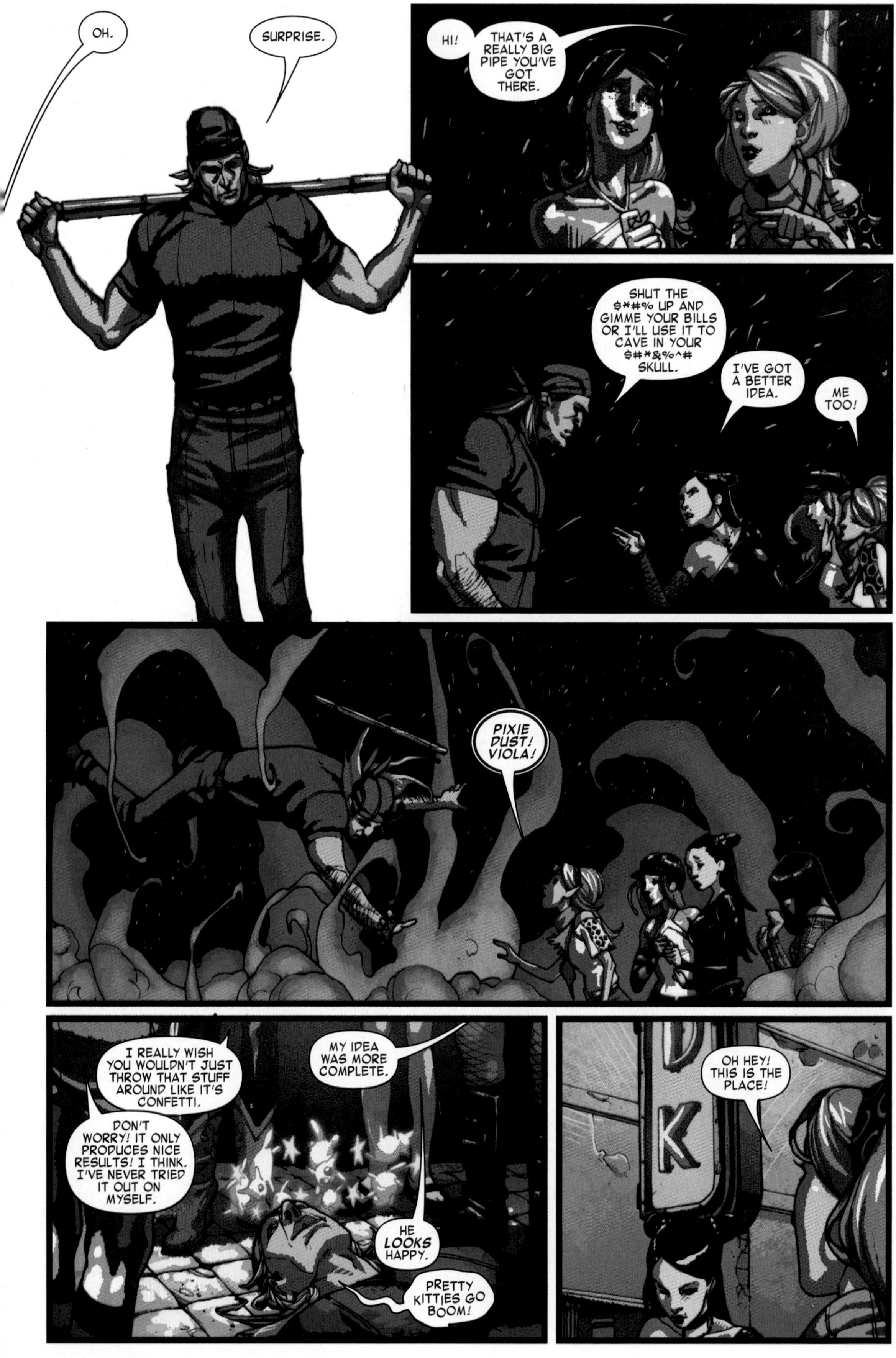
OH.
SURPRISE.
HI!
THAT'S A REALLY BIG PIPE YOU'VE GOT THERE.
SHUT THE $*#% UP AND GIMME YOUR BILLS OR I'LL USE IT TO CAVE IN YOUR $#*&%^# SKULL.
I'VE GOT A BETTER IDEA.
ME TOO!
PIXIE DUST! VIOLA!
I REALLY WISH YOU WOULDN'T JUST THROW THAT STUFF AROUND LIKE IT'S CONFETTI.
DON'T WORRY! IT ONLY PRODUCES NICE RESULTS! I THINK. I'VE NEVER TRIED IT OUT ON MYSELF.
MY IDEA WAS MORE COMPLETE.
HE LOOKS HAPPY.
PRETTY KITTIES GO BOOM!
OH HEY! THIS IS THE PLACE!
K

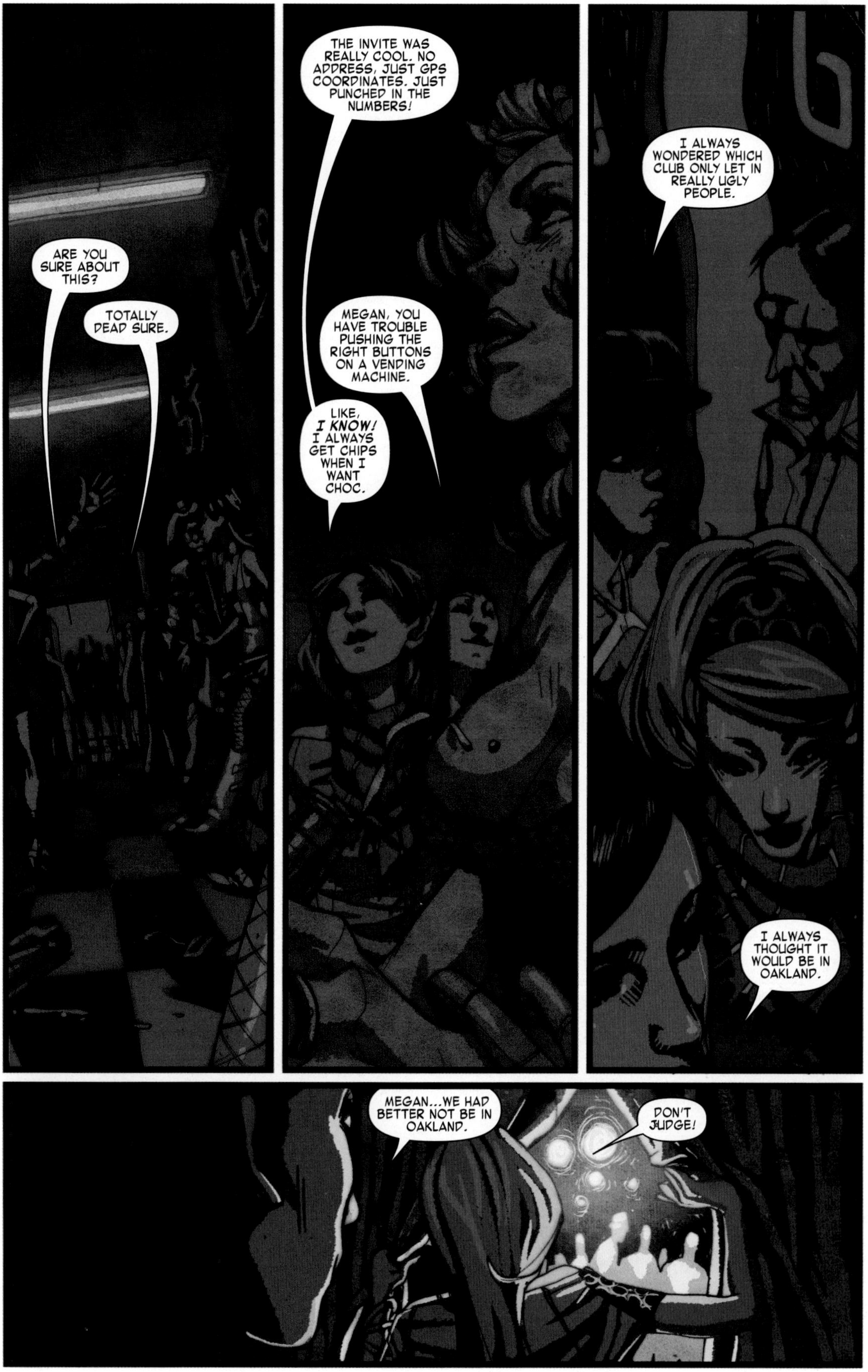
ARE YOU SURE ABOUT THIS?
TOTALLY DEAD SURE.
THE INVITE WAS REALLY COOL. NO ADDRESS, JUST GPS COORDINATES. JUST PUNCHED IN THE NUMBERS!
MEGAN, YOU HAVE TROUBLE PUSHING THE RIGHT BUTTONS ON A VENDING MACHINE.
LIKE, I KNOW! I ALWAYS GET CHIPS WHEN I WANT CHOC.
I ALWAYS WONDERED WHICH CLUB ONLY LET IN REALLY UGLY PEOPLE.
I ALWAYS THOUGHT IT WOULD BE IN OAKLAND.
MEGAN...WE HAD BETTER NOT BE IN OAKLAND.
DON'T JUDGE!

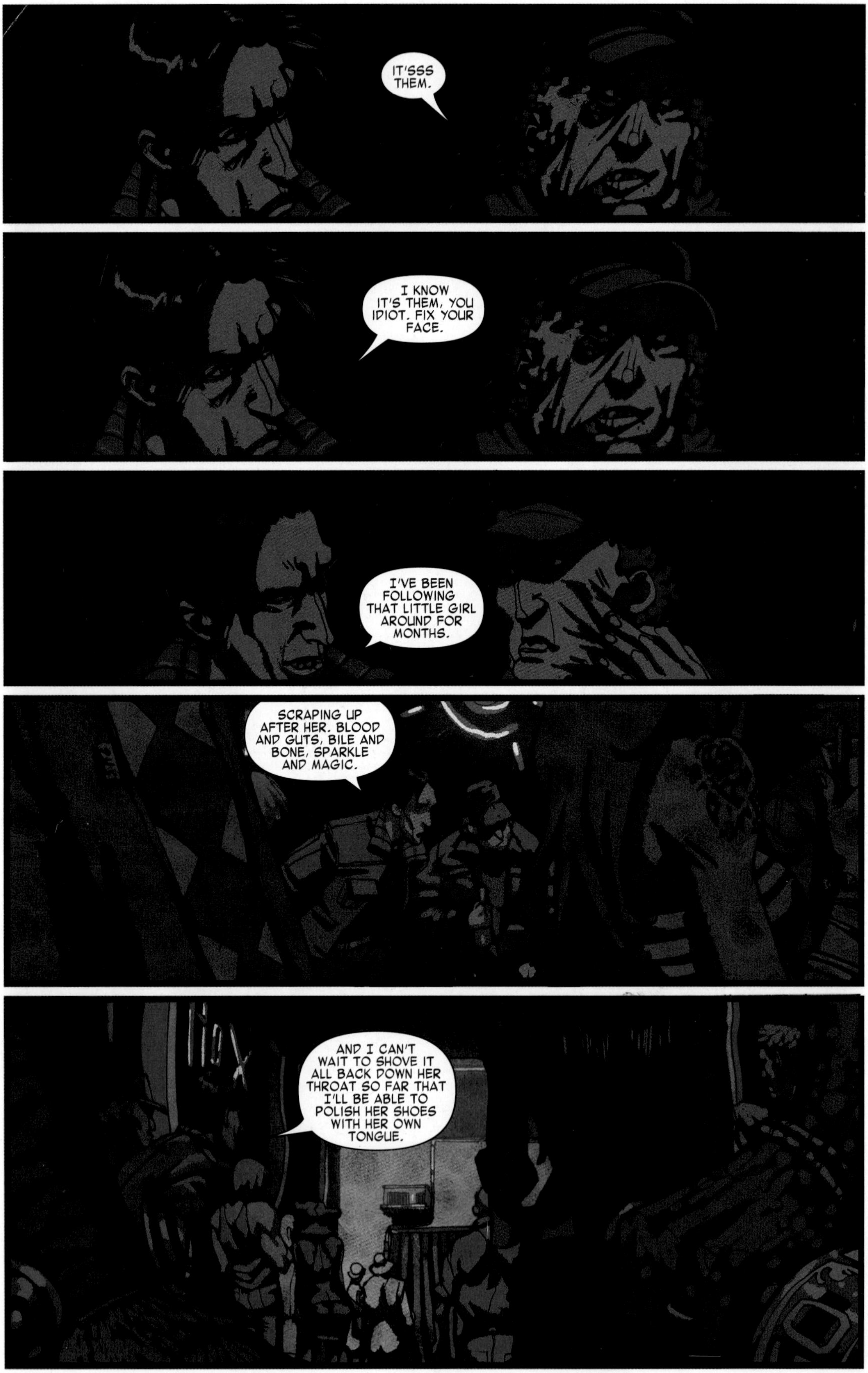
IT'SSS THEM.
I KNOW IT'S THEM, YOU IDIOT. FIX YOUR FACE.
I'VE BEEN FOLLOWING THAT LITTLE GIRL AROUND FOR MONTHS.
SCRAPING UP AFTER HER. BLOOD AND GUTS, BILE AND BONE, SPARKLE AND MAGIC.
AND I CAN'T WAIT TO SHOVE IT ALL BACK DOWN HER THROAT SO FAR THAT I'LL BE ABLE TO POLISH HER SHOES WITH HER OWN TONGUE.

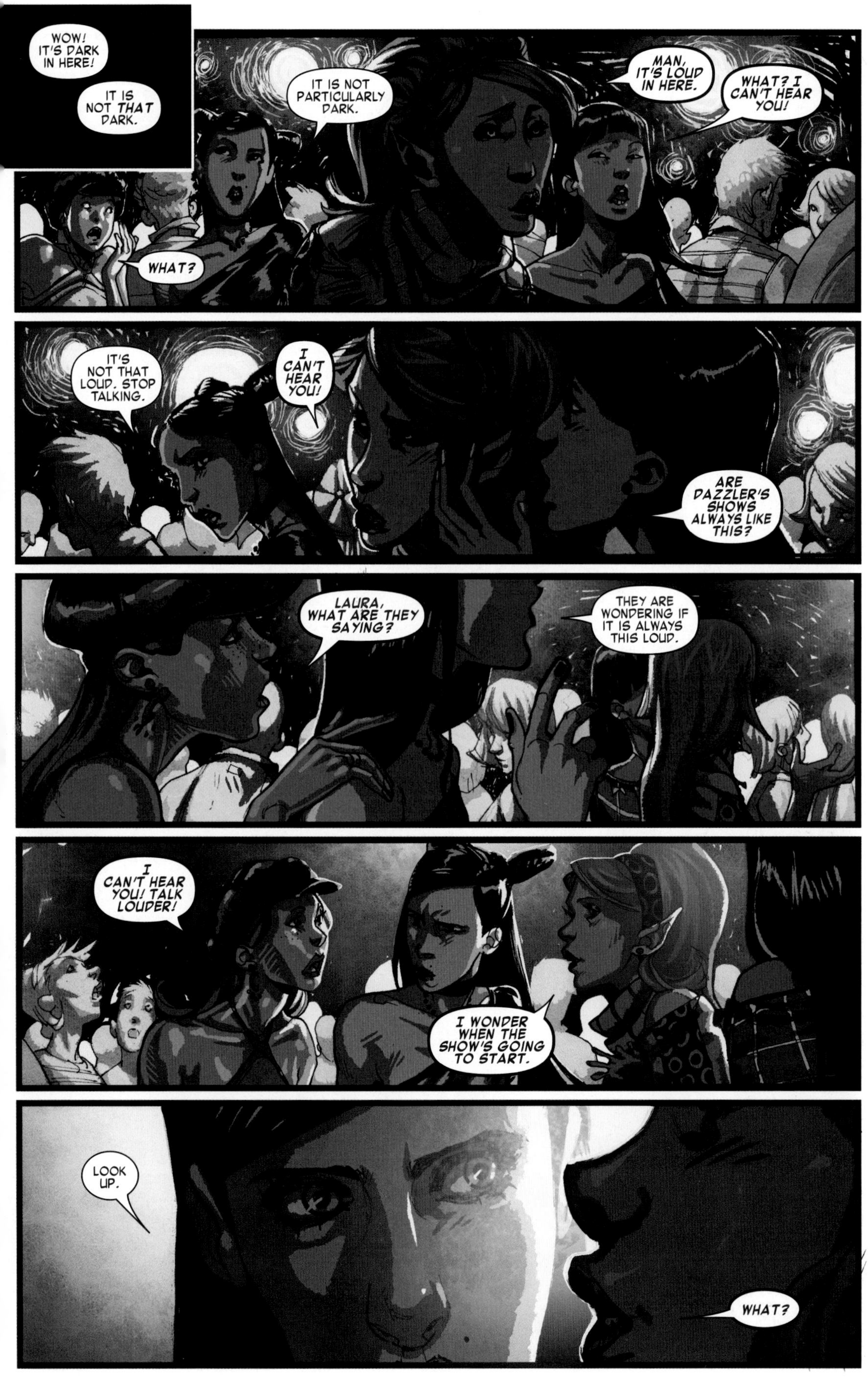
WOW! IT'S DARK IN HERE!
IT IS NOT THAT DARK.
IT IS NOT PARTICULARLY DARK.
MAN, IT'S LOUD IN HERE.
WHAT? I CAN'T HEAR YOU!
WHAT?
IT'S NOT THAT LOUD. STOP TALKING.
I CAN'T HEAR YOU!
ARE DAZZLER'S SHOWS ALWAYS LIKE THIS?
LAURA, WHAT ARE THEY SAYING?
THEY ARE WONDERING IF IT IS ALWAYS THIS LOUD.
I CAN'T HEAR YOU! TALK LOUDER!
I WONDER WHEN THE SHOW'S GOING TO START.
LOOK UP.
WHAT?

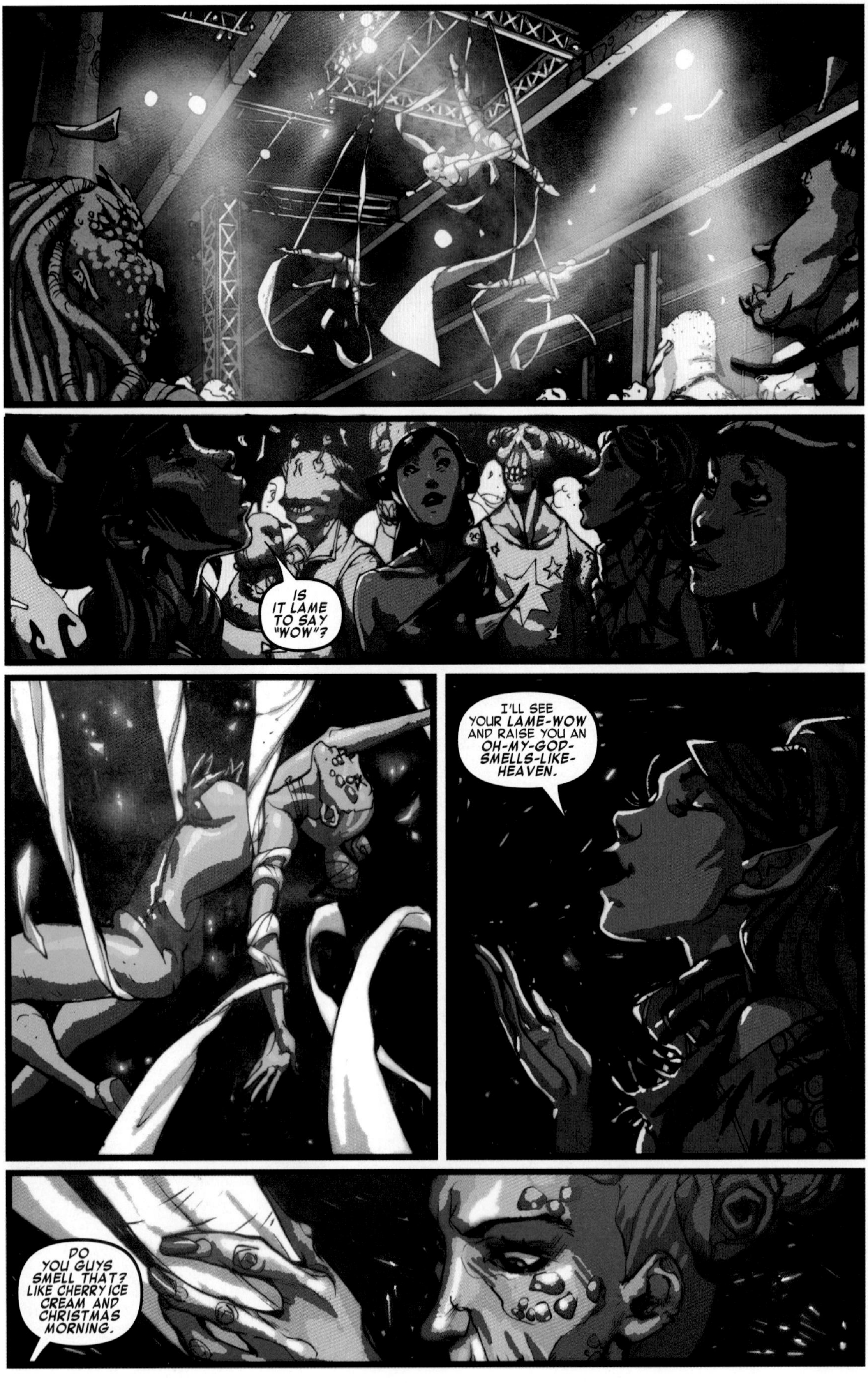
IS IT LAME TO SAY "WOW"?
I'LL SEE YOUR LAME-WOW AND RAISE YOU AN OH-MY-GOD-SMELLS-LIKE-HEAVEN.
DO YOU GUYS SMELL THAT? LIKE CHERRY ICE CREAM AND CHRISTMAS MORNING.

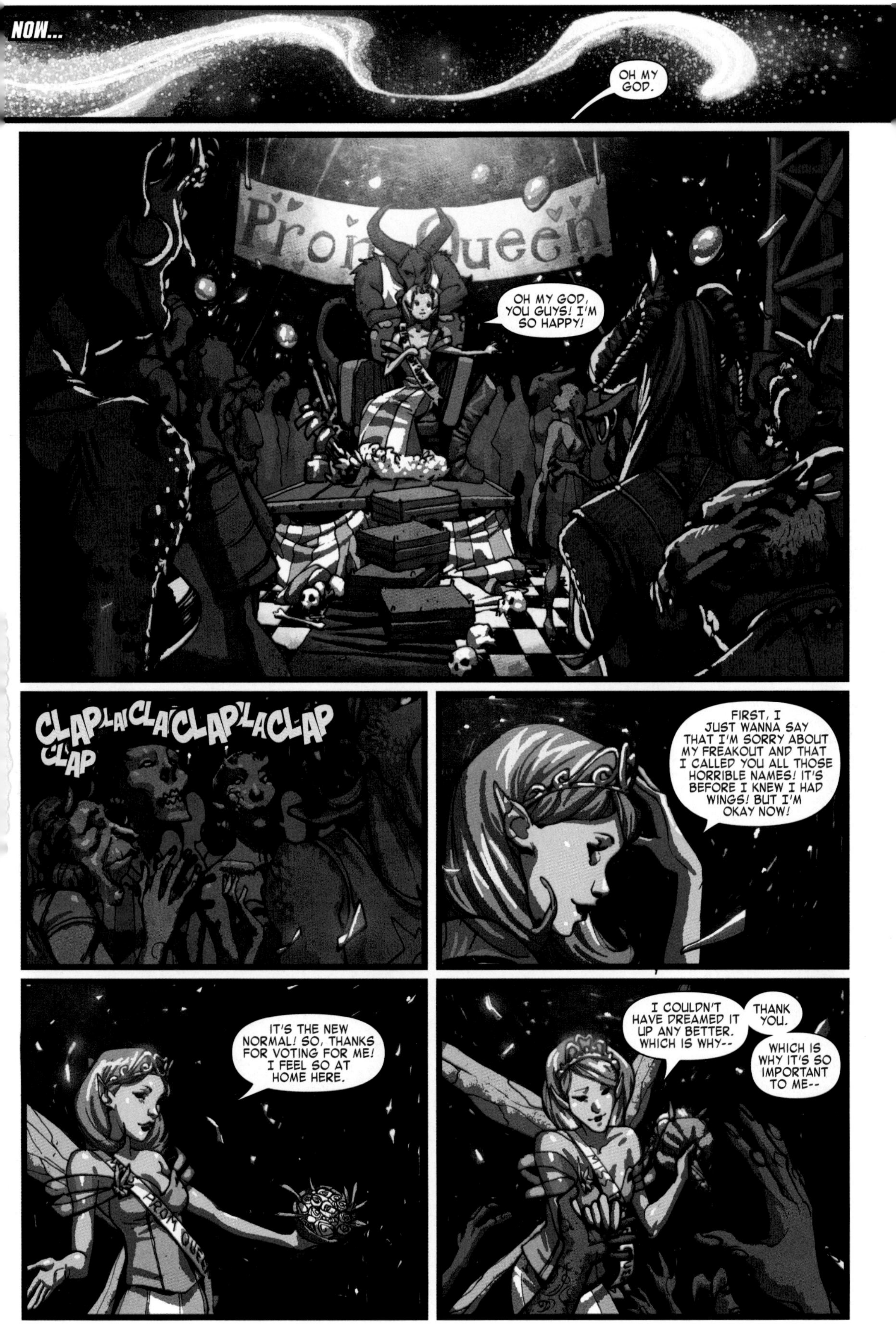
NOW...
OH MY GOD.
Prom Queen
OH MY GOD, YOU GUYS! I'M SO HAPPY!
CLAP CLA CLA CLAP CLA CLAP CLAP
FIRST, I JUST WANNA SAY THAT I'M SORRY ABOUT MY FREAKOUT AND THAT I CALLED YOU ALL THOSE HORRIBLE NAMES! IT'S BEFORE I KNEW I HAD WINGS! BUT I'M OKAY NOW!
IT'S THE NEW NORMAL! SO, THANKS FOR VOTING FOR ME! I FEEL SO AT HOME HERE.
I COULDN'T HAVE DREAMED IT UP ANY BETTER. WHICH IS WHY--
THANK YOU.
WHICH IS WHY IT'S SO IMPORTANT TO ME--

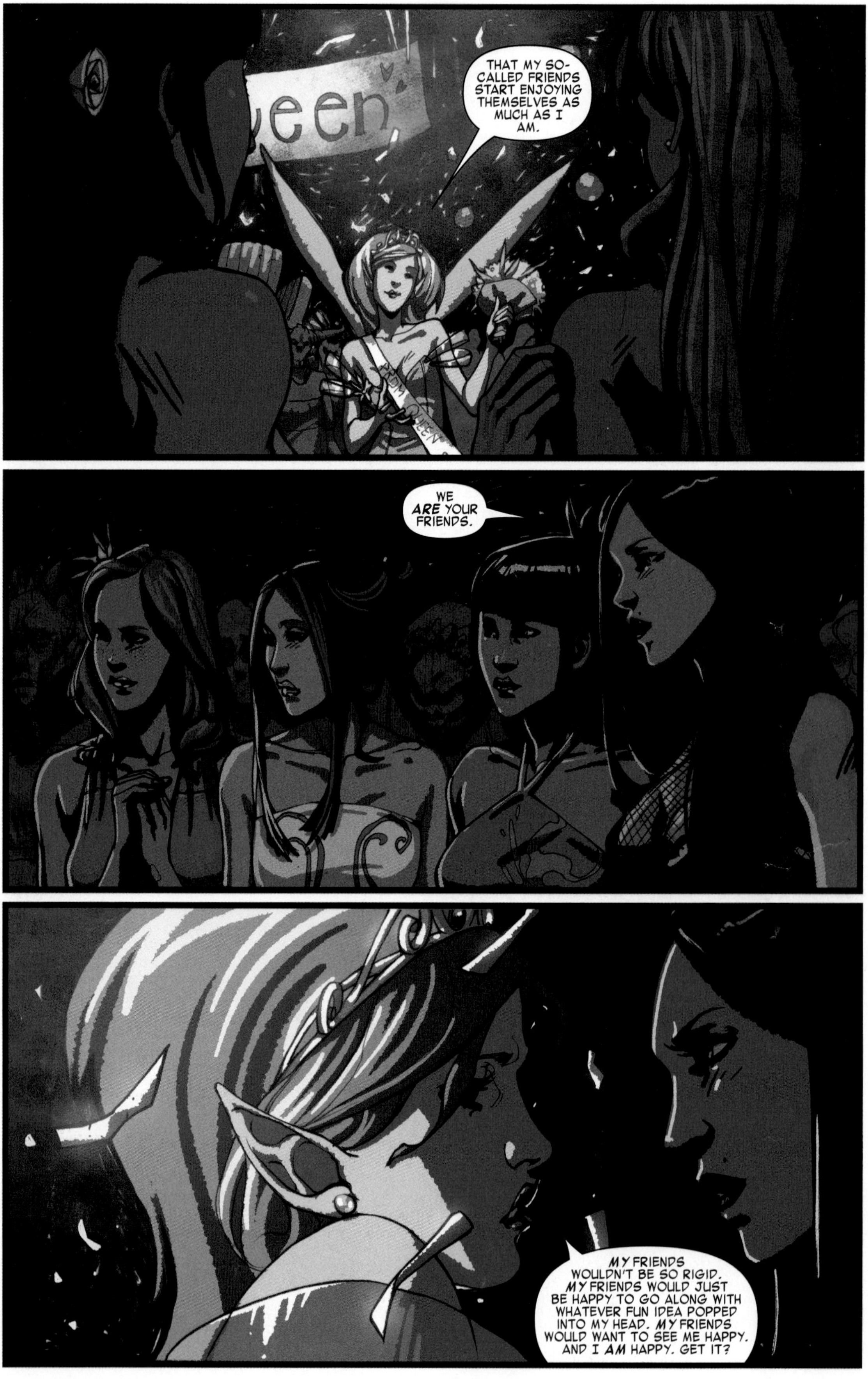
THAT MY SO-CALLED FRIENDS START ENJOYING THEMSELVES AS MUCH AS I AM.
WE *ARE* YOUR FRIENDS.
*MY* FRIENDS WOULDN'T BE SO RIGID. *MY* FRIENDS WOULD JUST BE HAPPY TO GO ALONG WITH WHATEVER FUN IDEA POPPED INTO MY HEAD. *MY* FRIENDS WOULD WANT TO SEE ME HAPPY. AND I *AM* HAPPY. GET IT?

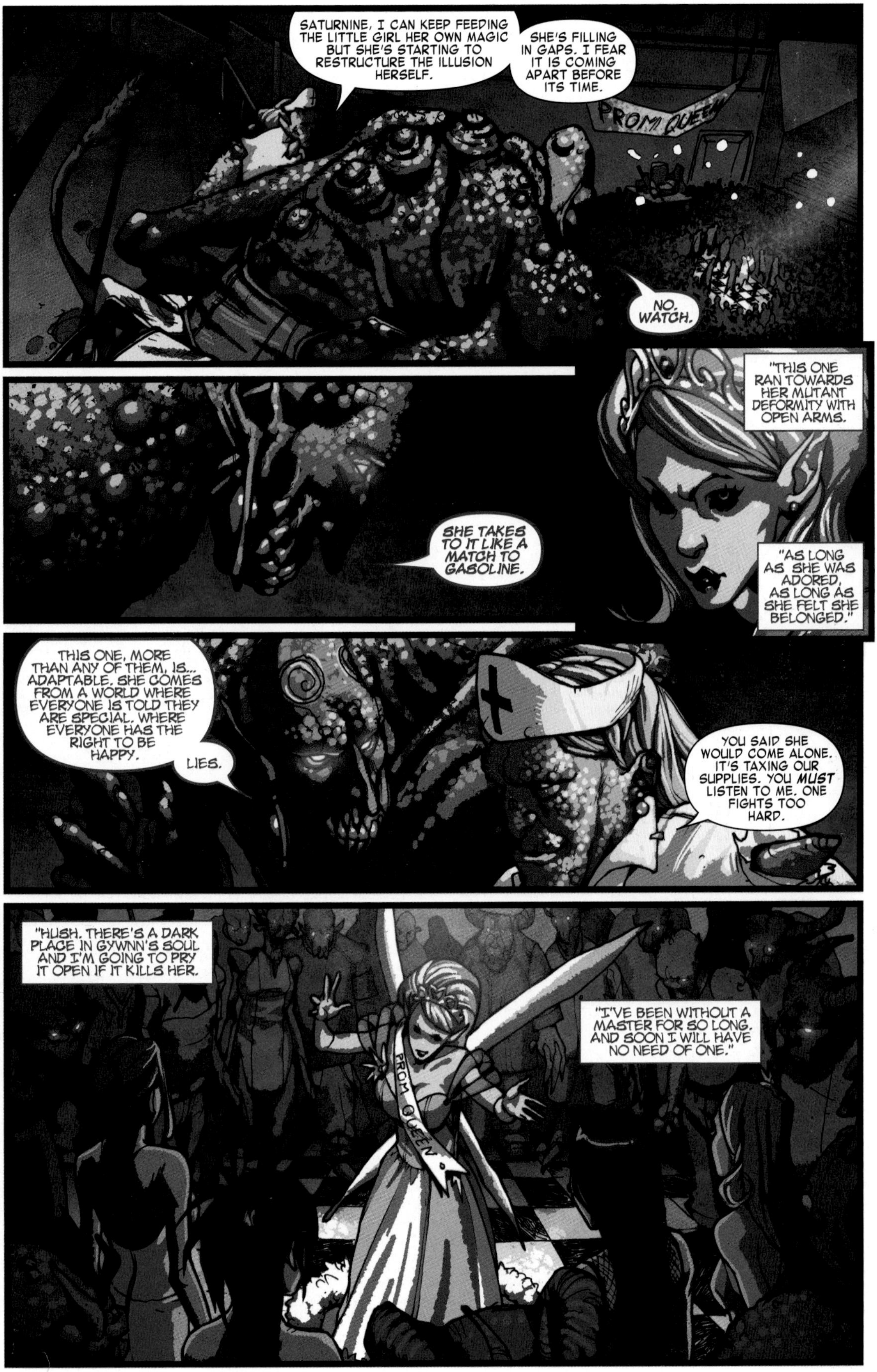
SATURNINE, I CAN KEEP FEEDING THE LITTLE GIRL HER OWN MAGIC BUT SHE'S STARTING TO RESTRUCTURE THE ILLUSION HERSELF.
SHE'S FILLING IN GAPS. I FEAR IT IS COMING APART BEFORE ITS TIME.
PROM QUEEN
NO. WATCH.
"THIS ONE RAN TOWARDS HER MUTANT DEFORMITY WITH OPEN ARMS.
SHE TAKES TO IT LIKE A MATCH TO GASOLINE.
"AS LONG AS SHE WAS ADORED, AS LONG AS SHE FELT SHE BELONGED."
THIS ONE, MORE THAN ANY OF THEM, IS... ADAPTABLE. SHE COMES FROM A WORLD WHERE EVERYONE IS TOLD THEY ARE SPECIAL. WHERE EVERYONE HAS THE RIGHT TO BE HAPPY.
LIES.
YOU SAID SHE WOULD COME ALONE. IT'S TAXING OUR SUPPLIES. YOU MUST LISTEN TO ME. ONE FIGHTS TOO HARD.
"HUSH. THERE'S A DARK PLACE IN GYWNN'S SOUL AND I'M GOING TO PRY IT OPEN IF IT KILLS HER.
"I'VE BEEN WITHOUT A MASTER FOR SO LONG. AND SOON I WILL HAVE NO NEED OF ONE."
PROM QUEEN

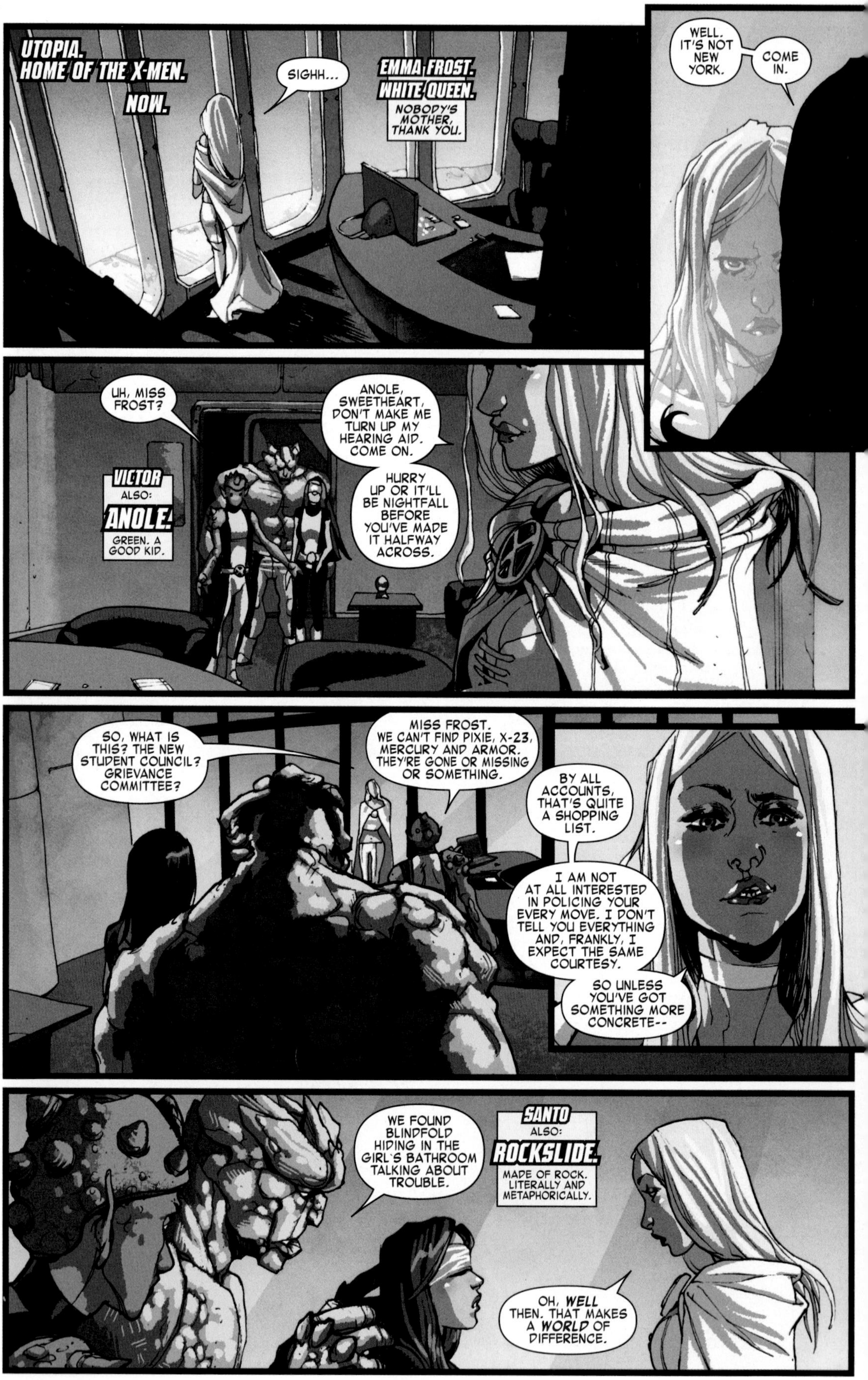
UTOPIA. HOME OF THE X-MEN.
NOW.
SIGHH...
EMMA FROST. WHITE QUEEN.
NOBODY'S MOTHER, THANK YOU.
WELL. IT'S NOT NEW YORK.
COME IN.
UH, MISS FROST?
VICTOR ALSO: ANOLE.
GREEN. A GOOD KID.
ANOLE, SWEETHEART, DON'T MAKE ME TURN UP MY HEARING AID. COME ON.
HURRY UP OR IT'LL BE NIGHTFALL BEFORE YOU'VE MADE IT HALFWAY ACROSS.
SO, WHAT IS THIS? THE NEW STUDENT COUNCIL? GRIEVANCE COMMITTEE?
MISS FROST. WE CAN'T FIND PIXIE, X-23, MERCURY AND ARMOR. THEY'RE GONE OR MISSING OR SOMETHING.
BY ALL ACCOUNTS, THAT'S QUITE A SHOPPING LIST.
I AM NOT AT ALL INTERESTED IN POLICING YOUR EVERY MOVE. I DON'T TELL YOU EVERYTHING AND, FRANKLY, I EXPECT THE SAME COURTESY.
SO UNLESS YOU'VE GOT SOMETHING MORE CONCRETE--
WE FOUND BLINDFOLD HIDING IN THE GIRL'S BATHROOM TALKING ABOUT TROUBLE.
SANTO ALSO: ROCKSLIDE.
MADE OF ROCK. LITERALLY AND METAPHORICALLY.
OH, WELL THEN. THAT MAKES A WORLD OF DIFFERENCE.

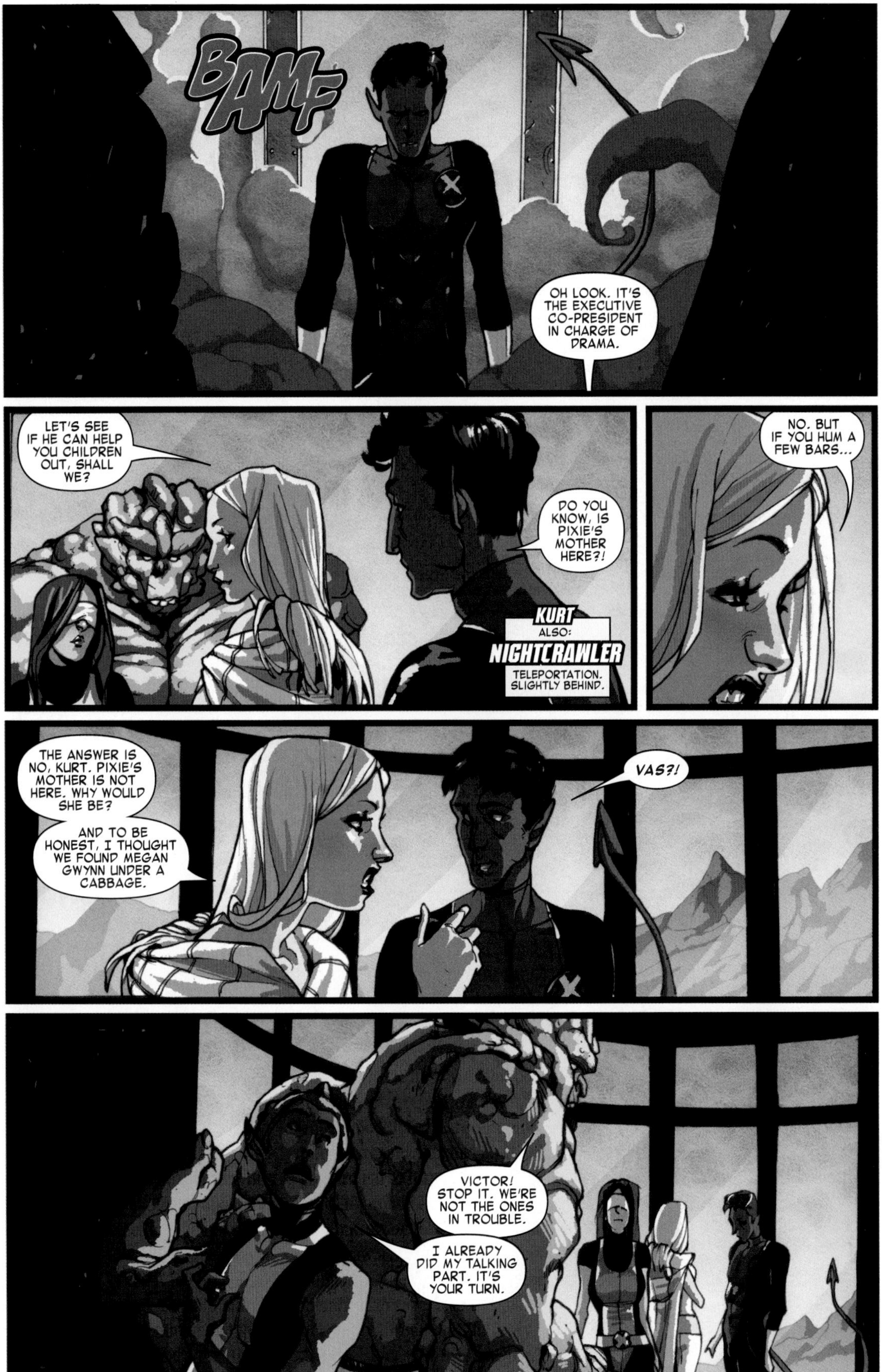
BAMF
OH LOOK. IT'S THE EXECUTIVE CO-PRESIDENT IN CHARGE OF DRAMA.
LET'S SEE IF HE CAN HELP YOU CHILDREN OUT, SHALL WE?
DO YOU KNOW, IS PIXIE'S MOTHER HERE?!
KURT
ALSO:
NIGHTCRAWLER
TELEPORTATION. SLIGHTLY BEHIND.
NO. BUT IF YOU HUM A FEW BARS...
THE ANSWER IS NO, KURT. PIXIE'S MOTHER IS NOT HERE. WHY WOULD SHE BE?
AND TO BE HONEST, I THOUGHT WE FOUND MEGAN GWYNN UNDER A CABBAGE.
VAS?!
VICTOR! STOP IT. WE'RE NOT THE ONES IN TROUBLE.
I ALREADY DID MY TALKING PART. IT'S YOUR TURN.

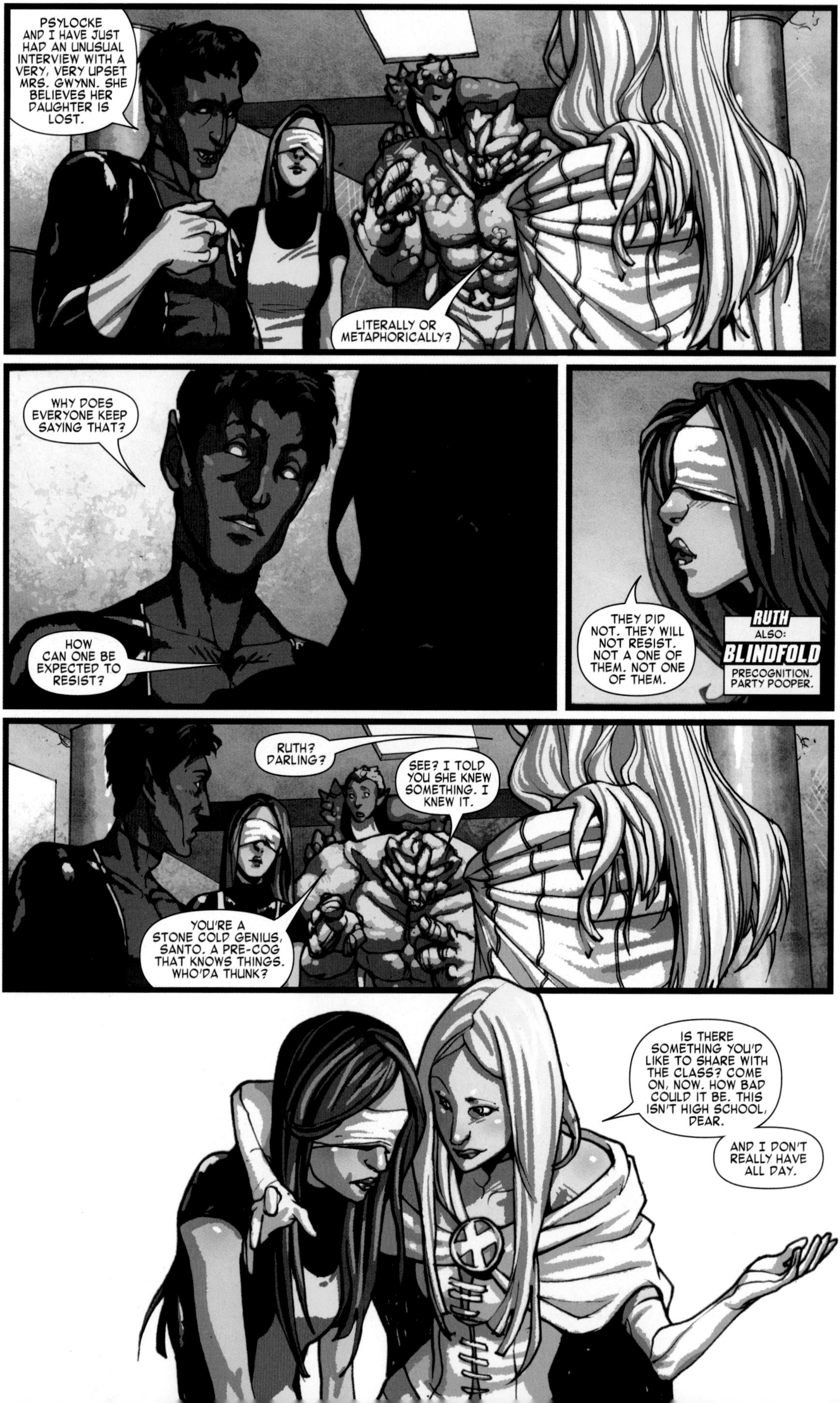
PSYLOCKE AND I HAVE JUST HAD AN UNUSUAL INTERVIEW WITH A VERY, VERY UPSET MRS. GWYNN. SHE BELIEVES HER DAUGHTER IS LOST.
LITERALLY OR METAPHORICALLY?
WHY DOES EVERYONE KEEP SAYING THAT?
HOW CAN ONE BE EXPECTED TO RESIST?
THEY DID NOT. THEY WILL NOT RESIST. NOT A ONE OF THEM. NOT ONE OF THEM.
RUTH
ALSO:
BLINDFOLD
PRECOGNITION. PARTY POOPER.
RUTH? DARLING?
SEE? I TOLD YOU SHE KNEW SOMETHING. I KNEW IT.
YOU'RE A STONE COLD GENIUS, SANTO. A PRE-COG THAT KNOWS THINGS. WHO'DA THUNK?
IS THERE SOMETHING YOU'D LIKE TO SHARE WITH THE CLASS? COME ON, NOW. HOW BAD COULD IT BE. THIS ISN'T HIGH SCHOOL, DEAR.
AND I DON'T REALLY HAVE ALL DAY.

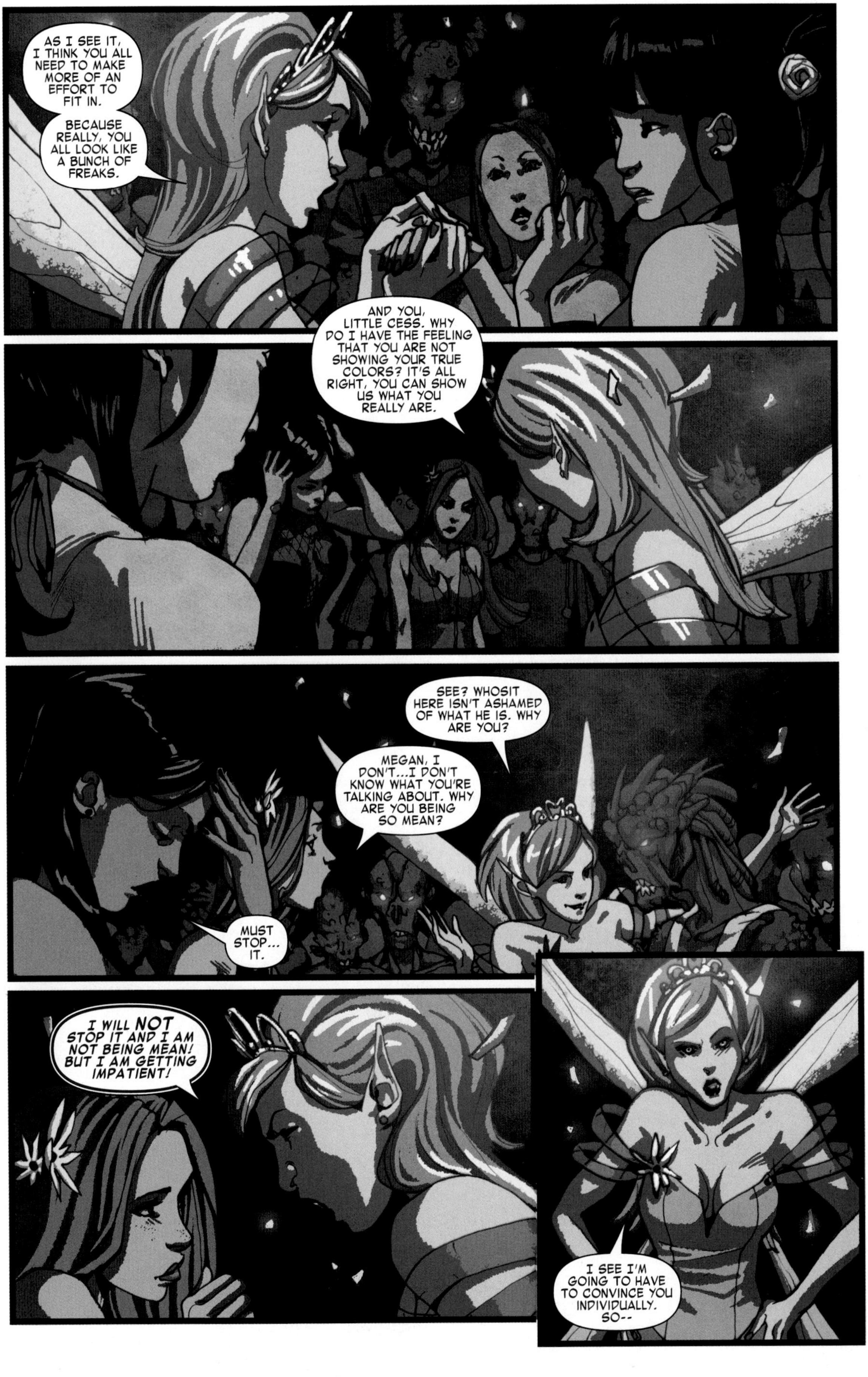
AS I SEE IT, I THINK YOU ALL NEED TO MAKE MORE OF AN EFFORT TO FIT IN.
BECAUSE REALLY, YOU ALL LOOK LIKE A BUNCH OF FREAKS.
AND YOU, LITTLE CESS. WHY DO I HAVE THE FEELING THAT YOU ARE NOT SHOWING YOUR TRUE COLORS? IT'S ALL RIGHT, YOU CAN SHOW US WHAT YOU REALLY ARE.
SEE? WHOSIT HERE ISN'T ASHAMED OF WHAT HE IS. WHY ARE YOU?
MEGAN, I DON'T...I DON'T KNOW WHAT YOU'RE TALKING ABOUT. WHY ARE YOU BEING SO MEAN?
MUST STOP... IT.
I WILL NOT STOP IT AND I AM NOT BEING MEAN! BUT I AM GETTING IMPATIENT!
I SEE I'M GOING TO HAVE TO CONVINCE YOU INDIVIDUALLY. SO--

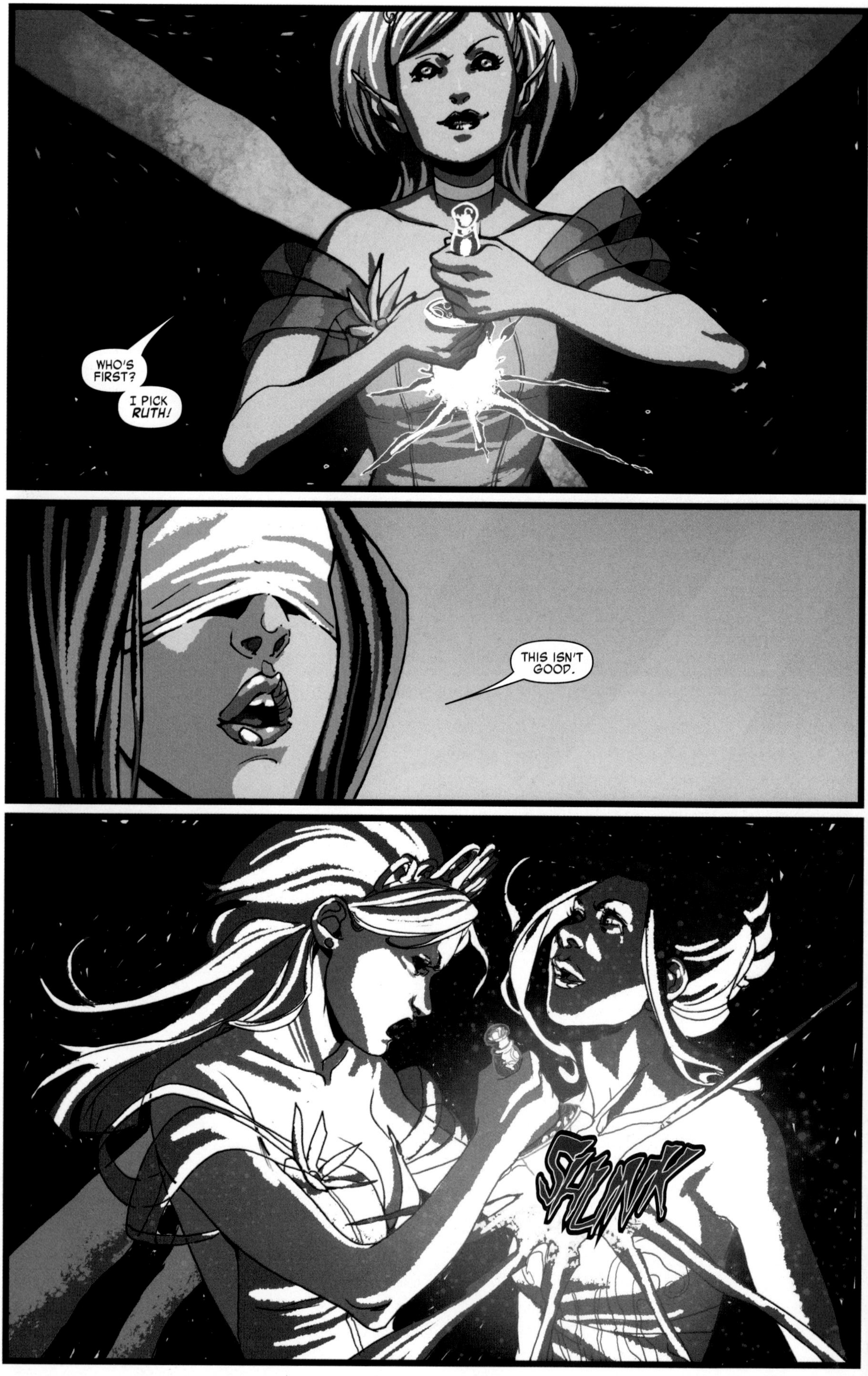
WHO'S FIRST?
I PICK RUTH!
THIS ISN'T GOOD.
SHUNK

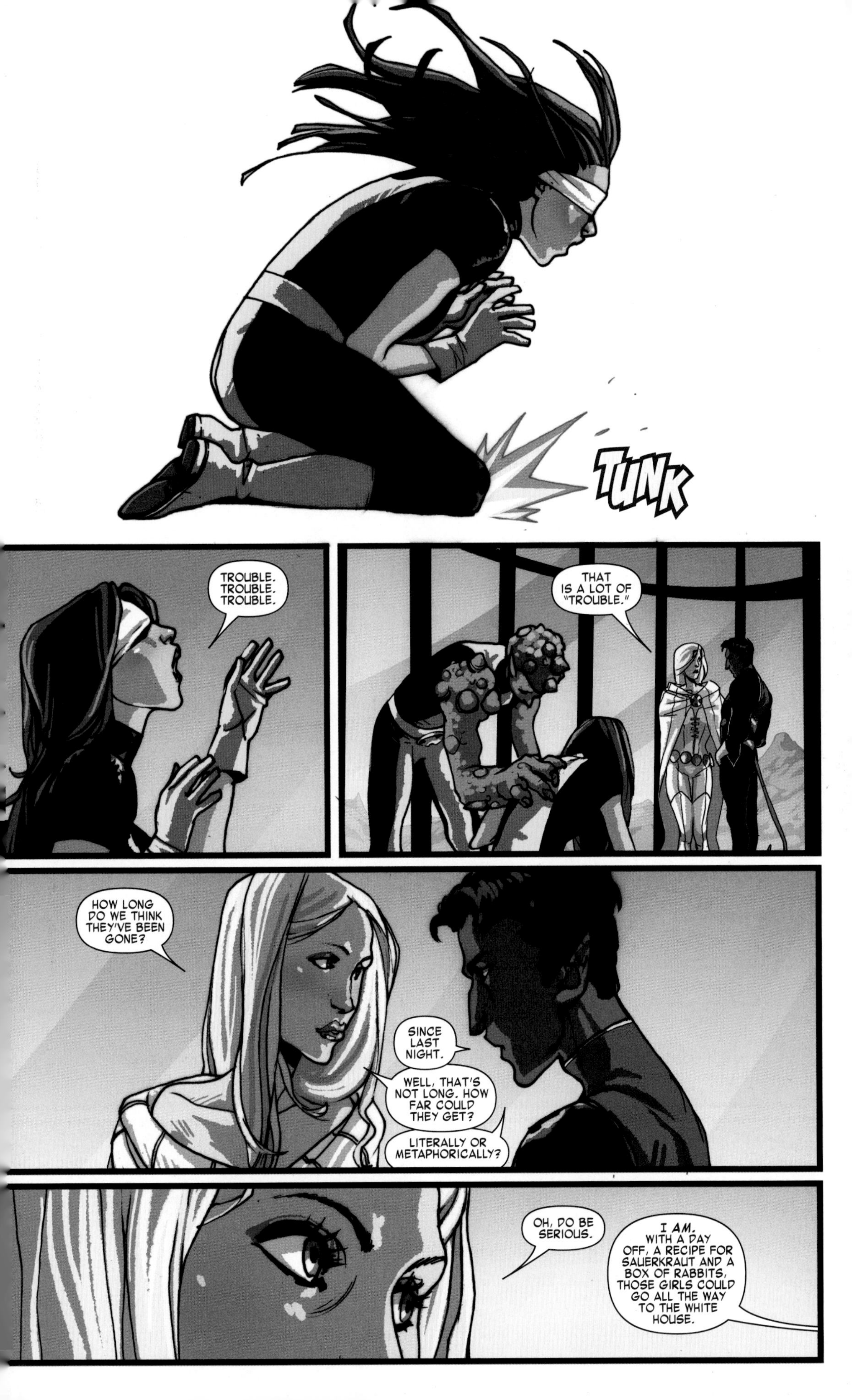
TUNK
TROUBLE. TROUBLE. TROUBLE.
THAT IS A LOT OF "TROUBLE."
HOW LONG DO WE THINK THEY'VE BEEN GONE?
SINCE LAST NIGHT.
WELL, THAT'S NOT LONG. HOW FAR COULD THEY GET?
LITERALLY OR METAPHORICALLY?
OH, DO BE SERIOUS.
I AM. WITH A DAY OFF, A RECIPE FOR SAUERKRAUT AND A BOX OF RABBITS, THOSE GIRLS COULD GO ALL THE WAY TO THE WHITE HOUSE.

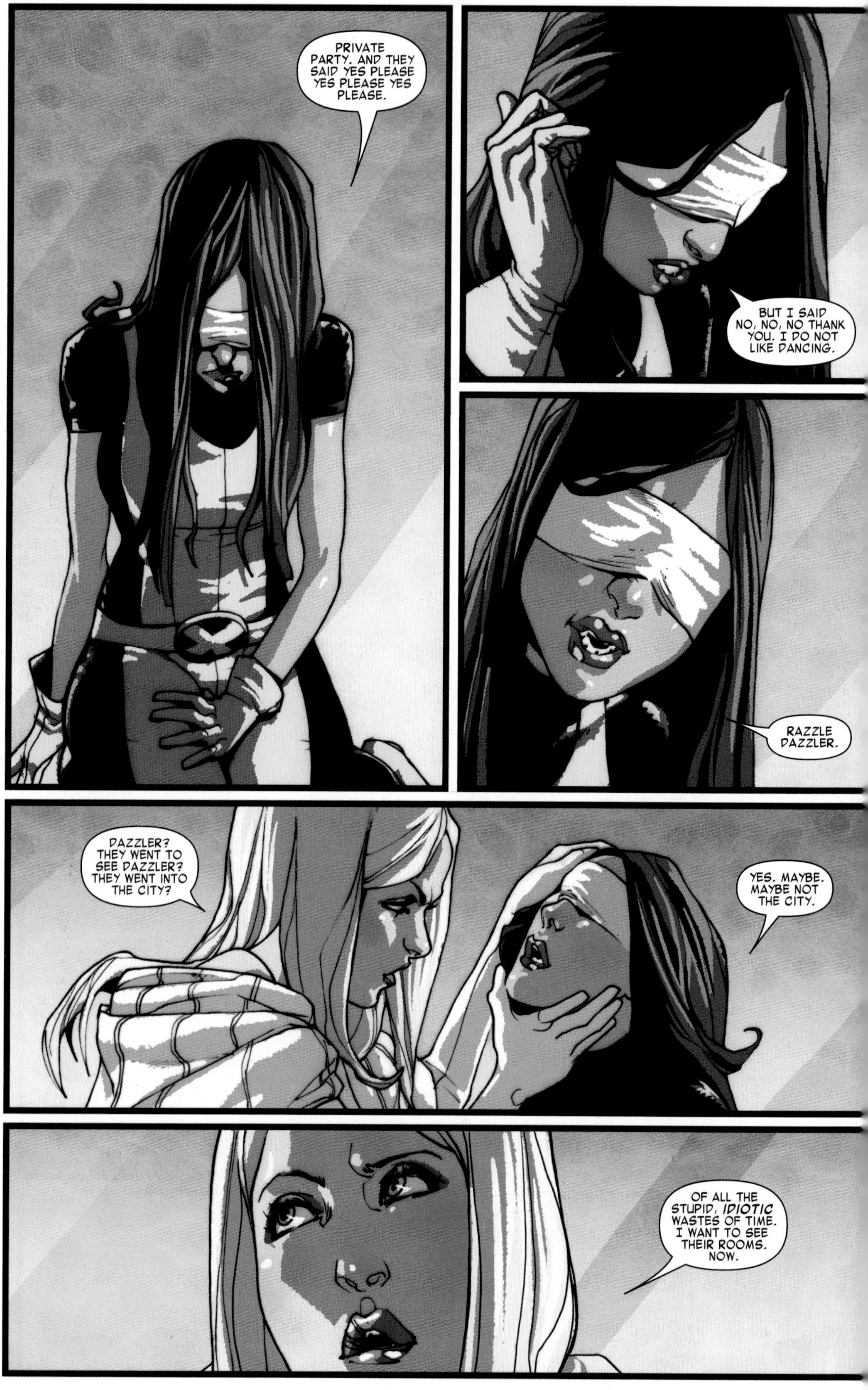
PRIVATE PARTY. AND THEY SAID YES PLEASE YES PLEASE YES PLEASE.
BUT I SAID NO, NO, NO THANK YOU. I DO NOT LIKE DANCING.
RAZZLE DAZZLER.
DAZZLER? THEY WENT TO SEE DAZZLER? THEY WENT INTO THE CITY?
YES. MAYBE. MAYBE NOT THE CITY.
OF ALL THE STUPID, *IDIOTIC* WASTES OF TIME. I WANT TO SEE THEIR ROOMS. NOW.

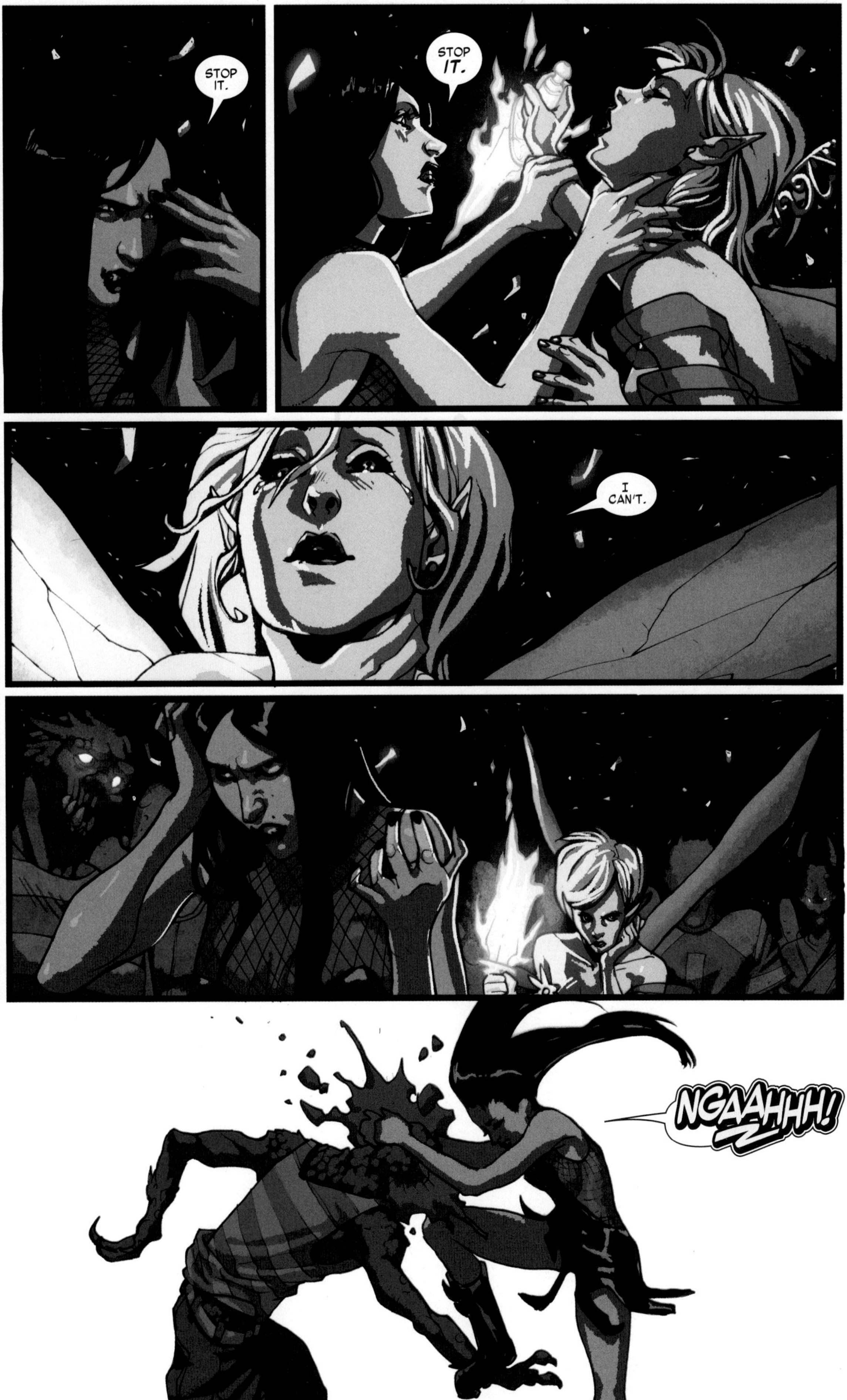
STOP IT.
STOP IT.
I CAN'T.
NGAAHHH!

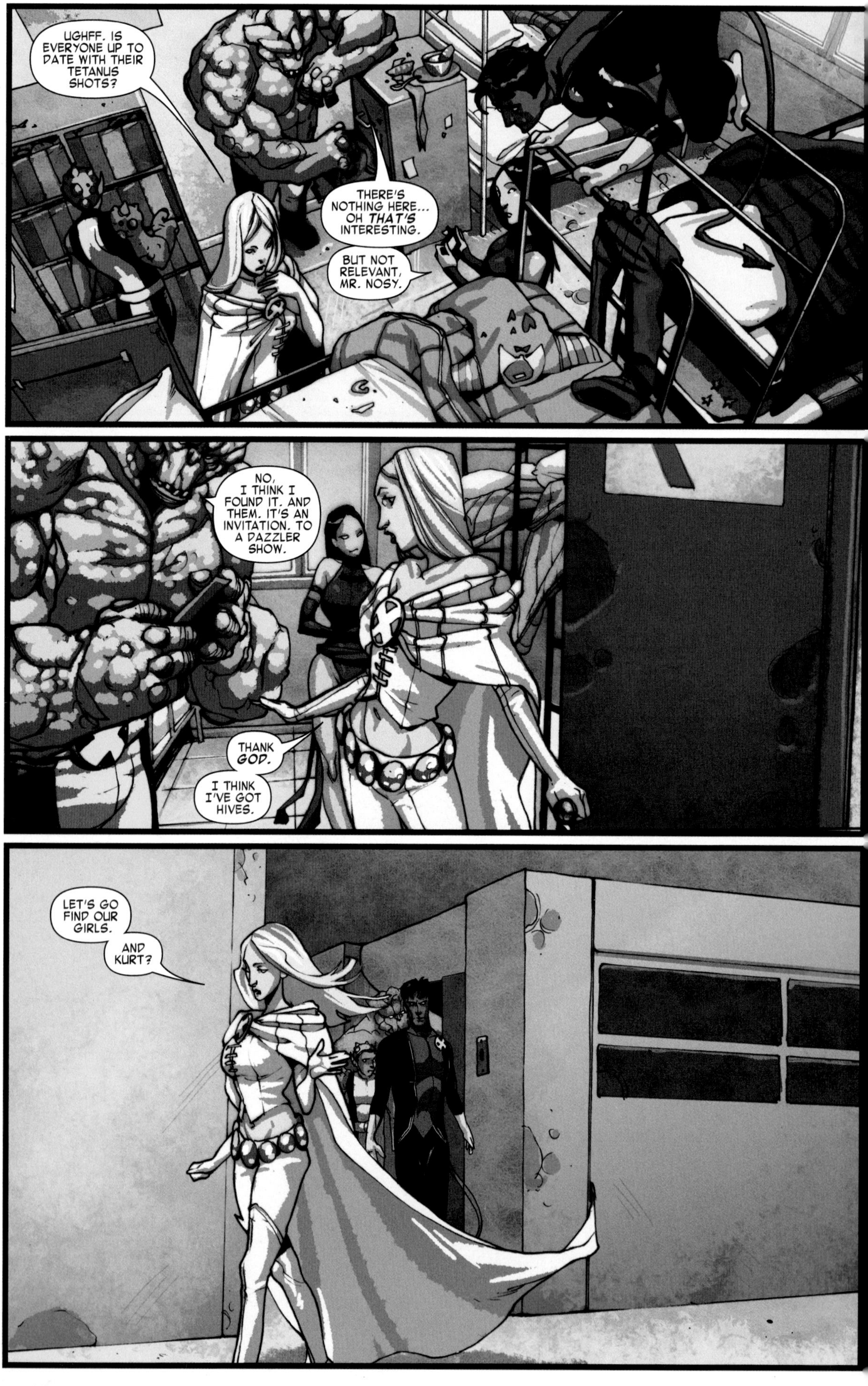
UGHFF. IS EVERYONE UP TO DATE WITH THEIR TETANUS SHOTS?
THERE'S NOTHING HERE... OH THAT'S INTERESTING.
BUT NOT RELEVANT, MR. NOSY.
NO, I THINK I FOUND IT. AND THEM. IT'S AN INVITATION. TO A DAZZLER SHOW.
THANK GOD.
I THINK I'VE GOT HIVES.
LET'S GO FIND OUR GIRLS.
AND KURT?

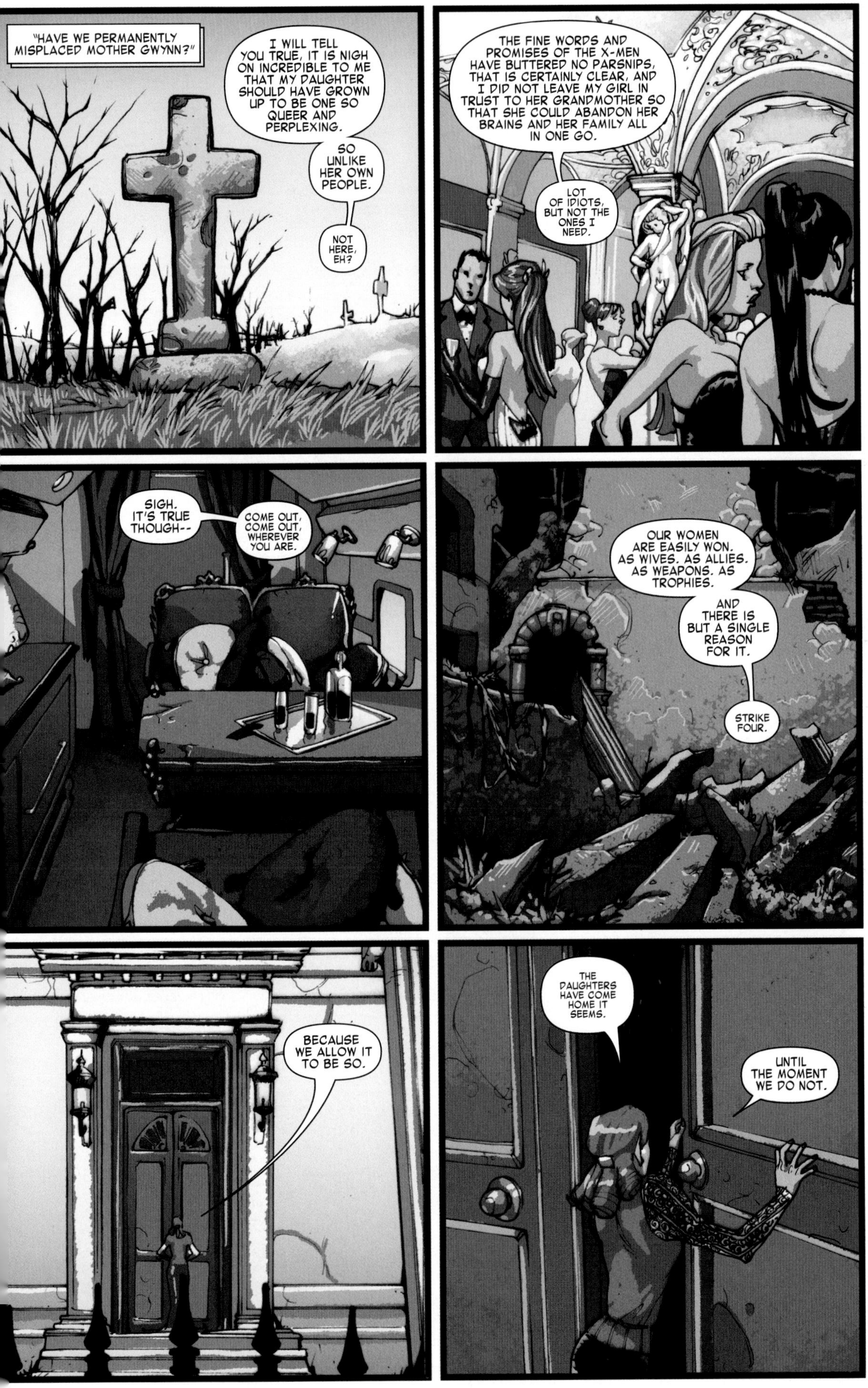
"HAVE WE PERMANENTLY MISPLACED MOTHER GWYNN?"
I WILL TELL YOU TRUE, IT IS NIGH ON INCREDIBLE TO ME THAT MY DAUGHTER SHOULD HAVE GROWN UP TO BE ONE SO QUEER AND PERPLEXING.
SO UNLIKE HER OWN PEOPLE.
NOT HERE, EH?
THE FINE WORDS AND PROMISES OF THE X-MEN HAVE BUTTERED NO PARSNIPS, THAT IS CERTAINLY CLEAR, AND I DID NOT LEAVE MY GIRL IN TRUST TO HER GRANDMOTHER SO THAT SHE COULD ABANDON HER BRAINS AND HER FAMILY ALL IN ONE GO.
LOT OF IDIOTS, BUT NOT THE ONES I NEED.
SIGH. IT'S TRUE THOUGH--
COME OUT, COME OUT, WHEREVER YOU ARE.
OUR WOMEN ARE EASILY WON. AS WIVES. AS ALLIES. AS WEAPONS. AS TROPHIES.
AND THERE IS BUT A SINGLE REASON FOR IT.
STRIKE FOUR.
BECAUSE WE ALLOW IT TO BE SO.
THE DAUGHTERS HAVE COME HOME IT SEEMS.
UNTIL THE MOMENT WE DO NOT.

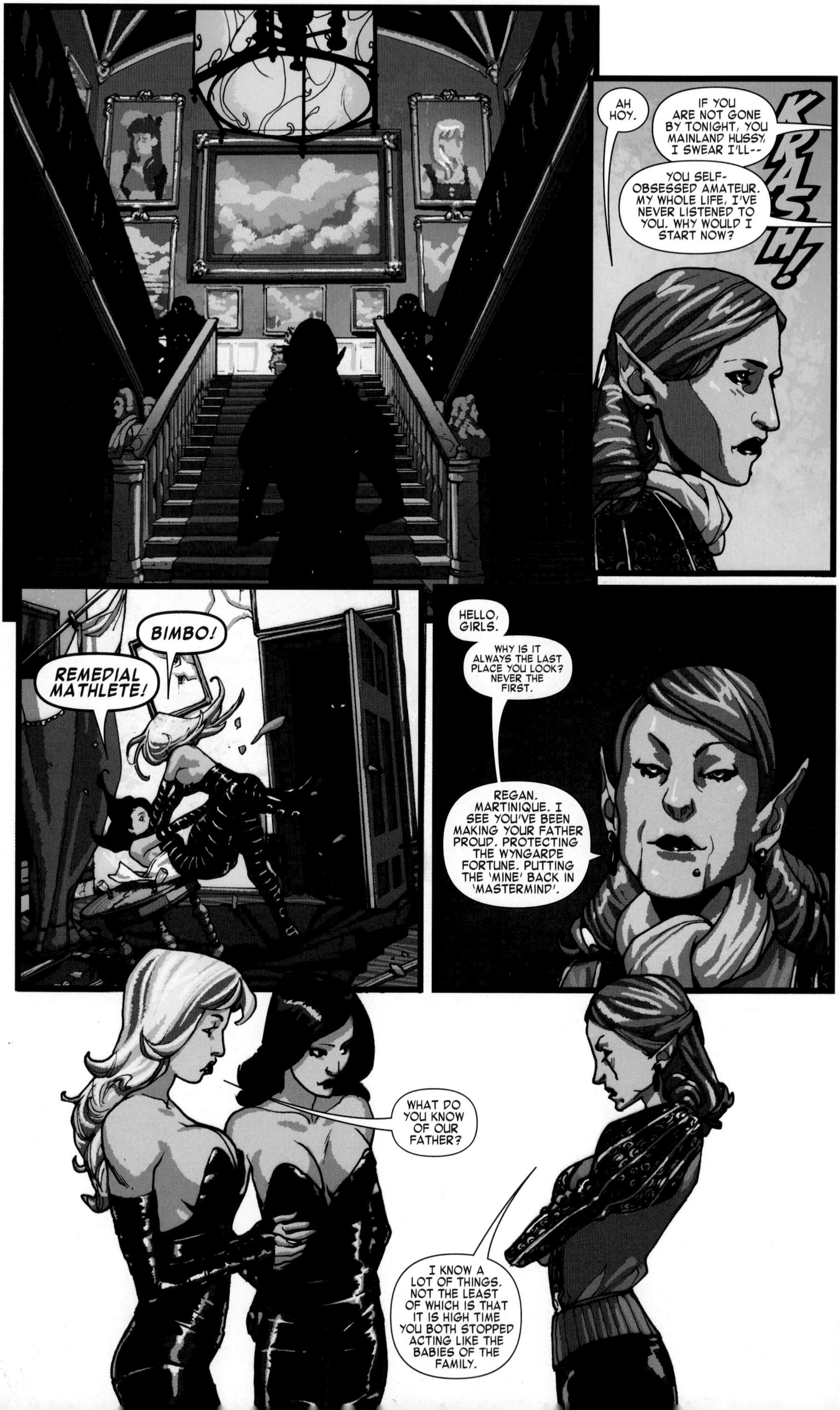
AH HOY.
IF YOU ARE NOT GONE BY TONIGHT, YOU MAINLAND HUSSY, I SWEAR I'LL--
YOU SELF-OBSESSED AMATEUR. MY WHOLE LIFE, I'VE NEVER LISTENED TO YOU. WHY WOULD I START NOW?
KRASH!
BIMBO!
REMEDIAL MATHLETE!
HELLO, GIRLS.
WHY IS IT ALWAYS THE LAST PLACE YOU LOOK? NEVER THE FIRST.
REGAN. MARTINIQUE. I SEE YOU'VE BEEN MAKING YOUR FATHER PROUD. PROTECTING THE WYNGARDE FORTUNE. PUTTING THE 'MINE' BACK IN 'MASTERMIND'.
WHAT DO YOU KNOW OF OUR FATHER?
I KNOW A LOT OF THINGS. NOT THE LEAST OF WHICH IS THAT IT IS HIGH TIME YOU BOTH STOPPED ACTING LIKE THE BABIES OF THE FAMILY.

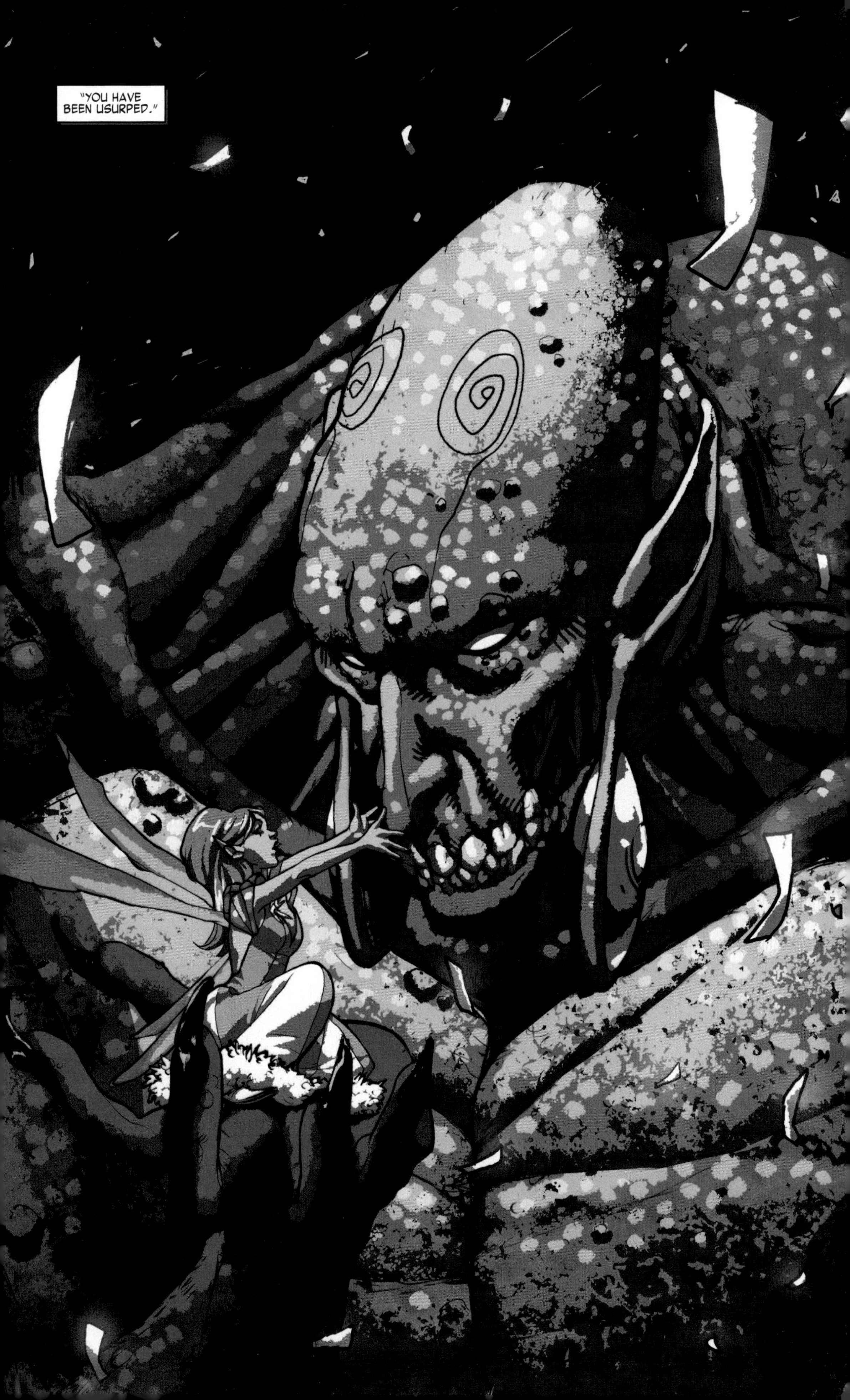
"YOU HAVE BEEN USURPED."

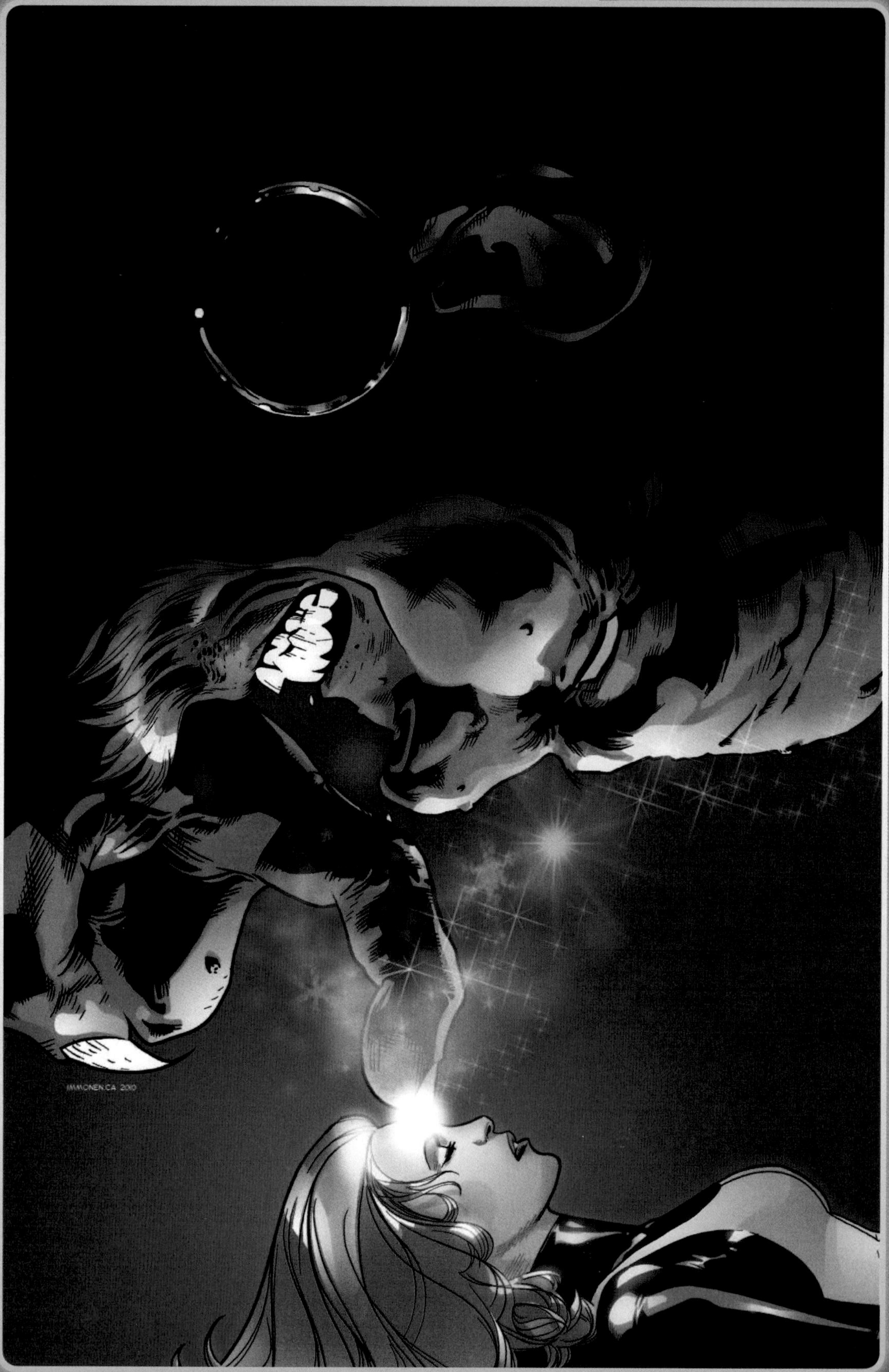
IMMONEN.CA 2010

# THREE

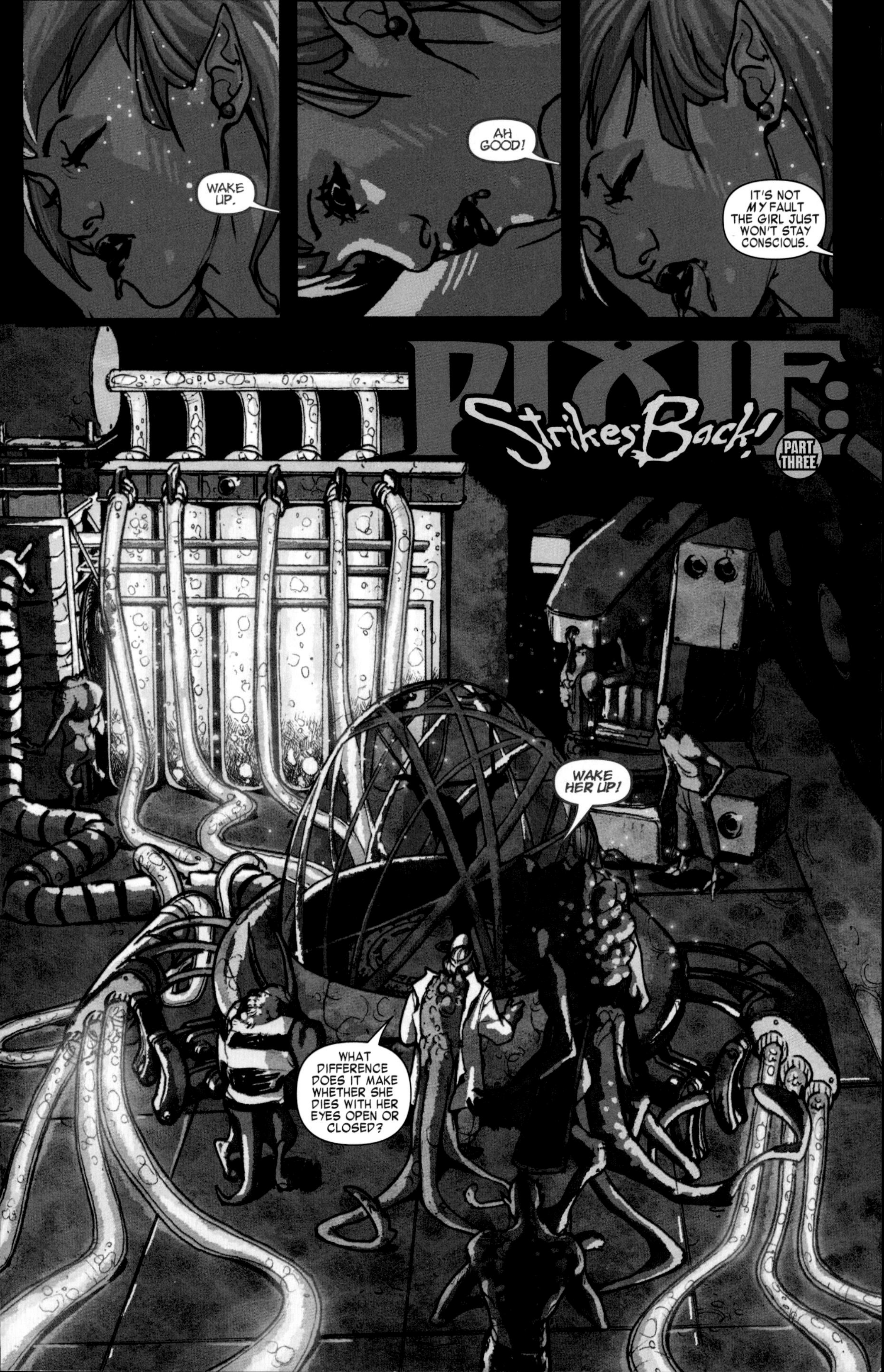
WAKE UP.
AH GOOD!
IT'S NOT MY FAULT THE GIRL JUST WON'T STAY CONSCIOUS.
PIXIE
Strikes Back!
PART THREE
WAKE HER UP!
WHAT DIFFERENCE DOES IT MAKE WHETHER SHE DIES WITH HER EYES OPEN OR CLOSED?

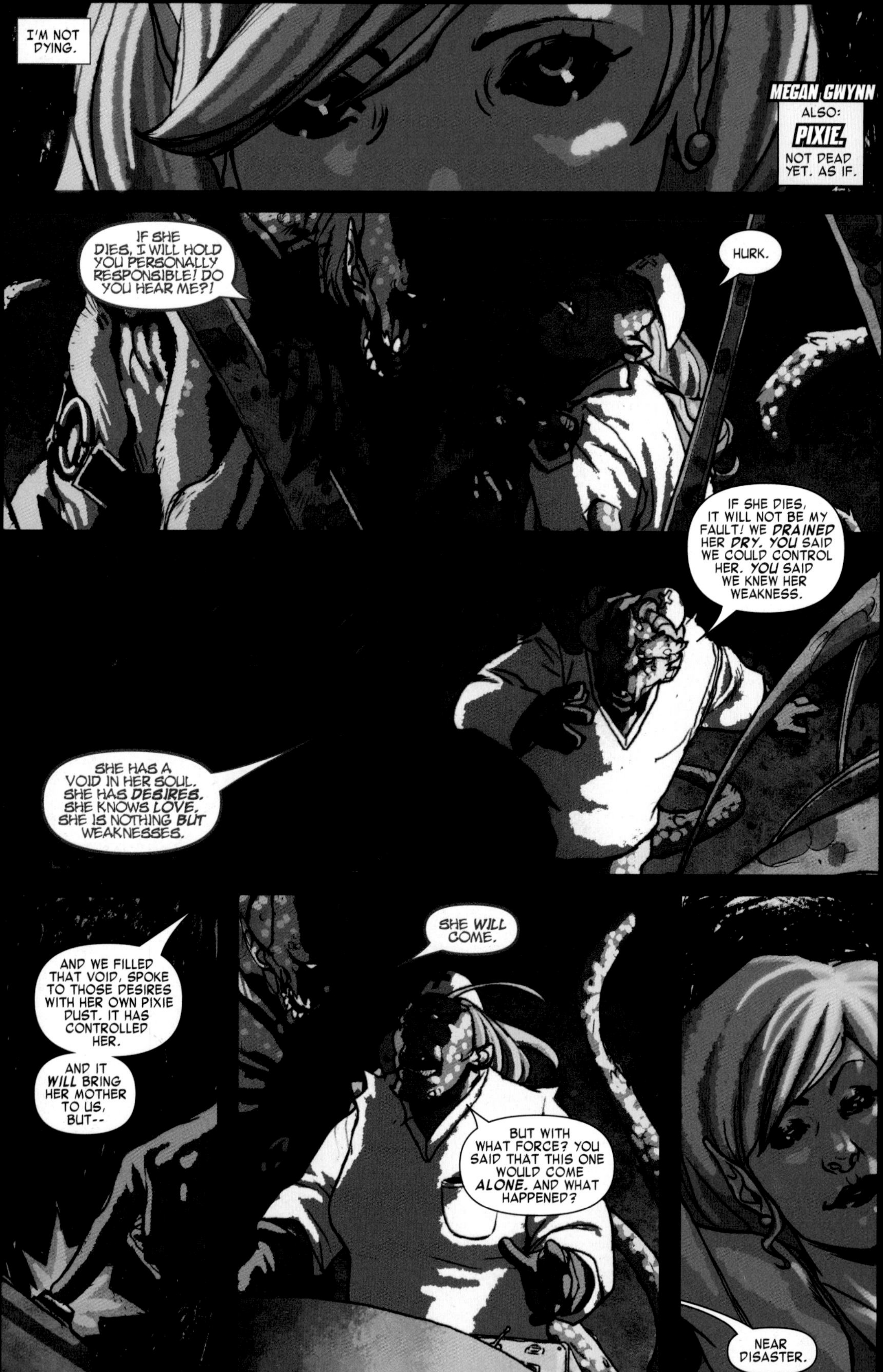

I'M NOT DYING.
MEGAN GWYNN
ALSO:
PIXIE.
NOT DEAD YET. AS IF.
IF SHE DIES, I WILL HOLD YOU PERSONALLY RESPONSIBLE! DO YOU HEAR ME?!
HURK.
IF SHE DIES, IT WILL NOT BE MY FAULT! WE DRAINED HER DRY. YOU SAID WE COULD CONTROL HER. YOU SAID WE KNEW HER WEAKNESS.
SHE HAS A VOID IN HER SOUL. SHE HAS DESIRES. SHE KNOWS LOVE. SHE IS NOTHING BUT WEAKNESSES.
AND WE FILLED THAT VOID, SPOKE TO THOSE DESIRES WITH HER OWN PIXIE DUST. IT HAS CONTROLLED HER.
AND IT WILL BRING HER MOTHER TO US, BUT--
SHE WILL COME.
BUT WITH WHAT FORCE? YOU SAID THAT THIS ONE WOULD COME ALONE. AND WHAT HAPPENED?
NEAR DISASTER.

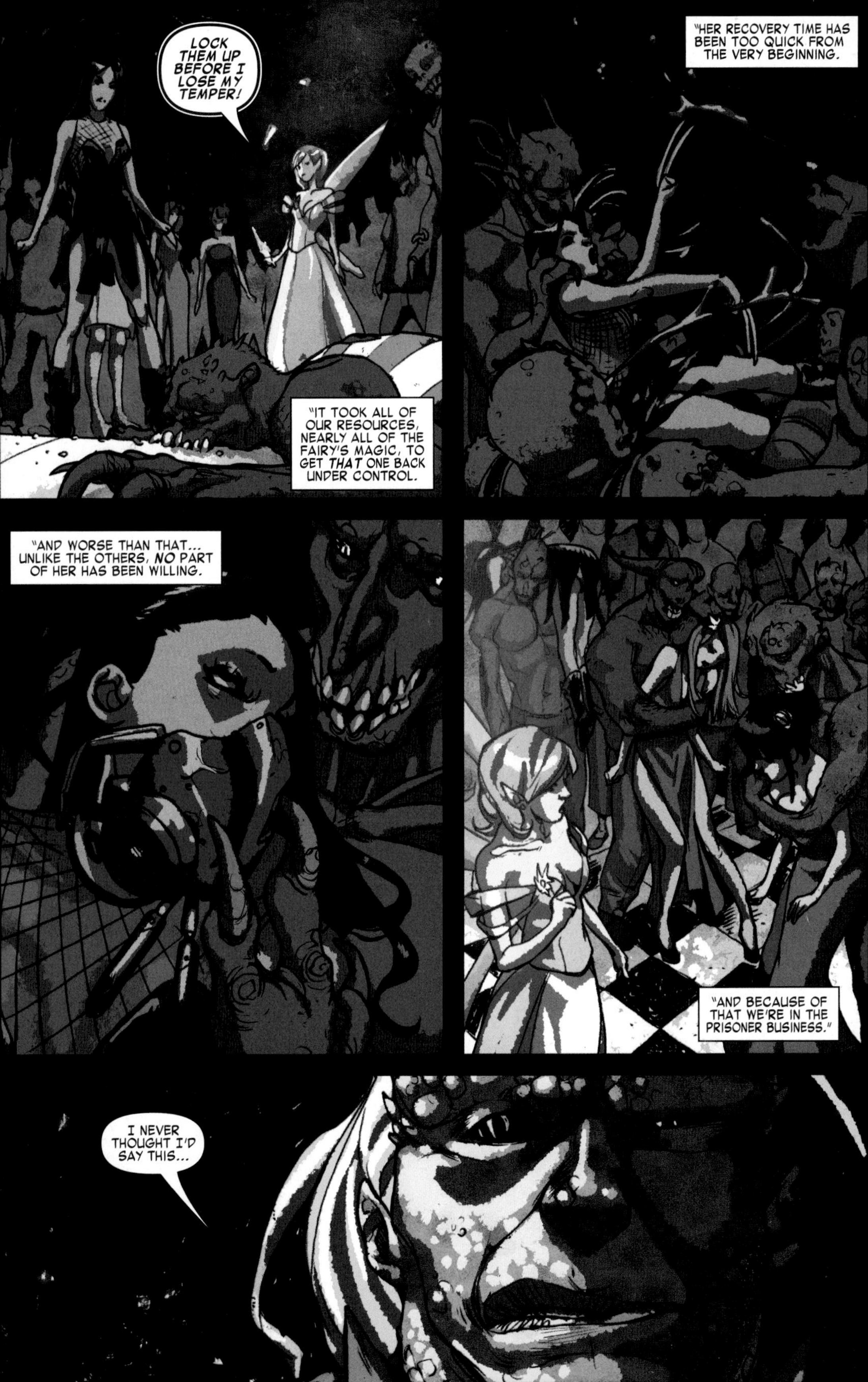
LOCK THEM UP BEFORE I LOSE MY TEMPER!
"IT TOOK ALL OF OUR RESOURCES, NEARLY ALL OF THE FAIRY'S MAGIC, TO GET THAT ONE BACK UNDER CONTROL.
"HER RECOVERY TIME HAS BEEN TOO QUICK FROM THE VERY BEGINNING.
"AND WORSE THAN THAT... UNLIKE THE OTHERS, NO PART OF HER HAS BEEN WILLING.
"AND BECAUSE OF THAT WE'RE IN THE PRISONER BUSINESS."
I NEVER THOUGHT I'D SAY THIS...

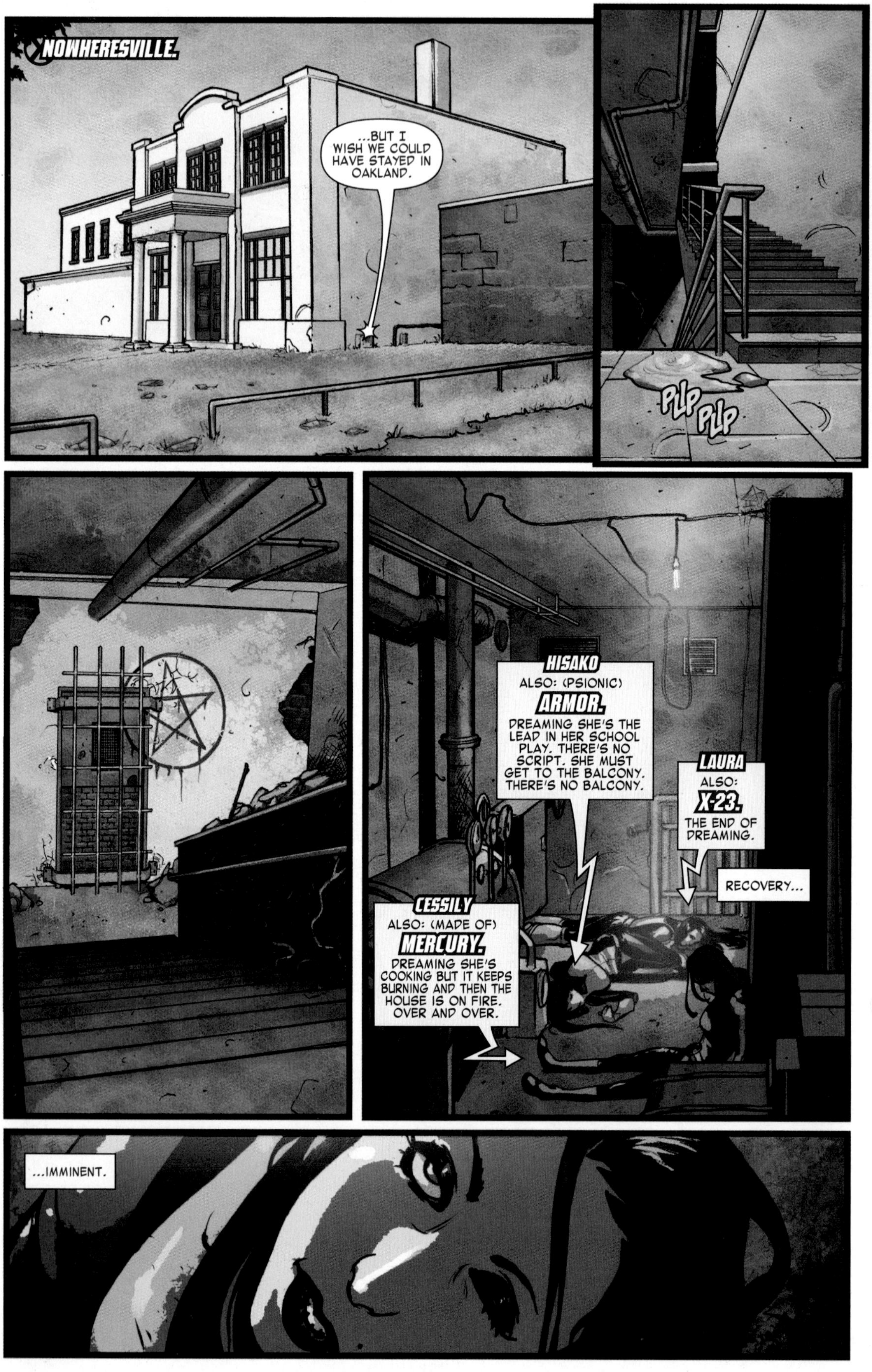
NOWHERESVILLE.
...BUT I WISH WE COULD HAVE STAYED IN OAKLAND.
PLIP PLIP
HISAKO
ALSO: (PSIONIC)
ARMOR.
DREAMING SHE'S THE LEAD IN HER SCHOOL PLAY. THERE'S NO SCRIPT. SHE MUST GET TO THE BALCONY. THERE'S NO BALCONY.
LAURA
ALSO:
X-23.
THE END OF DREAMING.
RECOVERY...
CESSILY
ALSO: (MADE OF)
MERCURY.
DREAMING SHE'S COOKING BUT IT KEEPS BURNING AND THEN THE HOUSE IS ON FIRE. OVER AND OVER.
...IMMINENT.

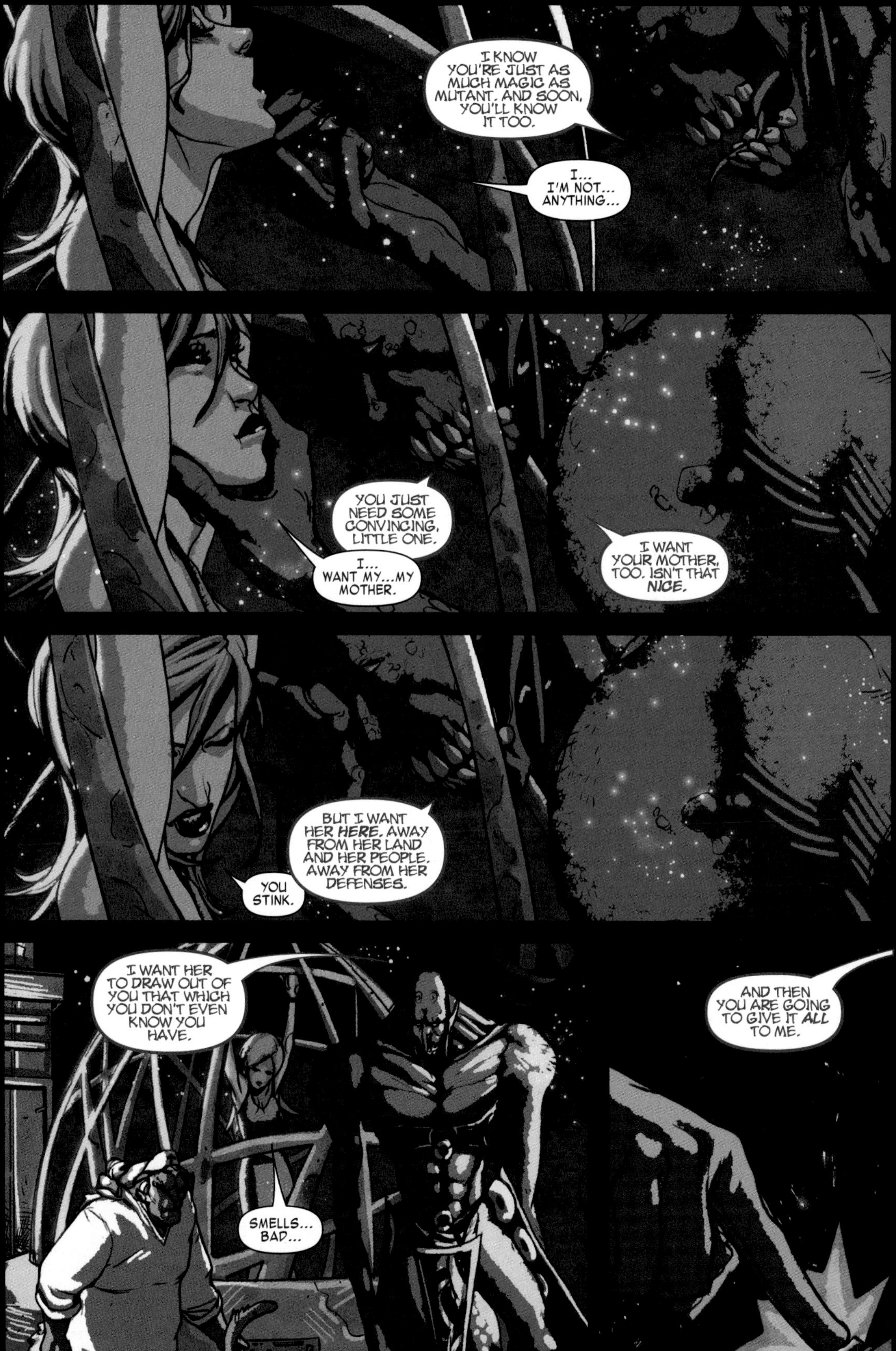
I KNOW YOU'RE JUST AS MUCH MAGIC AS MUTANT. AND SOON, YOU'LL KNOW IT TOO.
I... I'M NOT... ANYTHING...
YOU JUST NEED SOME CONVINCING, LITTLE ONE.
I... WANT MY...MY MOTHER.
I WANT YOUR MOTHER, TOO. ISN'T THAT NICE.
BUT I WANT HER HERE. AWAY FROM HER LAND AND HER PEOPLE. AWAY FROM HER DEFENSES.
YOU STINK.
I WANT HER TO DRAW OUT OF YOU THAT WHICH YOU DON'T EVEN KNOW YOU HAVE.
SMELLS... BAD...
AND THEN YOU ARE GOING TO GIVE IT ALL TO ME.

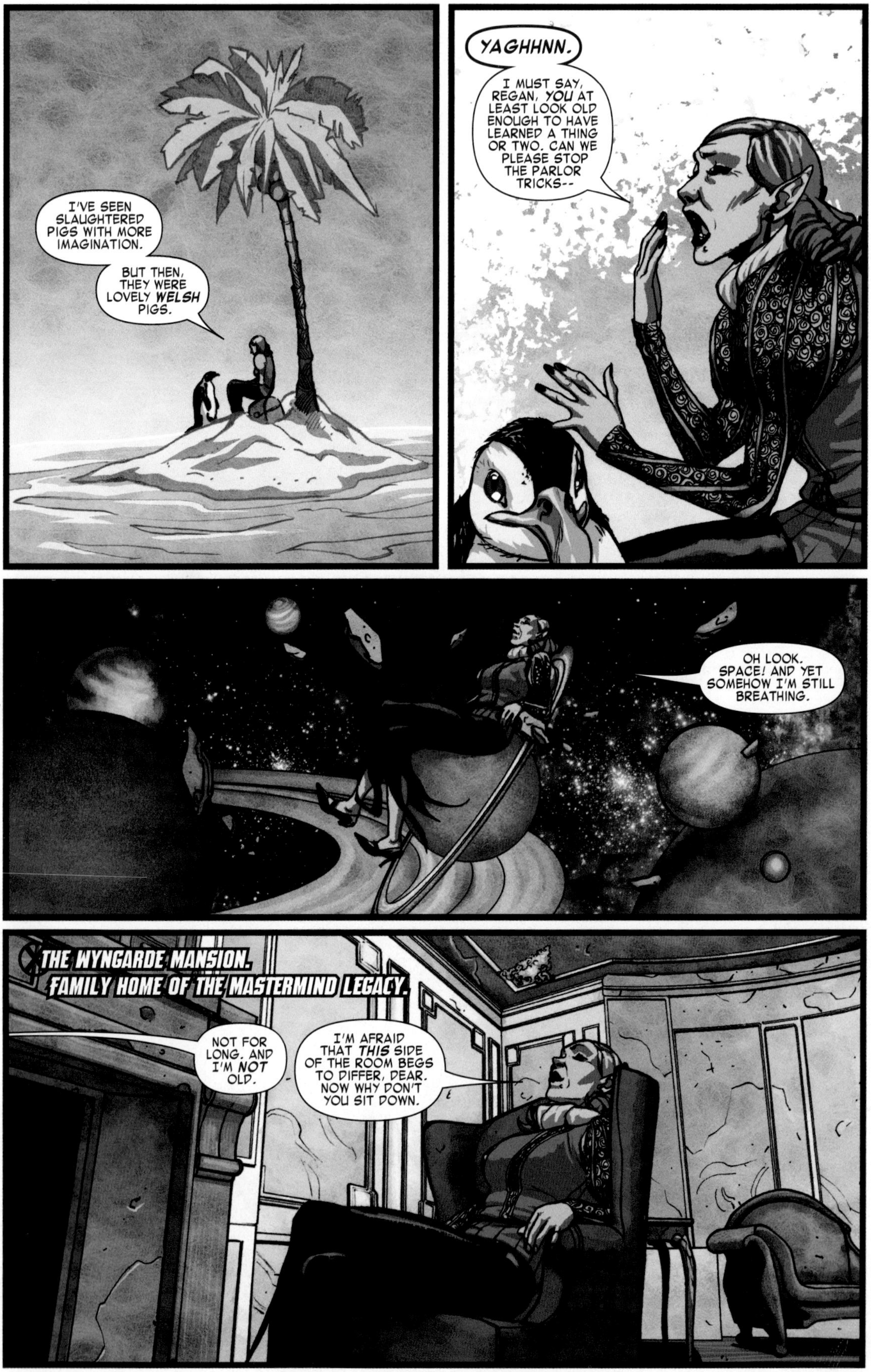
I'VE SEEN SLAUGHTERED PIGS WITH MORE IMAGINATION.
BUT THEN, THEY WERE LOVELY WELSH PIGS.
YAGHHNN.
I MUST SAY, REGAN, YOU AT LEAST LOOK OLD ENOUGH TO HAVE LEARNED A THING OR TWO. CAN WE PLEASE STOP THE PARLOR TRICKS--
OH LOOK. SPACE! AND YET SOMEHOW I'M STILL BREATHING.
THE WYNGARDE MANSION. FAMILY HOME OF THE MASTERMIND LEGACY.
NOT FOR LONG. AND I'M NOT OLD.
I'M AFRAID THAT THIS SIDE OF THE ROOM BEGS TO DIFFER, DEAR. NOW WHY DON'T YOU SIT DOWN.

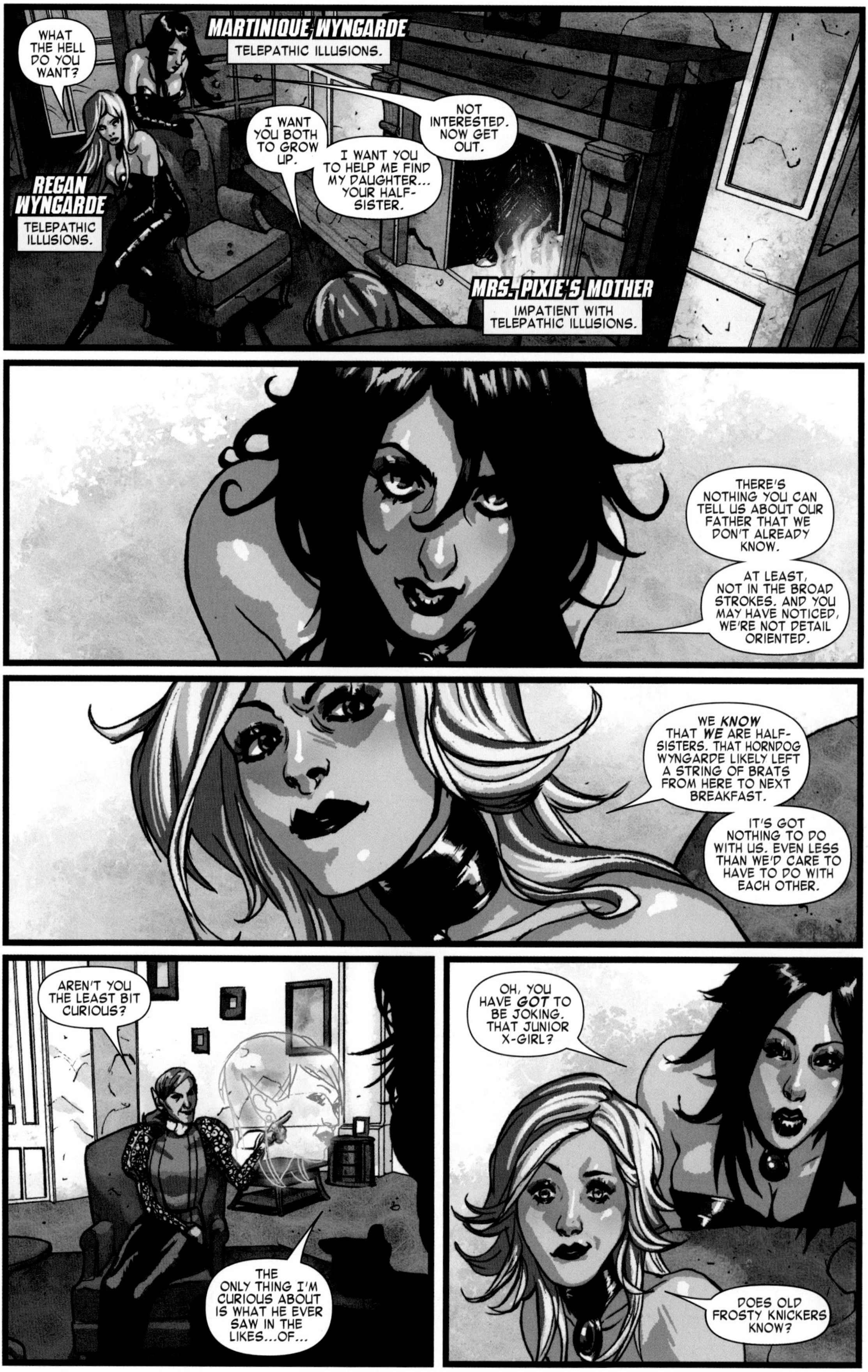
WHAT THE HELL DO YOU WANT?
MARTINIQUE WYNGARDE
TELEPATHIC ILLUSIONS.
REGAN WYNGARDE
TELEPATHIC ILLUSIONS.
I WANT YOU BOTH TO GROW UP.
NOT INTERESTED. NOW GET OUT.
I WANT YOU TO HELP ME FIND MY DAUGHTER... YOUR HALF-SISTER.
MRS. PIXIE'S MOTHER
IMPATIENT WITH TELEPATHIC ILLUSIONS.
THERE'S NOTHING YOU CAN TELL US ABOUT OUR FATHER THAT WE DON'T ALREADY KNOW.
AT LEAST, NOT IN THE BROAD STROKES. AND YOU MAY HAVE NOTICED, WE'RE NOT DETAIL ORIENTED.
WE KNOW THAT WE ARE HALF-SISTERS. THAT HORNDOG WYNGARDE LIKELY LEFT A STRING OF BRATS FROM HERE TO NEXT BREAKFAST.
IT'S GOT NOTHING TO DO WITH US. EVEN LESS THAN WE'D CARE TO HAVE TO DO WITH EACH OTHER.
AREN'T YOU THE LEAST BIT CURIOUS?
THE ONLY THING I'M CURIOUS ABOUT IS WHAT HE EVER SAW IN THE LIKES...OF...
OH, YOU HAVE GOT TO BE JOKING. THAT JUNIOR X-GIRL?
DOES OLD FROSTY KNICKERS KNOW?

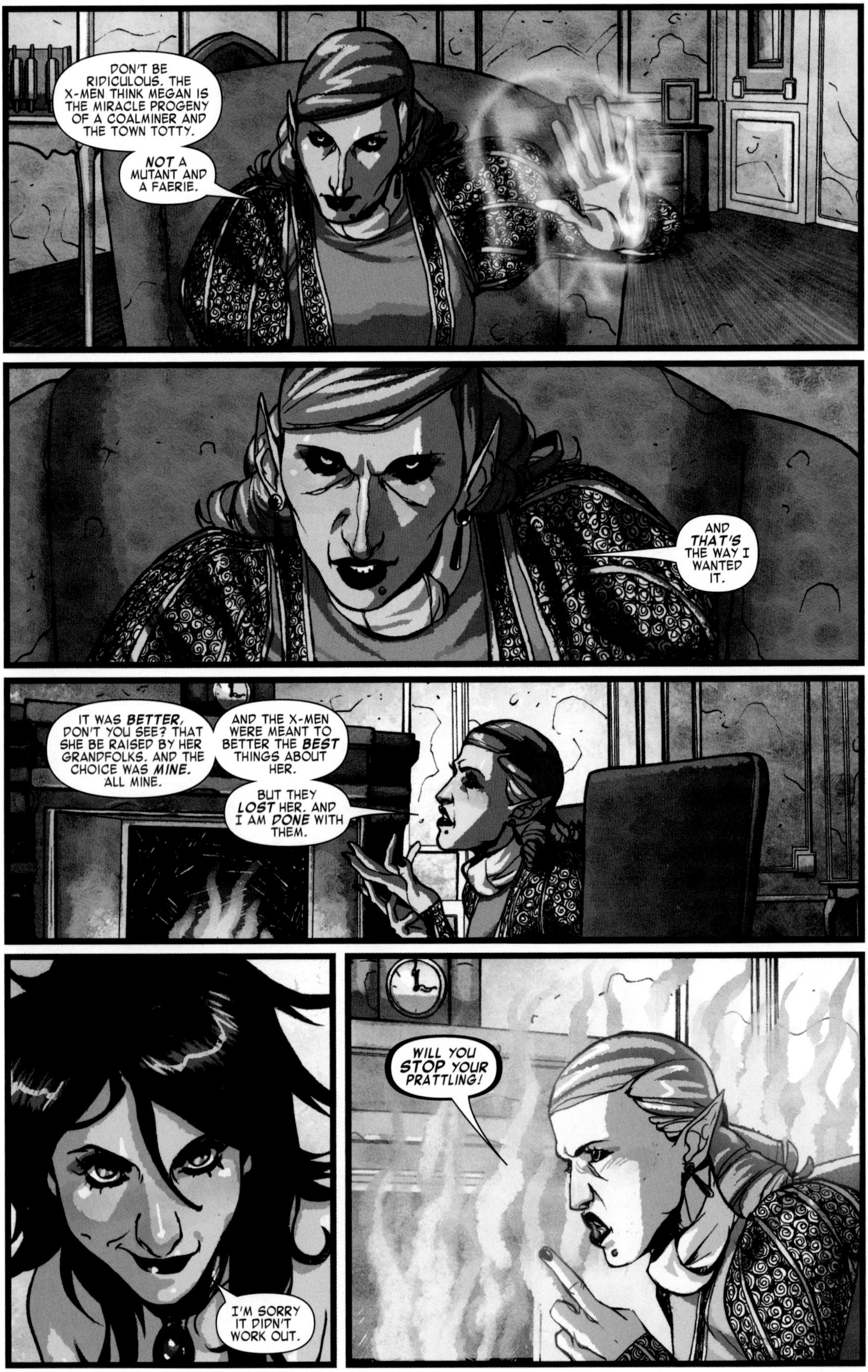
DON'T BE RIDICULOUS. THE X-MEN THINK MEGAN IS THE MIRACLE PROGENY OF A COALMINER AND THE TOWN TOTTY.
NOT A MUTANT AND A FAERIE.
AND THAT'S THE WAY I WANTED IT.
IT WAS BETTER, DON'T YOU SEE? THAT SHE BE RAISED BY HER GRANDFOLKS. AND THE CHOICE WAS MINE. ALL MINE.
AND THE X-MEN WERE MEANT TO BETTER THE BEST THINGS ABOUT HER.
BUT THEY LOST HER. AND I AM DONE WITH THEM.
I'M SORRY IT DIDN'T WORK OUT.
WILL YOU STOP YOUR PRATTLING!

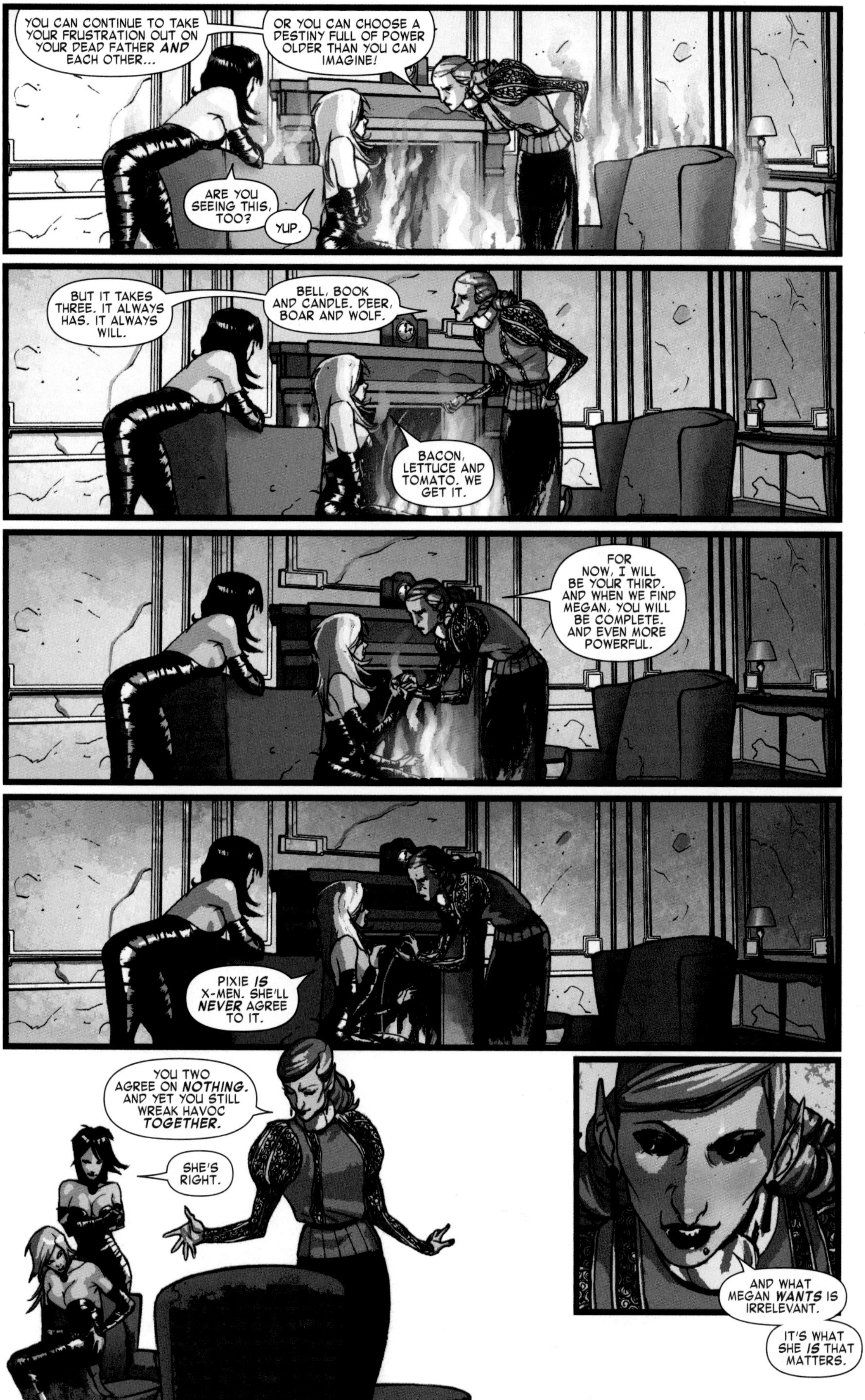

YOU CAN CONTINUE TO TAKE YOUR FRUSTRATION OUT ON YOUR DEAD FATHER AND EACH OTHER...
OR YOU CAN CHOOSE A DESTINY FULL OF POWER OLDER THAN YOU CAN IMAGINE!
ARE YOU SEEING THIS, TOO?
YUP.
BUT IT TAKES THREE. IT ALWAYS HAS. IT ALWAYS WILL.
BELL, BOOK AND CANDLE. DEER, BOAR AND WOLF.
BACON, LETTUCE AND TOMATO. WE GET IT.
FOR NOW, I WILL BE YOUR THIRD. AND WHEN WE FIND MEGAN, YOU WILL BE COMPLETE. AND EVEN MORE POWERFUL.
PIXIE IS X-MEN. SHE'LL NEVER AGREE TO IT.
YOU TWO AGREE ON NOTHING. AND YET YOU STILL WREAK HAVOC TOGETHER.
SHE'S RIGHT.
AND WHAT MEGAN WANTS IS IRRELEVANT.
IT'S WHAT SHE IS THAT MATTERS.

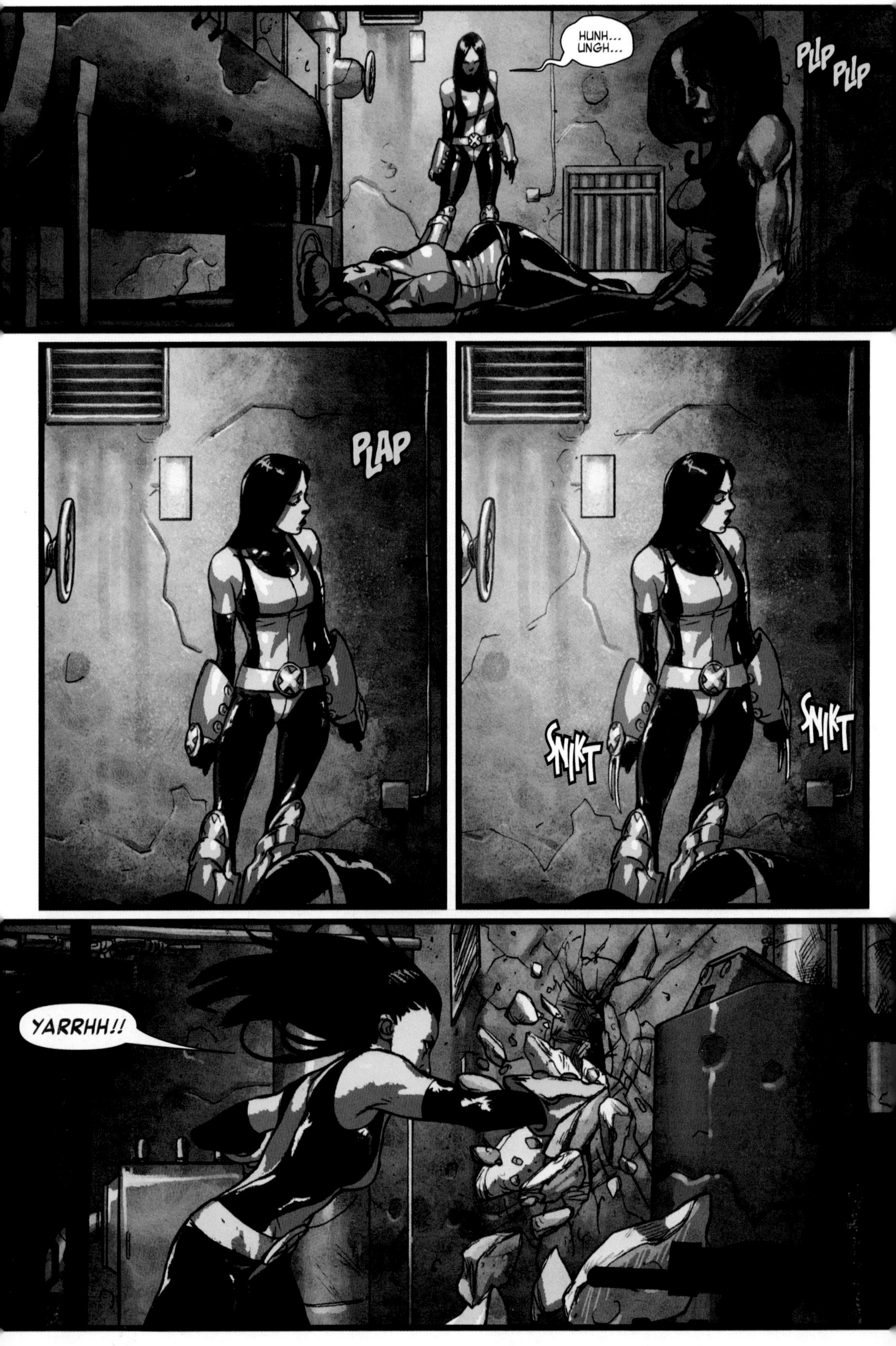
HUNH... UNGH...
PLIP PLIP
PLAP
SNIKT
SNIKT
YARRHH!!

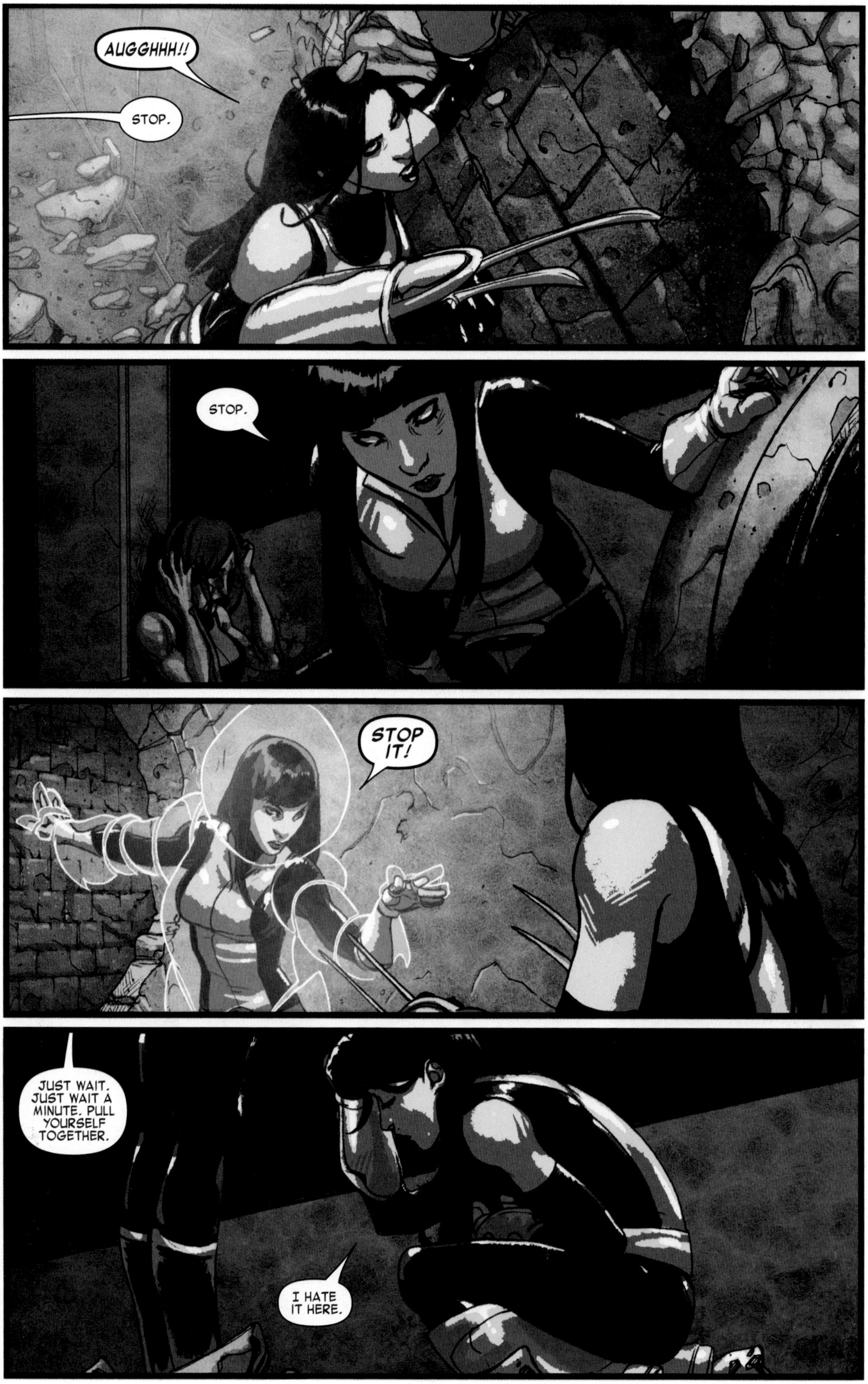
AUGGHHH!!
STOP.
STOP.
STOP IT!
JUST WAIT. JUST WAIT A MINUTE. PULL YOURSELF TOGETHER.
I HATE IT HERE.

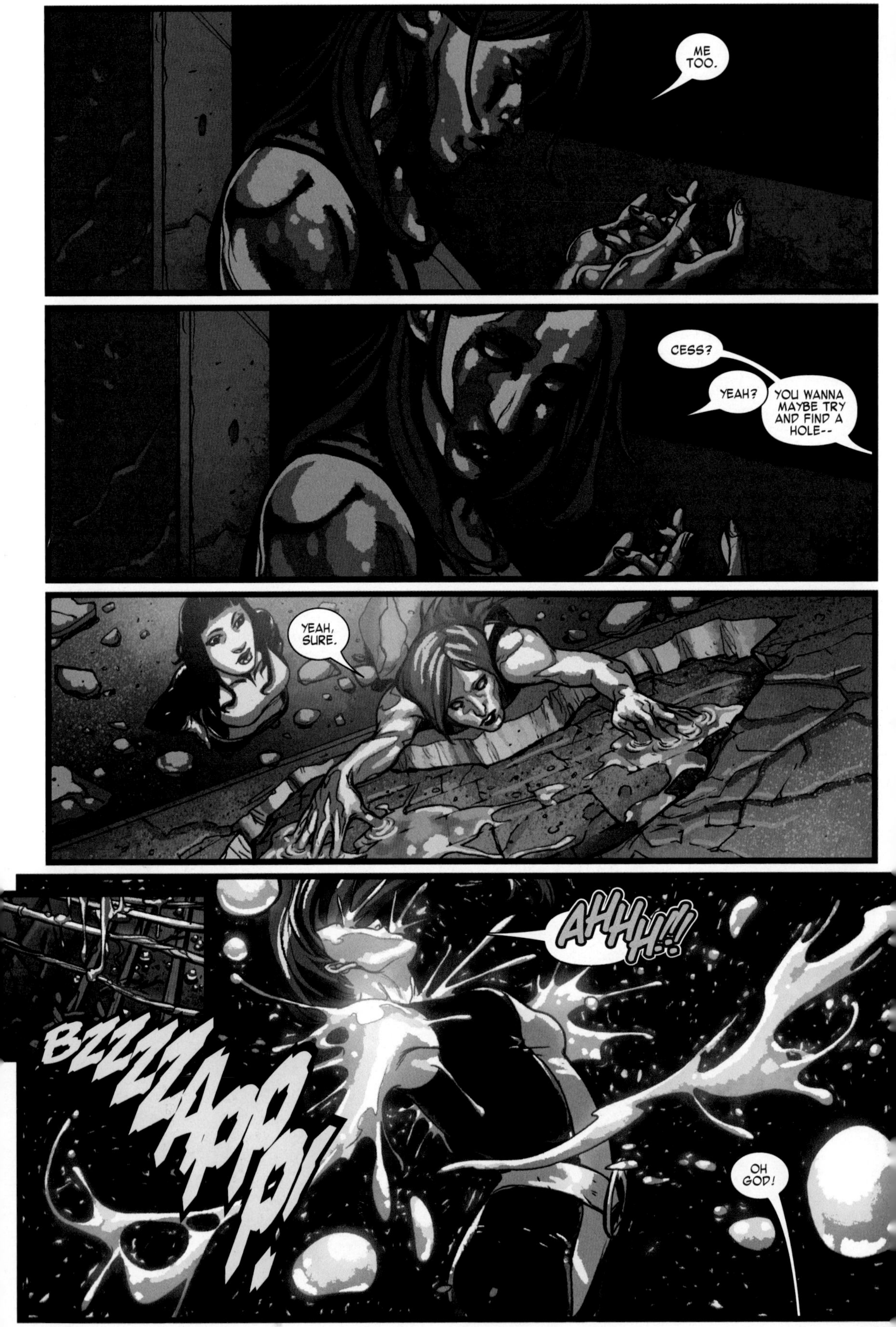

ME TOO.
CESS?
YEAH?
YOU WANNA MAYBE TRY AND FIND A HOLE--
YEAH, SURE.
AHHHH!!
BZZZZZAPPP!
OH GOD!

11/27/2020

# TAYLOR PATRICK SEAI

Item Number: 31901042055444

Contra Costa County Libraries are open for
front door pick up of holds. Masks and
social distancing are required. For faster
service, book an appointment at:
https://ccclib.org/front-door-service/
Book drops are available for returns.
All Contra Costa County Libraries will be
closed on November 11th and 26th, and will
close by 6:00 pm on November 25th. Prewett
Library will also be closed November 27th.
In addition, Concord Library will be closed
for building repairs November 9th - 29th.
Pinole Library and Ygnacio Valley Library
remain temporarily closed.

Hold Shelf Slip

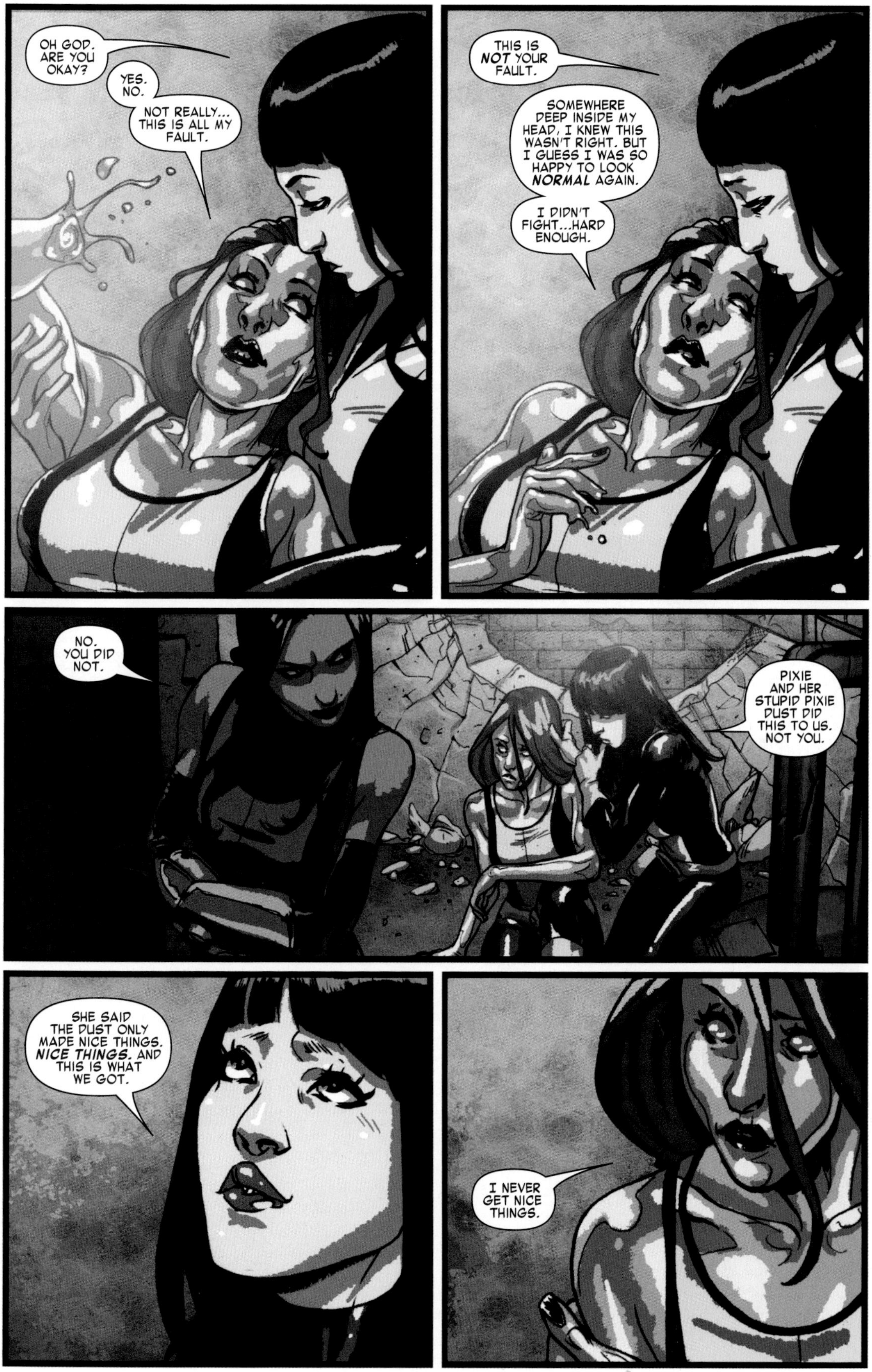
OH GOD. ARE YOU OKAY?
YES. NO.
NOT REALLY... THIS IS ALL MY FAULT.
THIS IS NOT YOUR FAULT.
SOMEWHERE DEEP INSIDE MY HEAD, I KNEW THIS WASN'T RIGHT. BUT I GUESS I WAS SO HAPPY TO LOOK NORMAL AGAIN.
I DIDN'T FIGHT...HARD ENOUGH.
NO. YOU DID NOT.
PIXIE AND HER STUPID PIXIE DUST DID THIS TO US. NOT YOU.
SHE SAID THE DUST ONLY MADE NICE THINGS. NICE THINGS. AND THIS IS WHAT WE GOT.
I NEVER GET NICE THINGS.

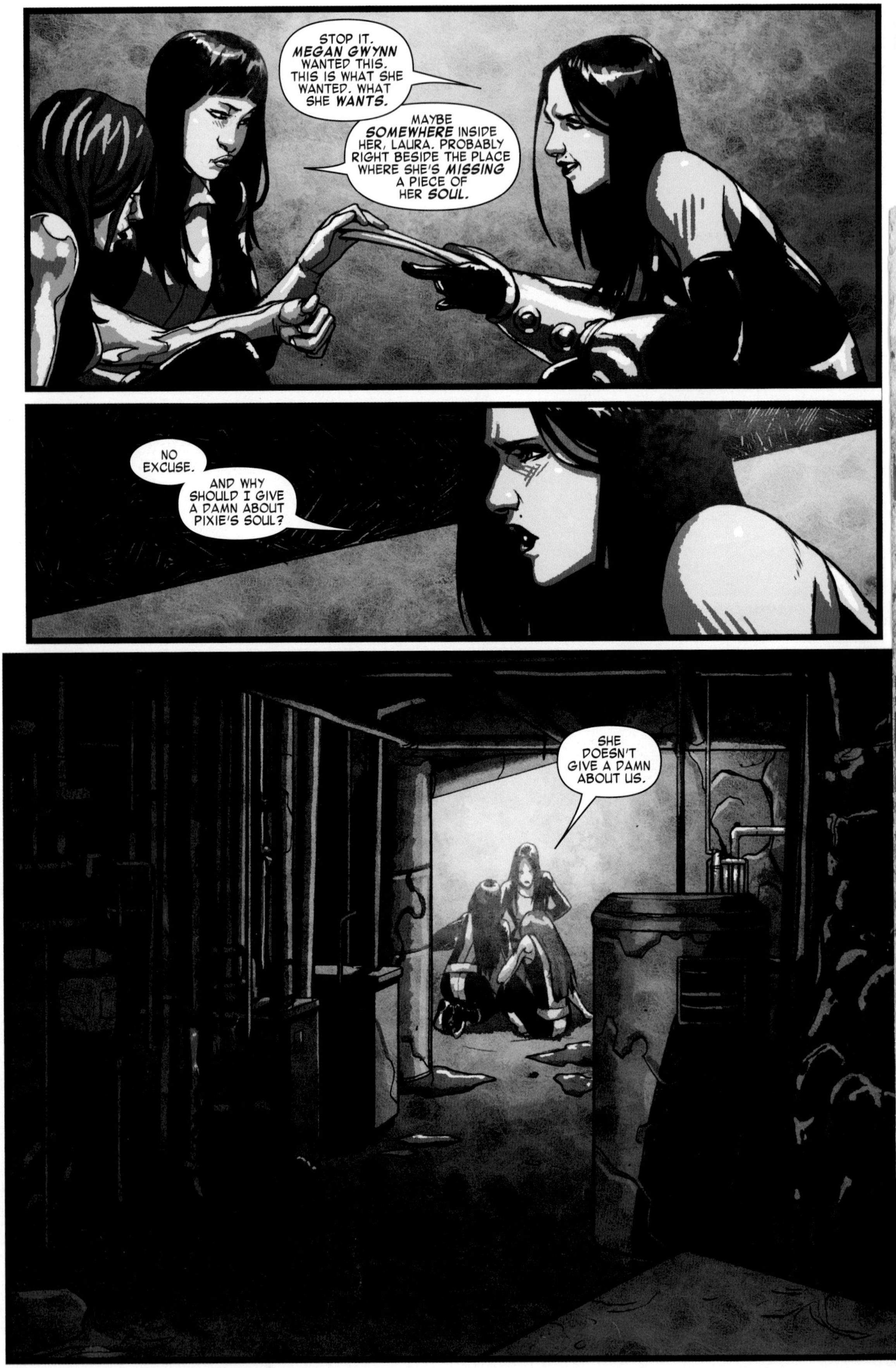
STOP IT. MEGAN GWYNN WANTED THIS. THIS IS WHAT SHE WANTED. WHAT SHE WANTS.
MAYBE SOMEWHERE INSIDE HER, LAURA. PROBABLY RIGHT BESIDE THE PLACE WHERE SHE'S MISSING A PIECE OF HER SOUL.
NO EXCUSE.
AND WHY SHOULD I GIVE A DAMN ABOUT PIXIE'S SOUL?
SHE DOESN'T GIVE A DAMN ABOUT US.

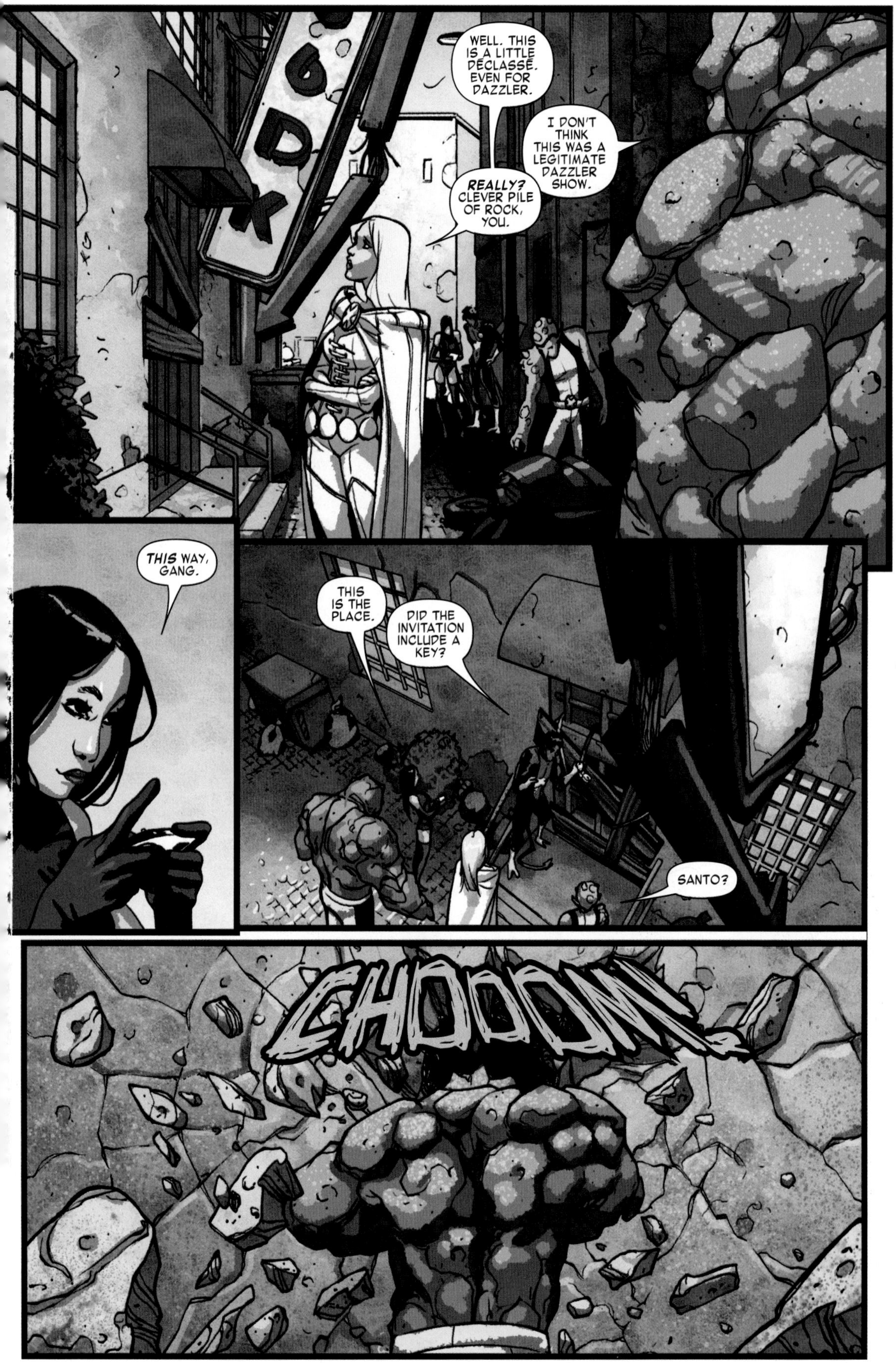
WELL. THIS IS A LITTLE DÉCLASSÉ. EVEN FOR DAZZLER.
I DON'T THINK THIS WAS A LEGITIMATE DAZZLER SHOW.
REALLY? CLEVER PILE OF ROCK, YOU.
THIS WAY, GANG.
THIS IS THE PLACE.
DID THE INVITATION INCLUDE A KEY?
SANTO?
CHOOOM!

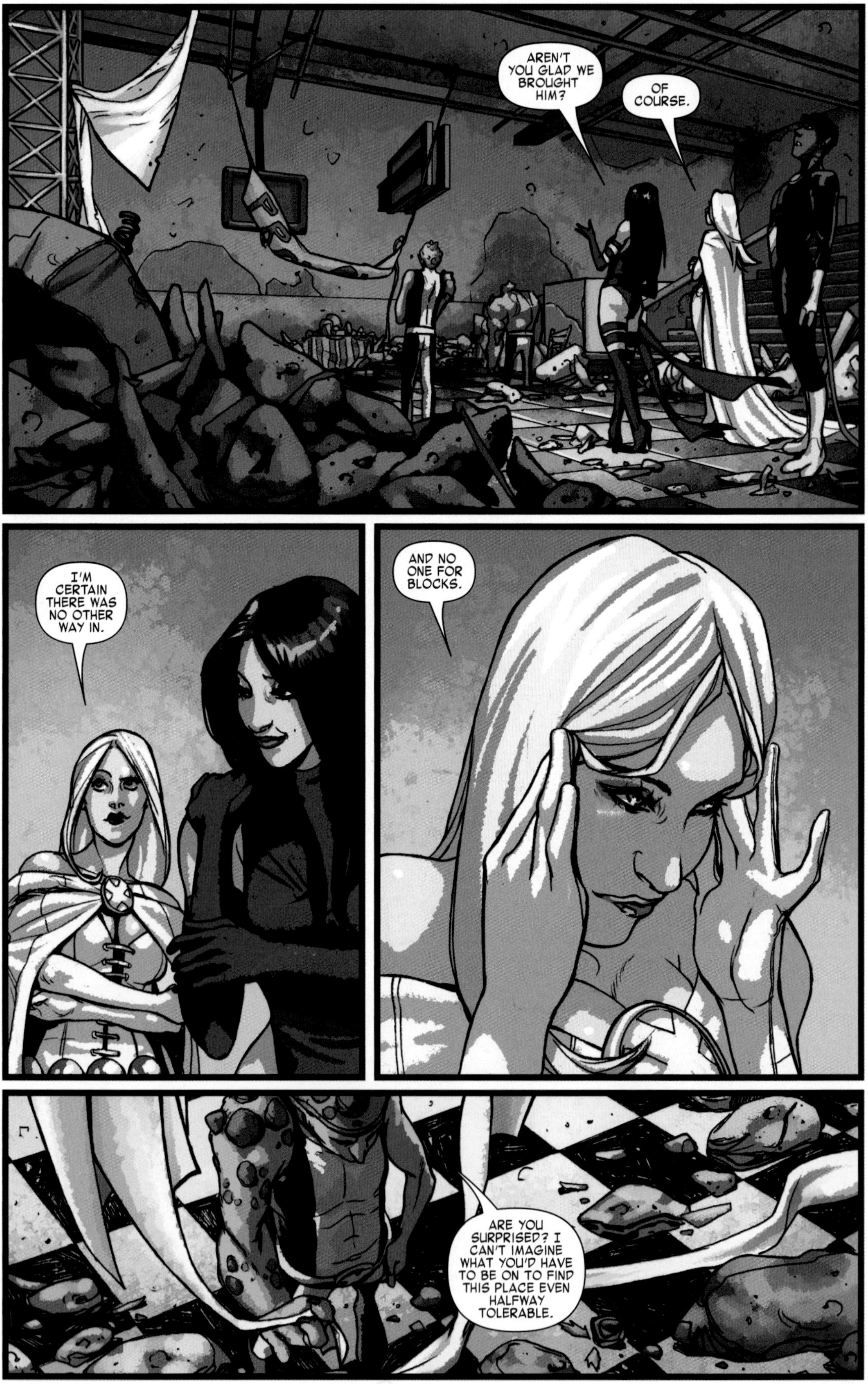
AREN'T YOU GLAD WE BROUGHT HIM?
OF COURSE.
I'M CERTAIN THERE WAS NO OTHER WAY IN.
AND NO ONE FOR BLOCKS.
ARE YOU SURPRISED? I CAN'T IMAGINE WHAT YOU'D HAVE TO BE ON TO FIND THIS PLACE EVEN HALFWAY TOLERABLE.

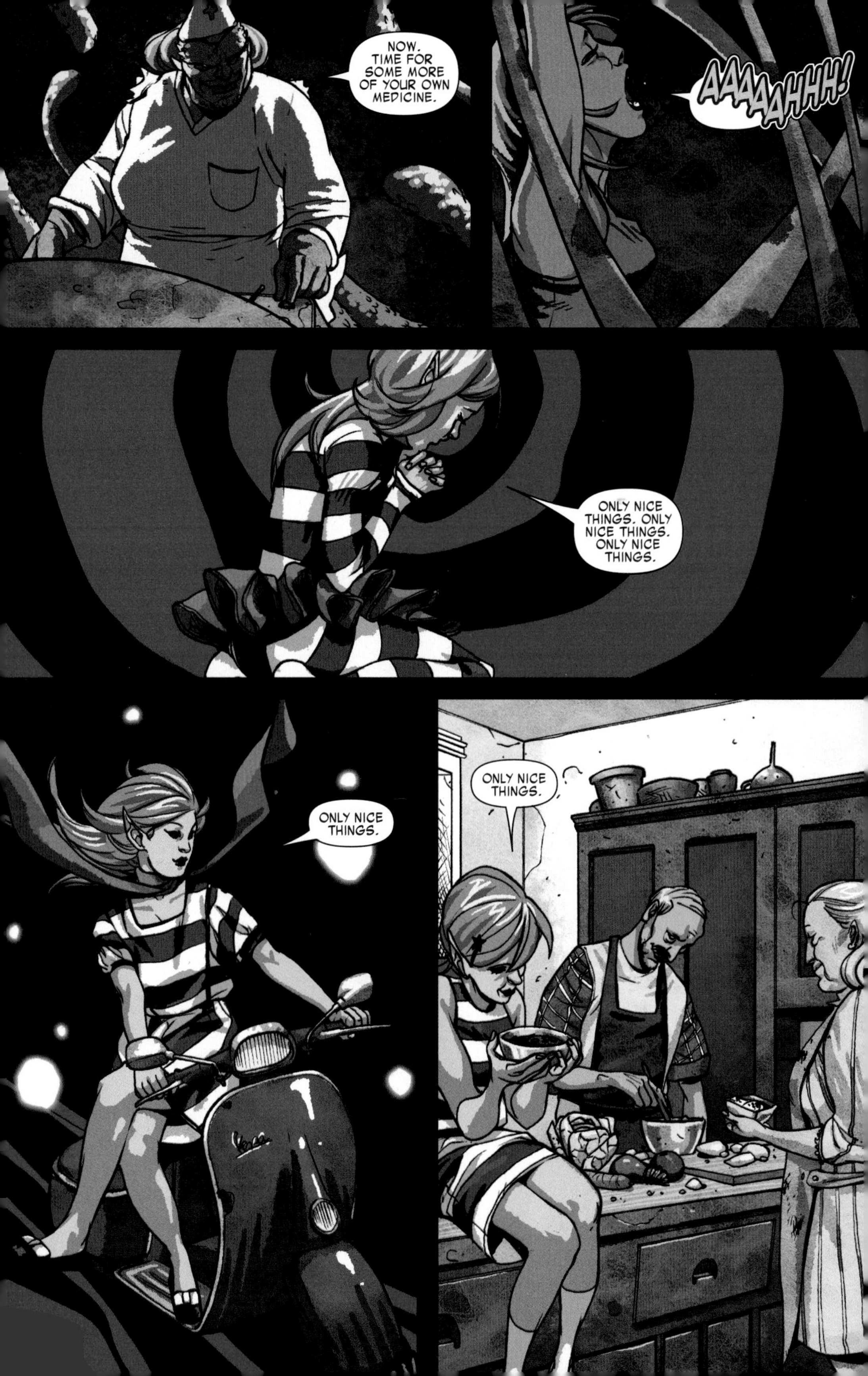
NOW. TIME FOR SOME MORE OF YOUR OWN MEDICINE.
AAAAAHHH!
ONLY NICE THINGS. ONLY NICE THINGS. ONLY NICE THINGS.
ONLY NICE THINGS.
ONLY NICE THINGS.

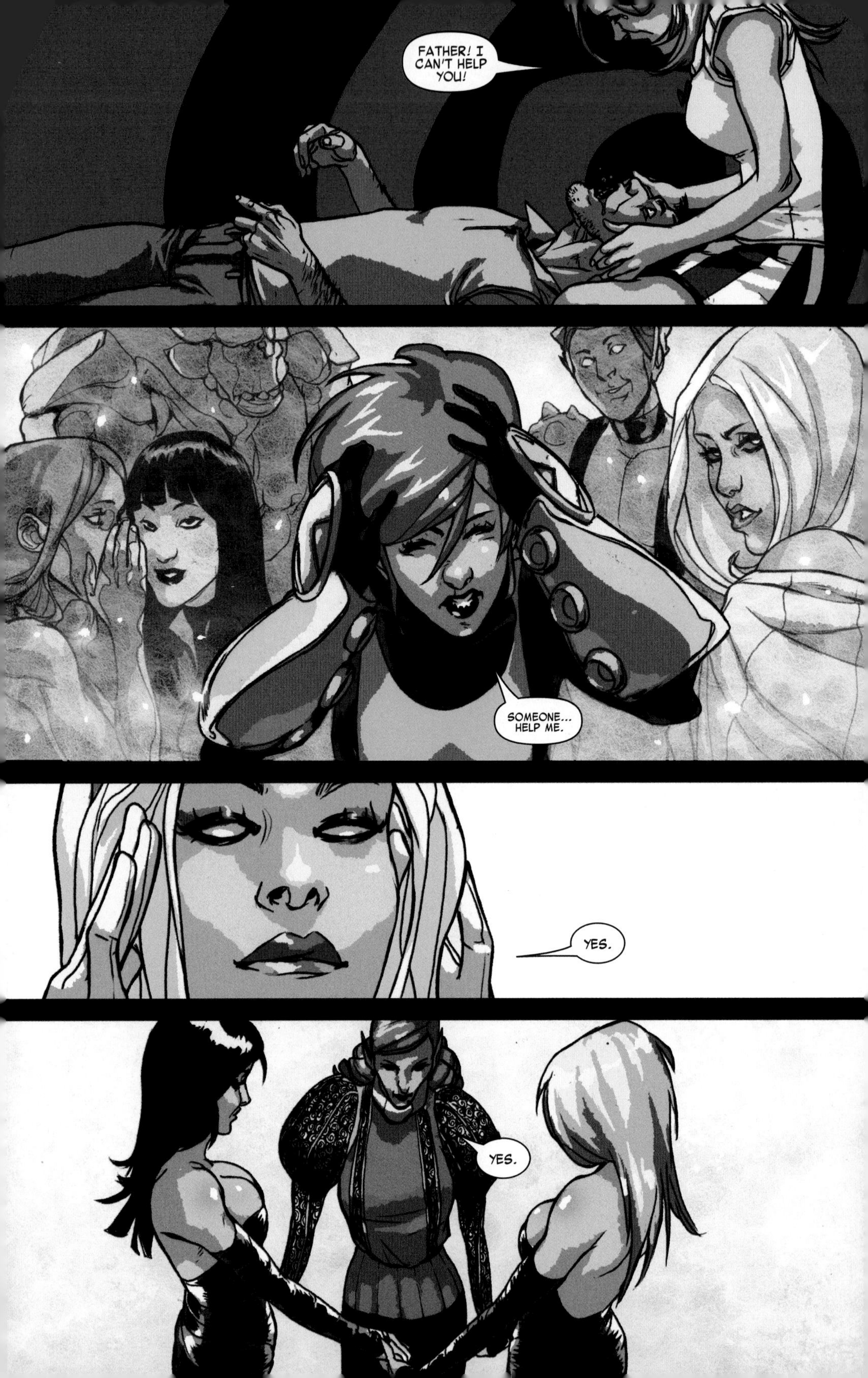
FATHER! I CAN'T HELP YOU!
SOMEONE... HELP ME.
YES.
YES.

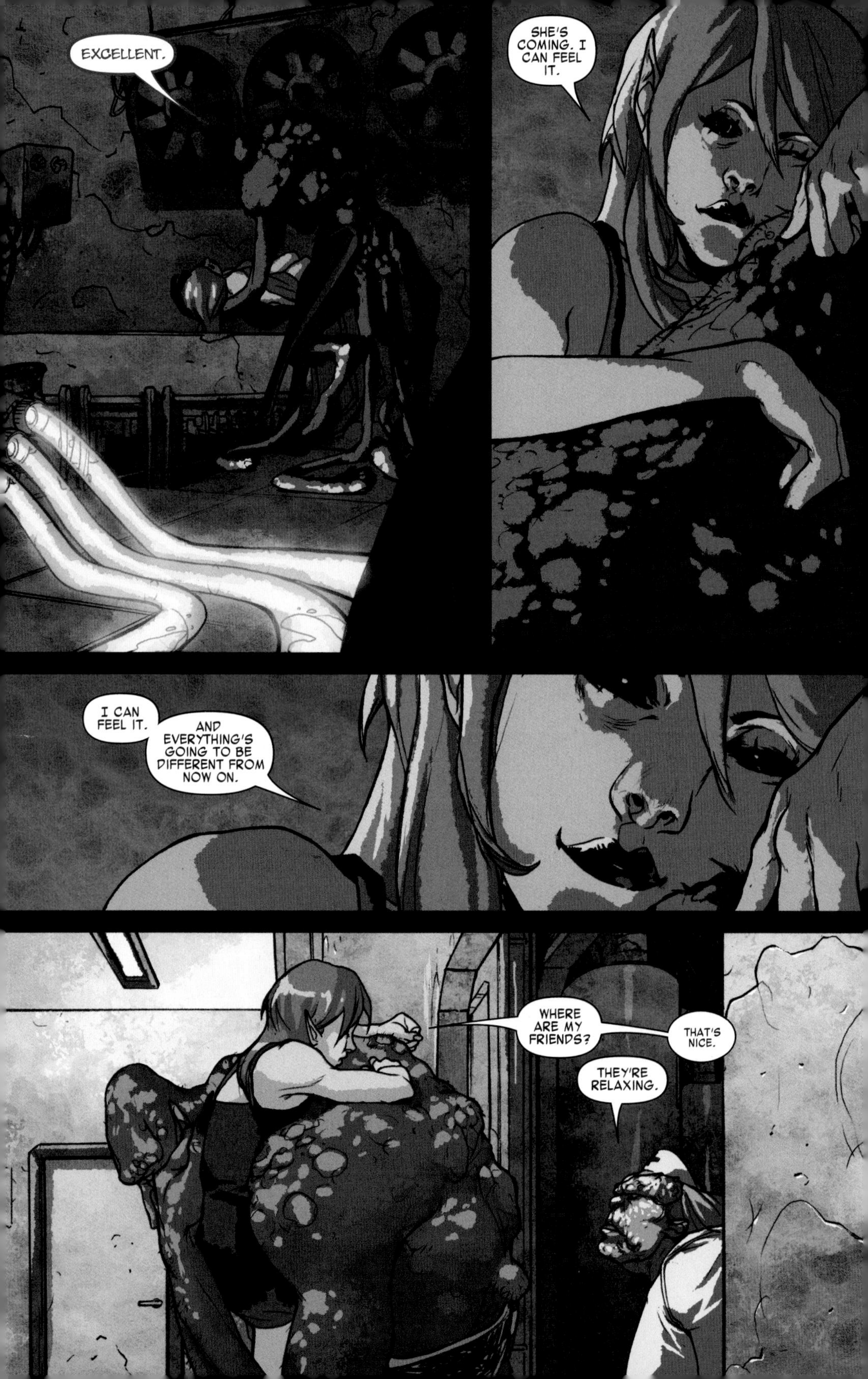
EXCELLENT.
SHE'S COMING. I CAN FEEL IT.
I CAN FEEL IT.
AND EVERYTHING'S GOING TO BE DIFFERENT FROM NOW ON.
WHERE ARE MY FRIENDS?
THEY'RE RELAXING.
THAT'S NICE.

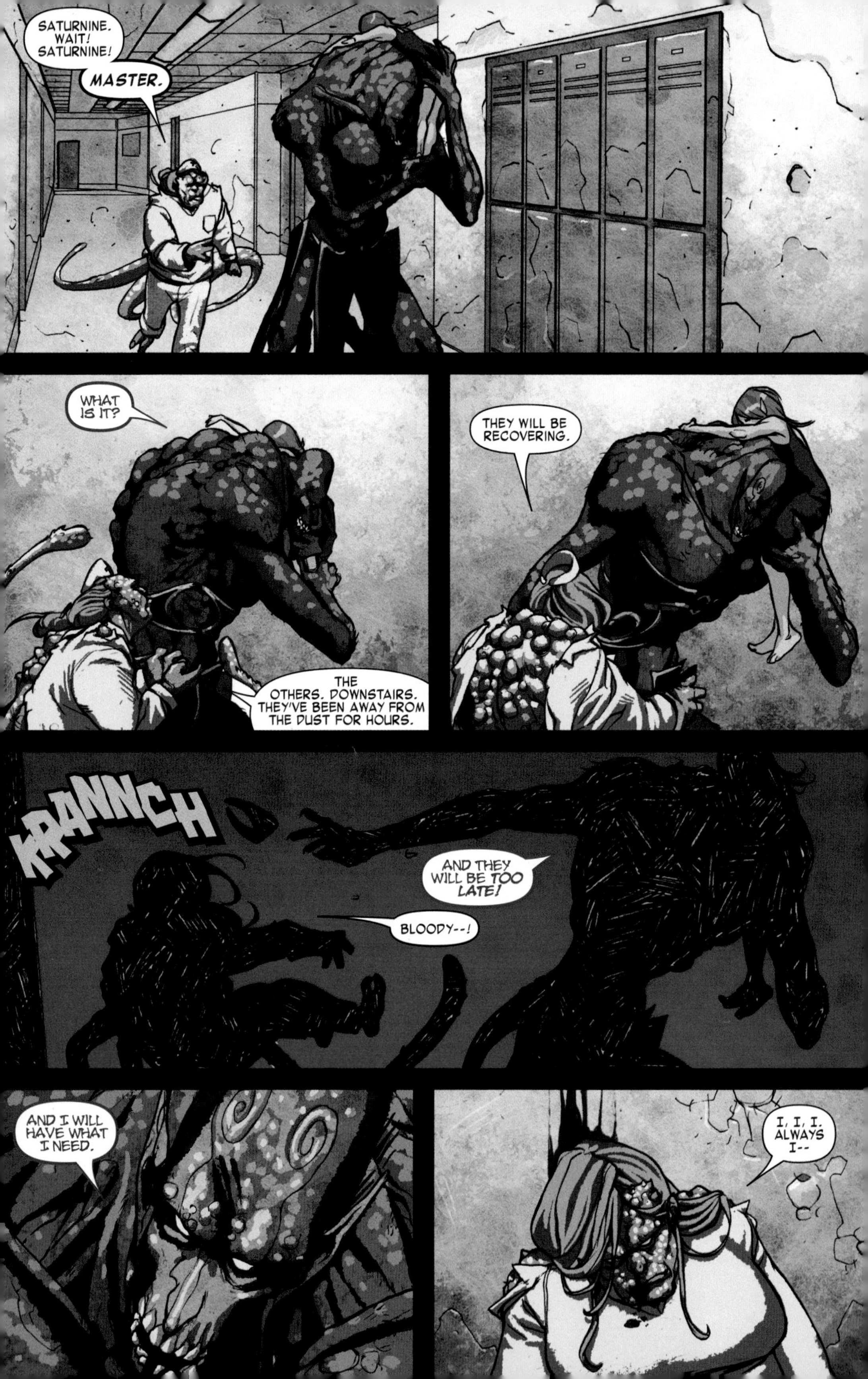
SATURNINE. WAIT! SATURNINE!
MASTER.
WHAT IS IT?
THE OTHERS. DOWNSTAIRS. THEY'VE BEEN AWAY FROM THE DUST FOR HOURS.
THEY WILL BE RECOVERING.
KRANNCH
AND THEY WILL BE TOO LATE!
BLOODY--!
AND I WILL HAVE WHAT I NEED.
I, I, I. ALWAYS I--

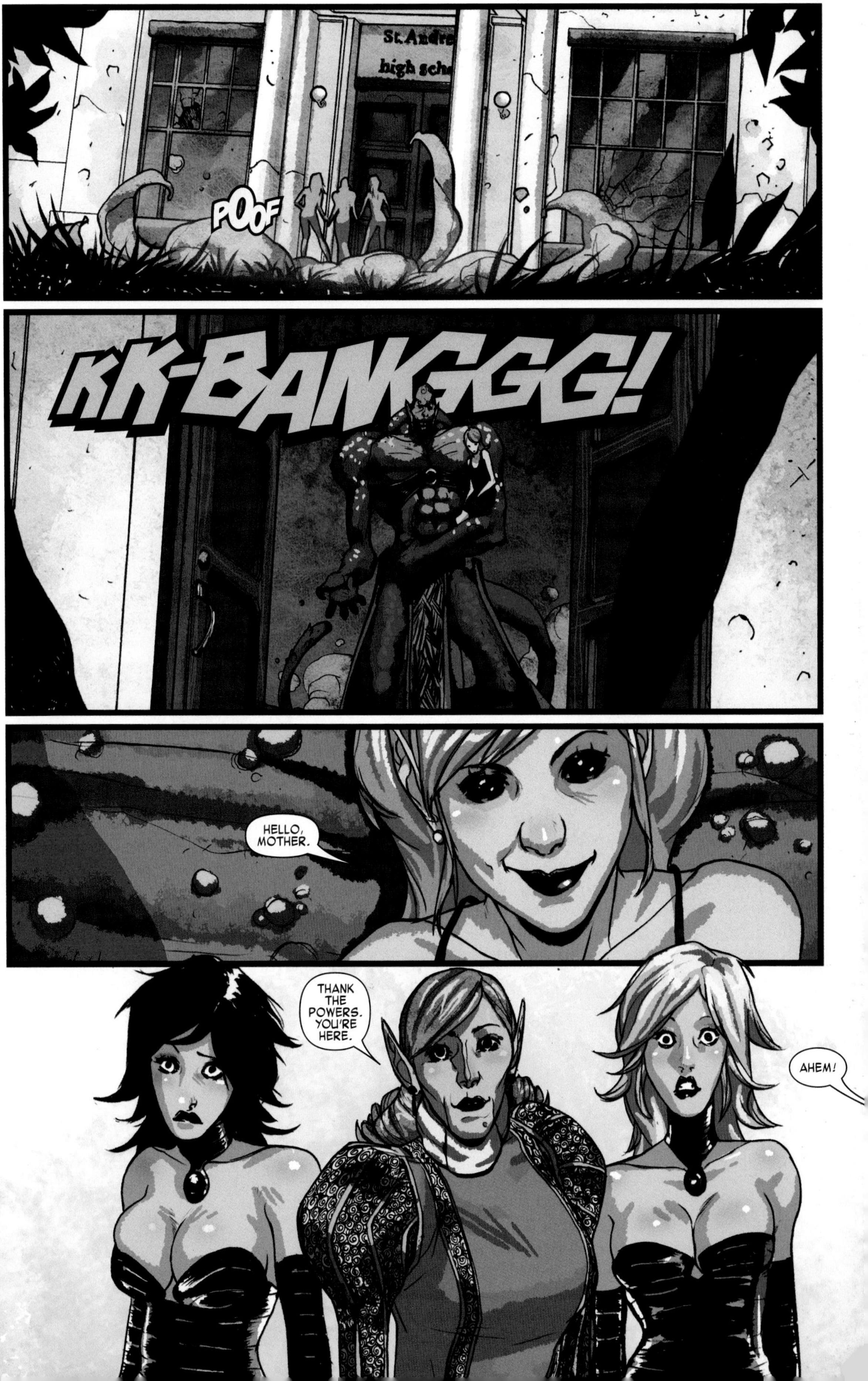
POOF
KK-BANGGG!
HELLO, MOTHER.
THANK THE POWERS. YOU'RE HERE.
AHEM!

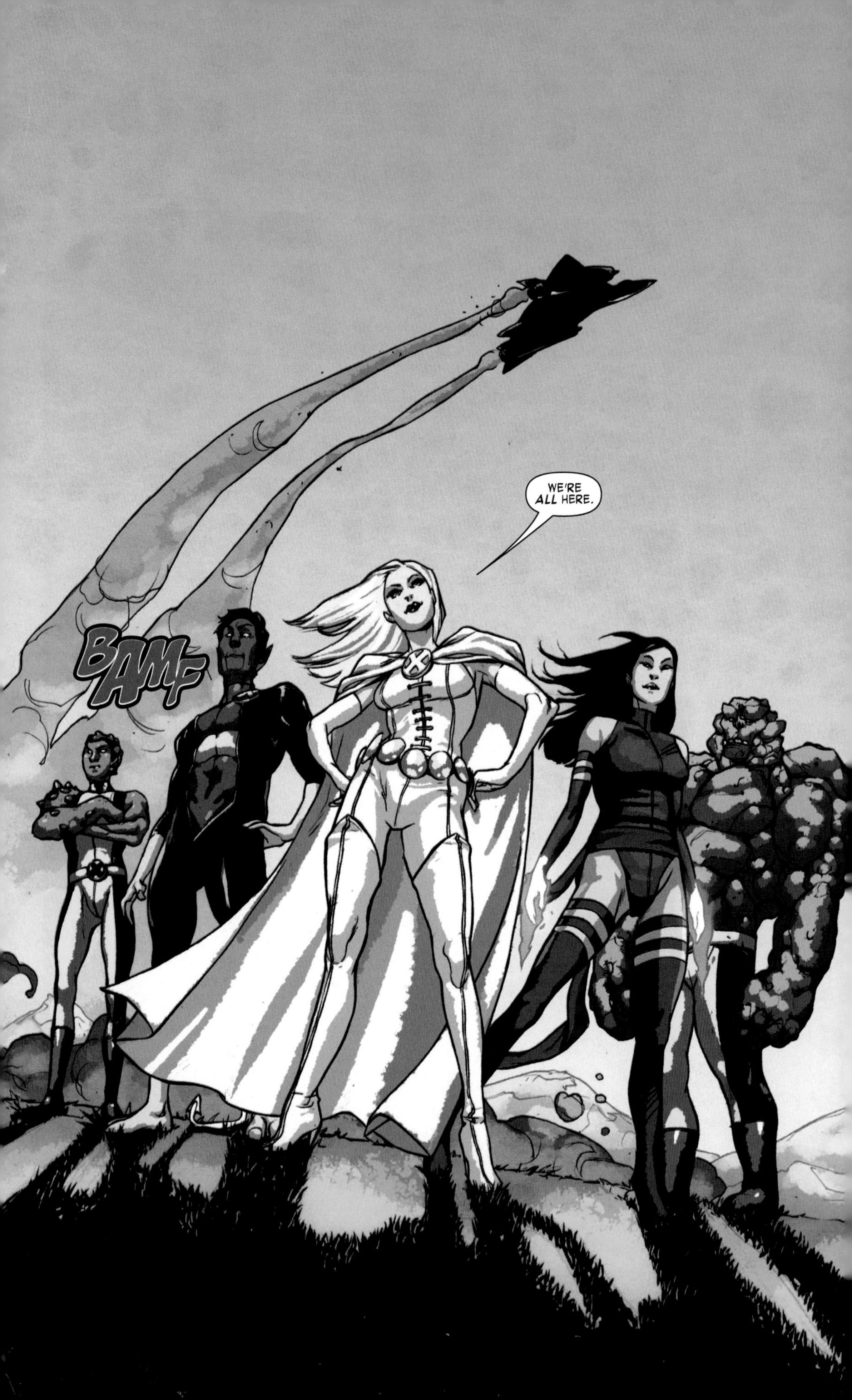
BAMF
WE'RE ALL HERE.

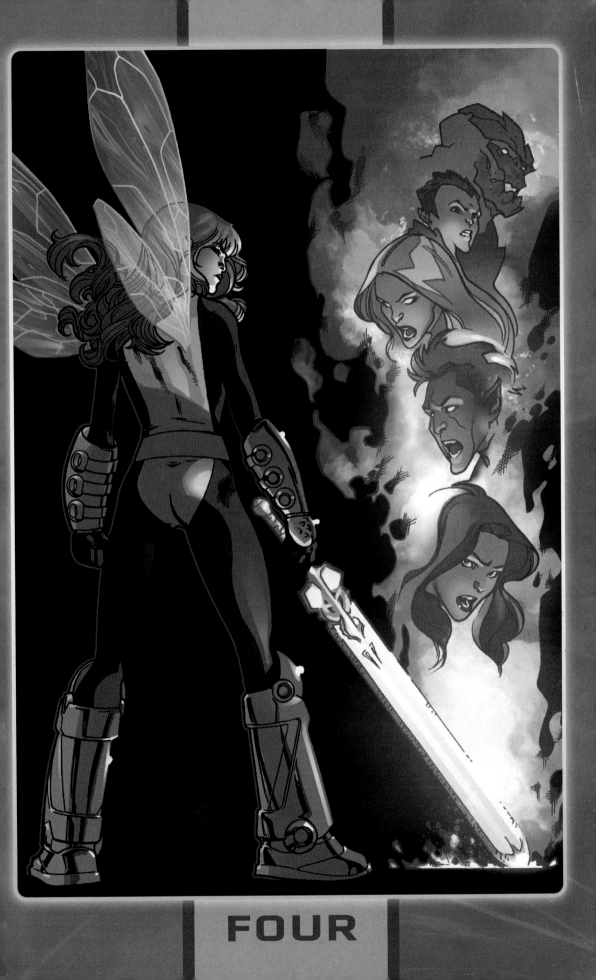

FOUR

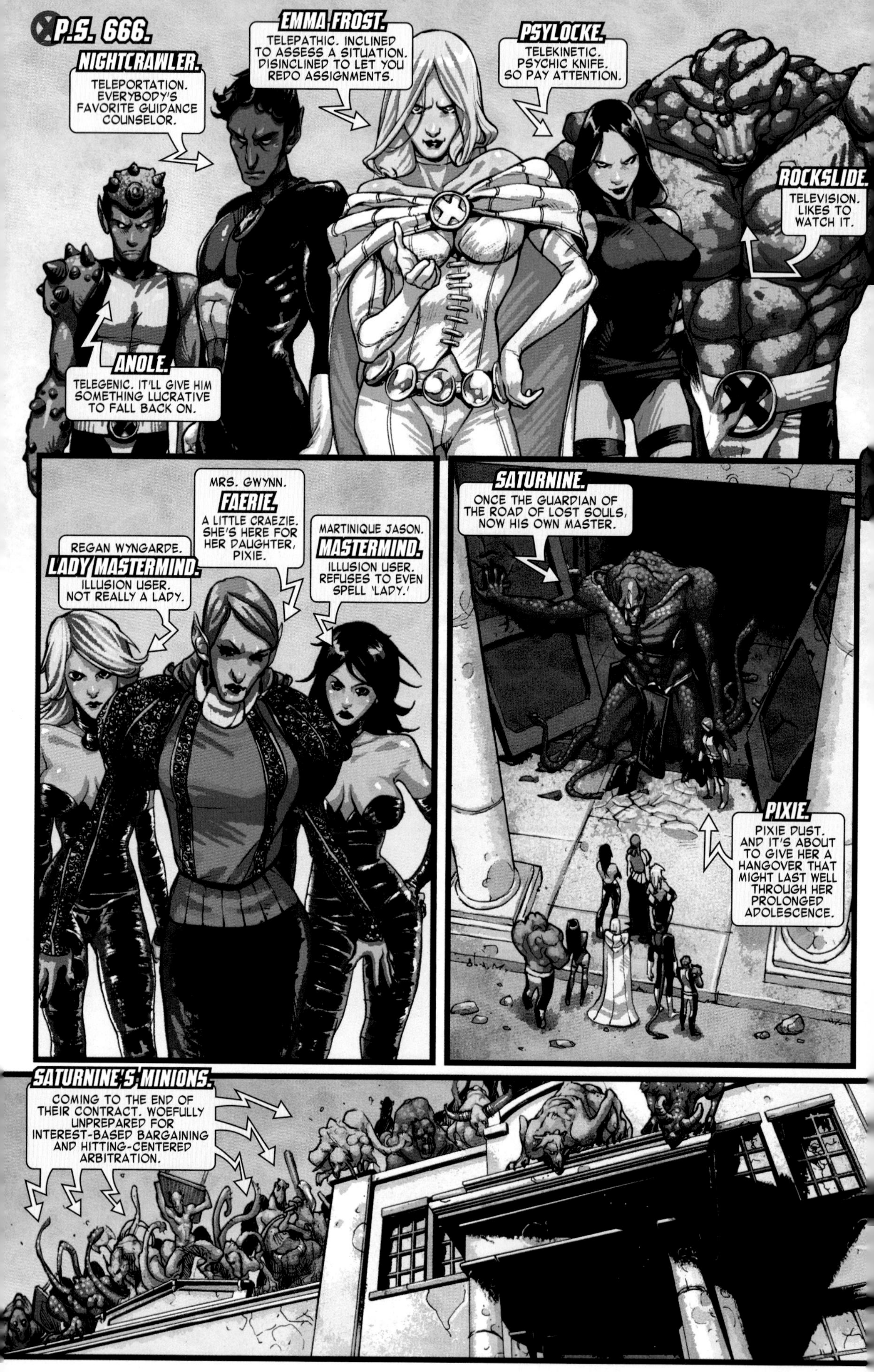
P.S. 666.
NIGHTCRAWLER.
TELEPORTATION. EVERYBODY'S FAVORITE GUIDANCE COUNSELOR.
EMMA FROST.
TELEPATHIC. INCLINED TO ASSESS A SITUATION. DISINCLINED TO LET YOU REDO ASSIGNMENTS.
PSYLOCKE.
TELEKINETIC. PSYCHIC KNIFE. SO PAY ATTENTION.
ROCKSLIDE.
TELEVISION. LIKES TO WATCH IT.
ANOLE.
TELEGENIC. IT'LL GIVE HIM SOMETHING LUCRATIVE TO FALL BACK ON.
REGAN WYNGARDE.
LADY MASTERMIND.
ILLUSION USER. NOT REALLY A LADY.
MRS. GWYNN.
FAERIE.
A LITTLE CRAEZIE. SHE'S HERE FOR HER DAUGHTER, PIXIE.
MARTINIQUE JASON.
MASTERMIND.
ILLUSION USER. REFUSES TO EVEN SPELL 'LADY.'
SATURNINE.
ONCE THE GUARDIAN OF THE ROAD OF LOST SOULS, NOW HIS OWN MASTER.
PIXIE.
PIXIE DUST. AND IT'S ABOUT TO GIVE HER A HANGOVER THAT MIGHT LAST WELL THROUGH HER PROLONGED ADOLESCENCE.
SATURNINE'S MINIONS.
COMING TO THE END OF THEIR CONTRACT. WOEFULLY UNPREPARED FOR INTEREST-BASED BARGAINING AND HITTING-CENTERED ARBITRATION.

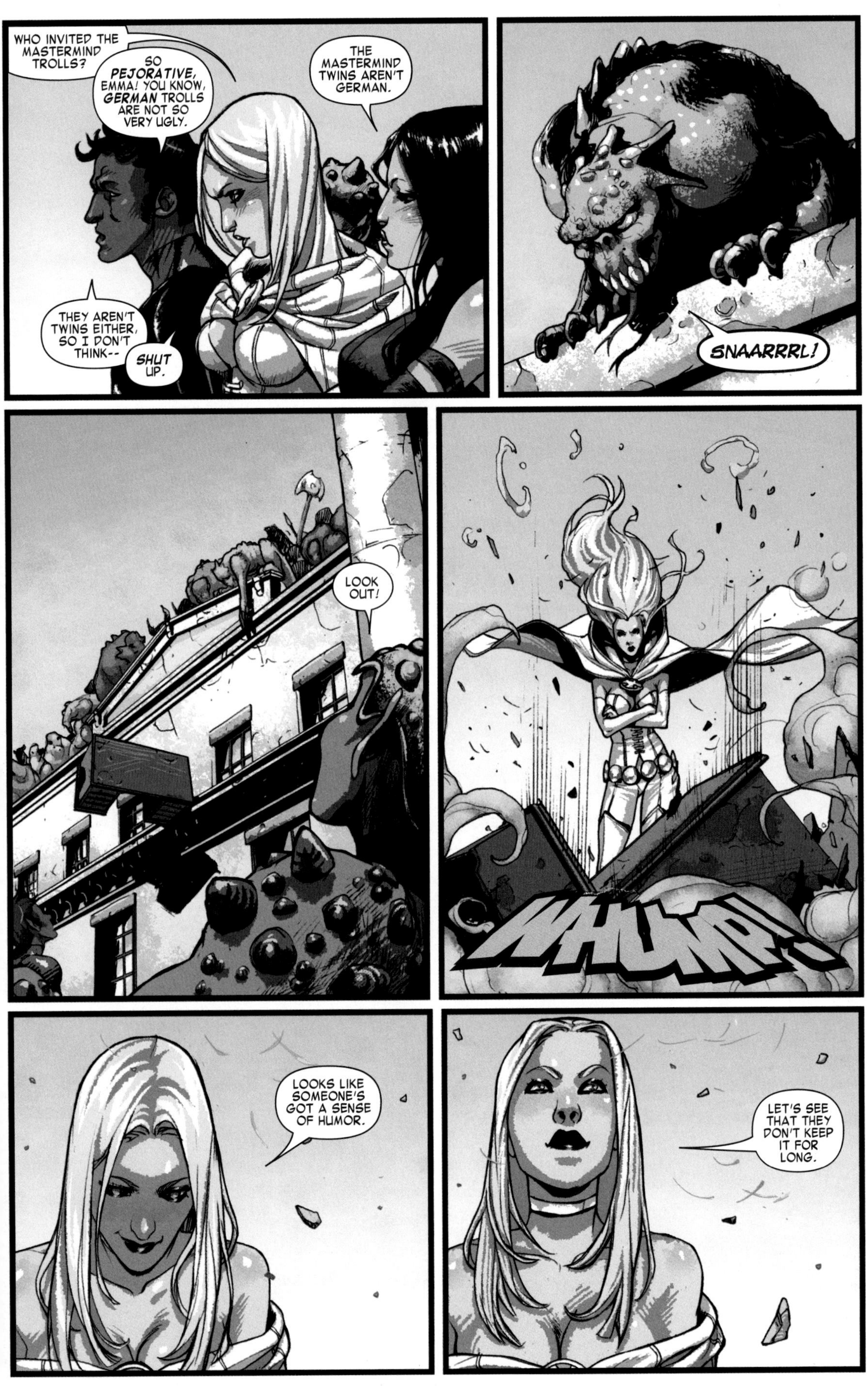
WHO INVITED THE MASTERMIND TROLLS?
SO PEJORATIVE, EMMA! YOU KNOW, GERMAN TROLLS ARE NOT SO VERY UGLY.
THE MASTERMIND TWINS AREN'T GERMAN.
THEY AREN'T TWINS EITHER, SO I DON'T THINK--
SHUT UP.
SNAARRRL!
LOOK OUT!
WHUMP!
LOOKS LIKE SOMEONE'S GOT A SENSE OF HUMOR.
LET'S SEE THAT THEY DON'T KEEP IT FOR LONG.

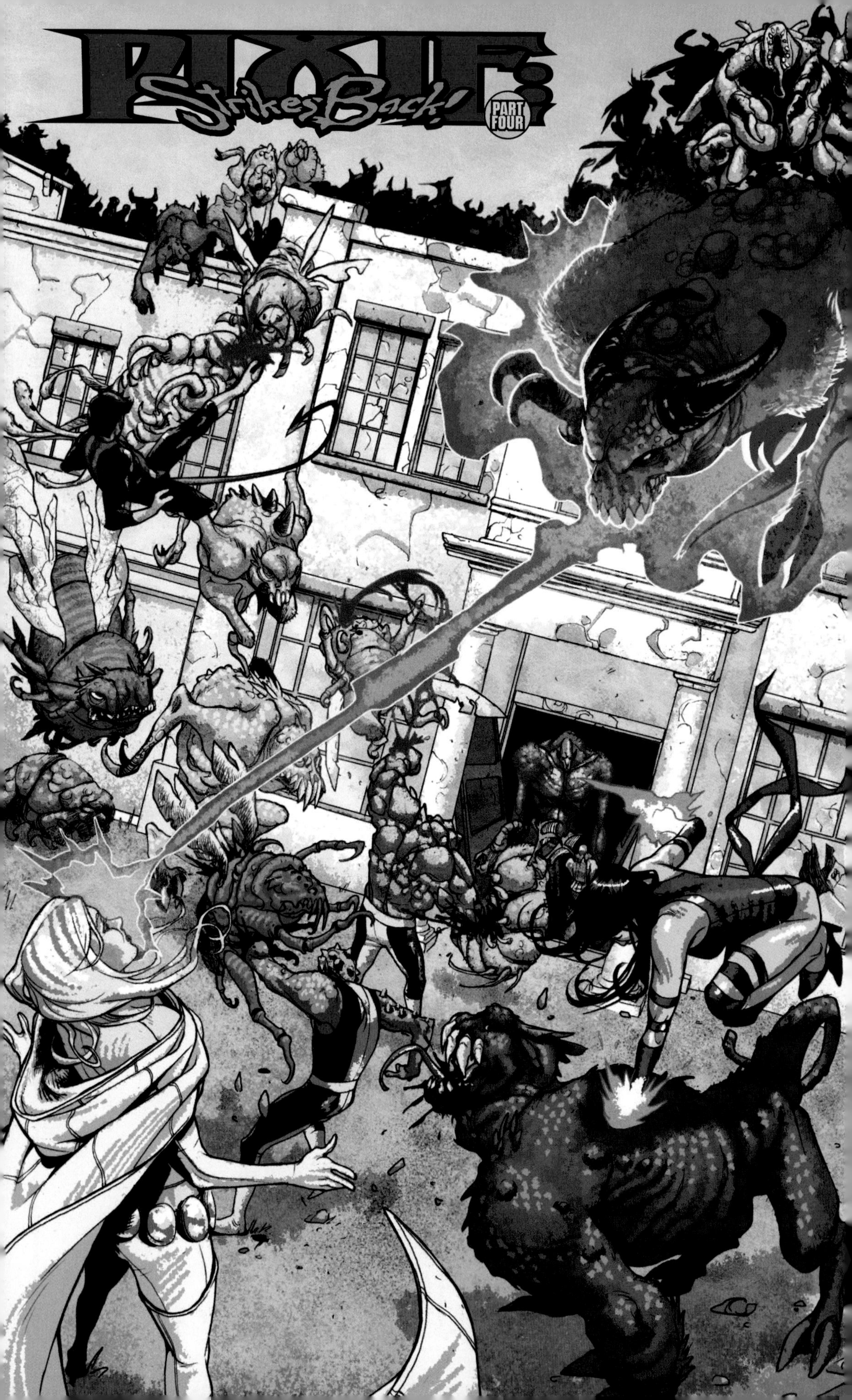
PIXIE
Strikes Back!
PART FOUR

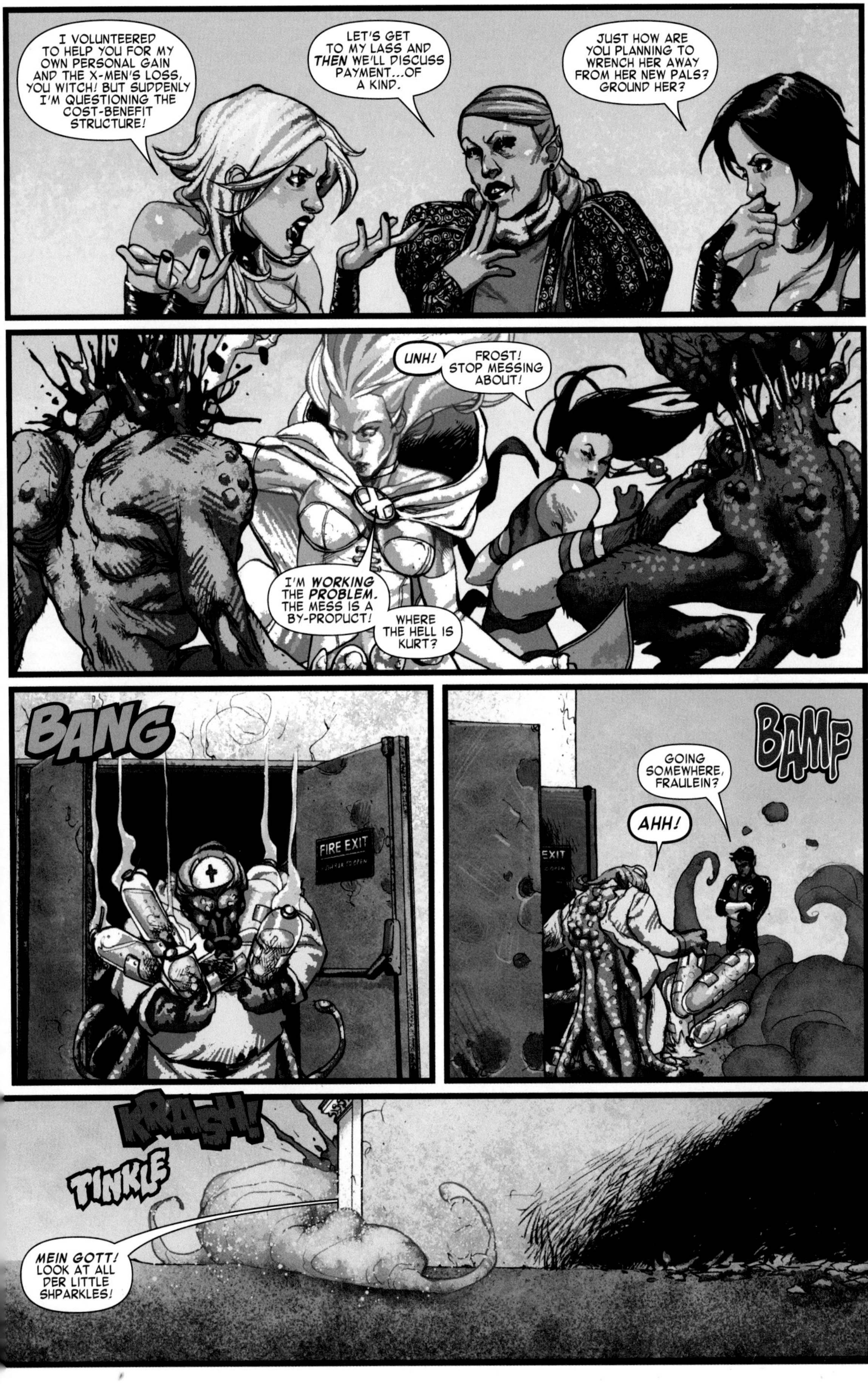
I VOLUNTEERED TO HELP YOU FOR MY OWN PERSONAL GAIN AND THE X-MEN'S LOSS, YOU WITCH! BUT SUDDENLY I'M QUESTIONING THE COST-BENEFIT STRUCTURE!
LET'S GET TO MY LASS AND *THEN* WE'LL DISCUSS PAYMENT...OF A KIND.
JUST HOW ARE YOU PLANNING TO WRENCH HER AWAY FROM HER NEW PALS? GROUND HER?
UNH!
FROST! STOP MESSING ABOUT!
I'M *WORKING* THE *PROBLEM*. THE MESS IS A BY-PRODUCT!
WHERE THE HELL IS KURT?
BANG
FIRE EXIT
BAMF
GOING SOMEWHERE, FRAULEIN?
AHH!
KRASH!
TINKLE
*MEIN GOTT!* LOOK AT ALL DER LITTLE SHPARKLES!

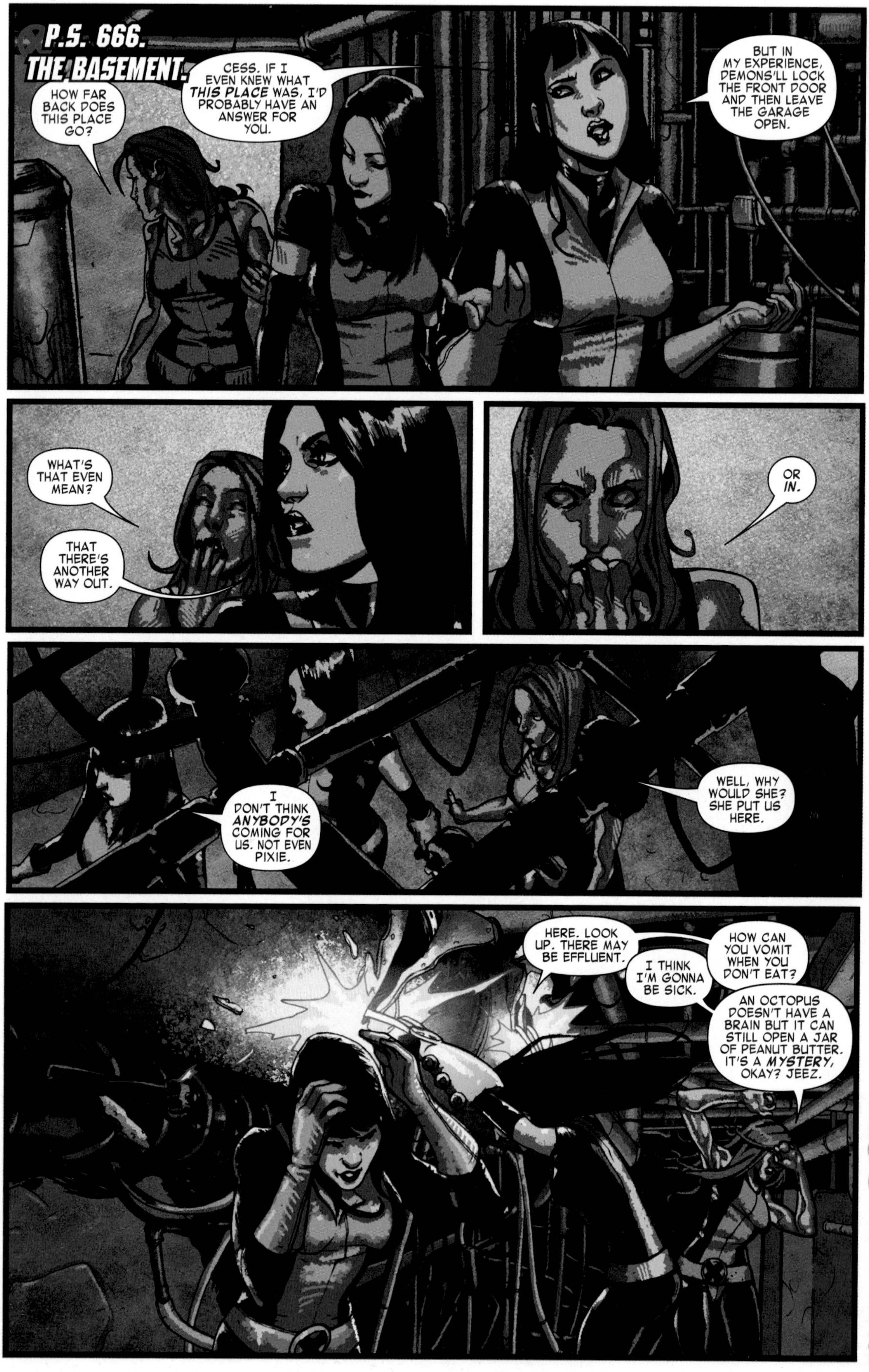
P.S. 666.
THE BASEMENT.
HOW FAR BACK DOES THIS PLACE GO?
CESS. IF I EVEN KNEW WHAT THIS PLACE WAS, I'D PROBABLY HAVE AN ANSWER FOR YOU.
BUT IN MY EXPERIENCE, DEMONS'LL LOCK THE FRONT DOOR AND THEN LEAVE THE GARAGE OPEN.
WHAT'S THAT EVEN MEAN?
THAT THERE'S ANOTHER WAY OUT.
OR IN.
I DON'T THINK ANYBODY'S COMING FOR US. NOT EVEN PIXIE.
WELL, WHY WOULD SHE? SHE PUT US HERE.
HERE. LOOK UP. THERE MAY BE EFFLUENT.
I THINK I'M GONNA BE SICK.
HOW CAN YOU VOMIT WHEN YOU DON'T EAT?
AN OCTOPUS DOESN'T HAVE A BRAIN BUT IT CAN STILL OPEN A JAR OF PEANUT BUTTER. IT'S A MYSTERY, OKAY? JEEZ.

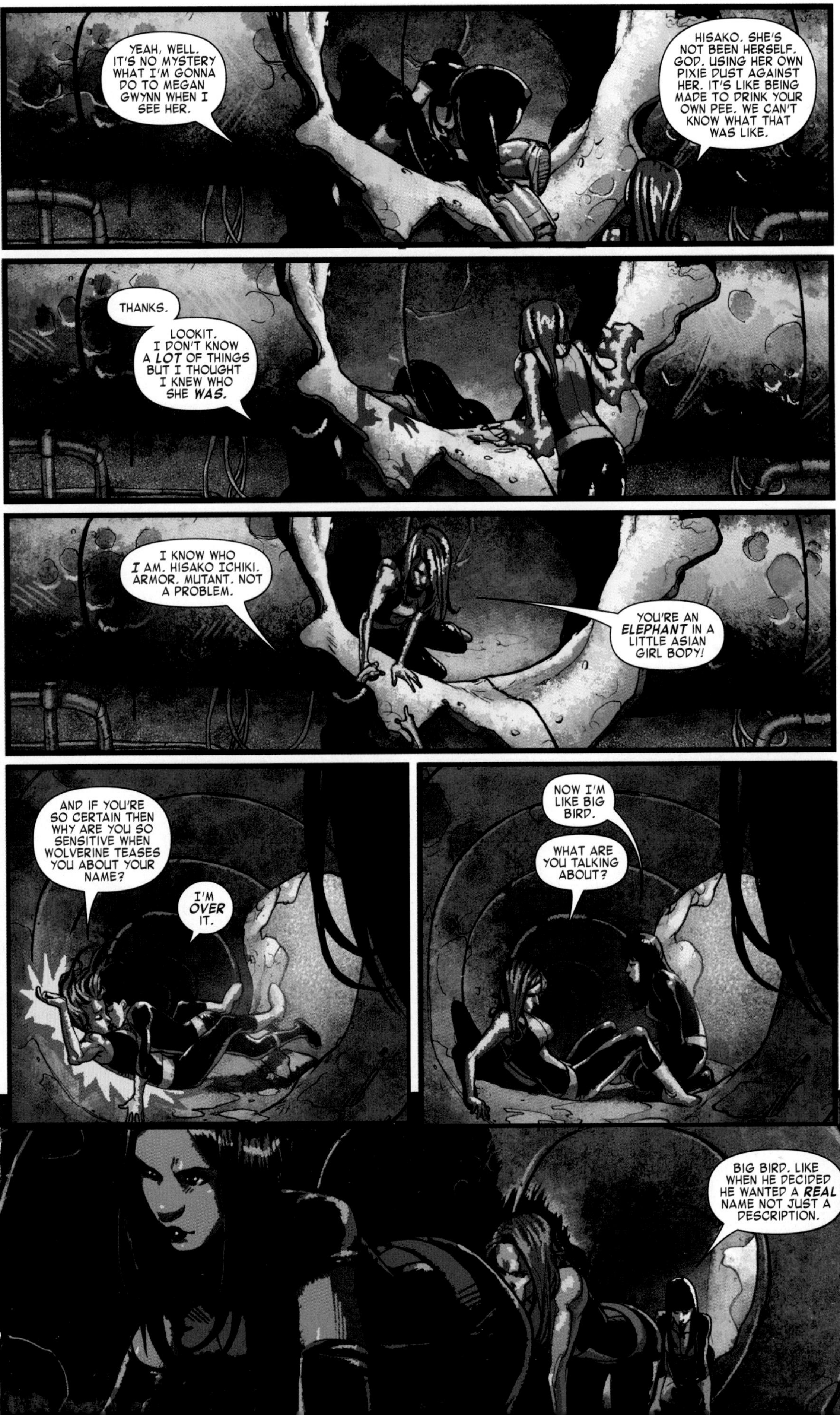
YEAH, WELL. IT'S NO MYSTERY WHAT I'M GONNA DO TO MEGAN GWYNN WHEN I SEE HER.
HISAKO. SHE'S NOT BEEN HERSELF. GOD. USING HER OWN PIXIE DUST AGAINST HER. IT'S LIKE BEING MADE TO DRINK YOUR OWN PEE. WE CAN'T KNOW WHAT THAT WAS LIKE.
THANKS.
LOOKIT. I DON'T KNOW A LOT OF THINGS BUT I THOUGHT I KNEW WHO SHE WAS.
I KNOW WHO I AM. HISAKO ICHIKI. ARMOR. MUTANT. NOT A PROBLEM.
YOU'RE AN ELEPHANT IN A LITTLE ASIAN GIRL BODY!
AND IF YOU'RE SO CERTAIN THEN WHY ARE YOU SO SENSITIVE WHEN WOLVERINE TEASES YOU ABOUT YOUR NAME?
I'M OVER IT.
NOW I'M LIKE BIG BIRD.
WHAT ARE YOU TALKING ABOUT?
BIG BIRD. LIKE WHEN HE DECIDED HE WANTED A REAL NAME NOT JUST A DESCRIPTION.

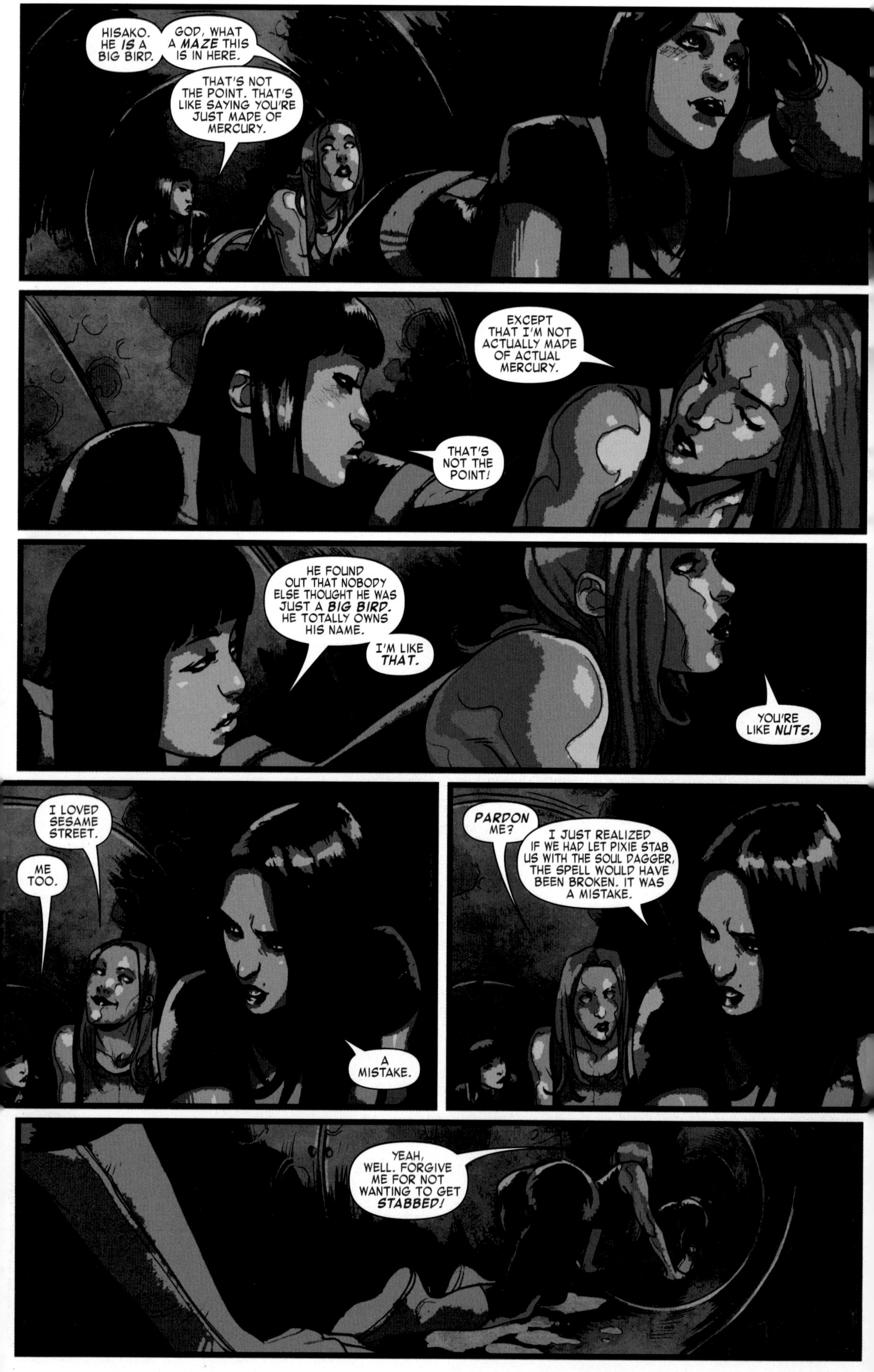
HISAKO. HE IS A BIG BIRD.
GOD, WHAT A MAZE THIS IS IN HERE.
THAT'S NOT THE POINT. THAT'S LIKE SAYING YOU'RE JUST MADE OF MERCURY.
EXCEPT THAT I'M NOT ACTUALLY MADE OF ACTUAL MERCURY.
THAT'S NOT THE POINT!
HE FOUND OUT THAT NOBODY ELSE THOUGHT HE WAS JUST A BIG BIRD. HE TOTALLY OWNS HIS NAME.
I'M LIKE THAT.
YOU'RE LIKE NUTS.
I LOVED SESAME STREET.
ME TOO.
A MISTAKE.
PARDON ME?
I JUST REALIZED IF WE HAD LET PIXIE STAB US WITH THE SOUL DAGGER, THE SPELL WOULD HAVE BEEN BROKEN. IT WAS A MISTAKE.
YEAH, WELL. FORGIVE ME FOR NOT WANTING TO GET STABBED!

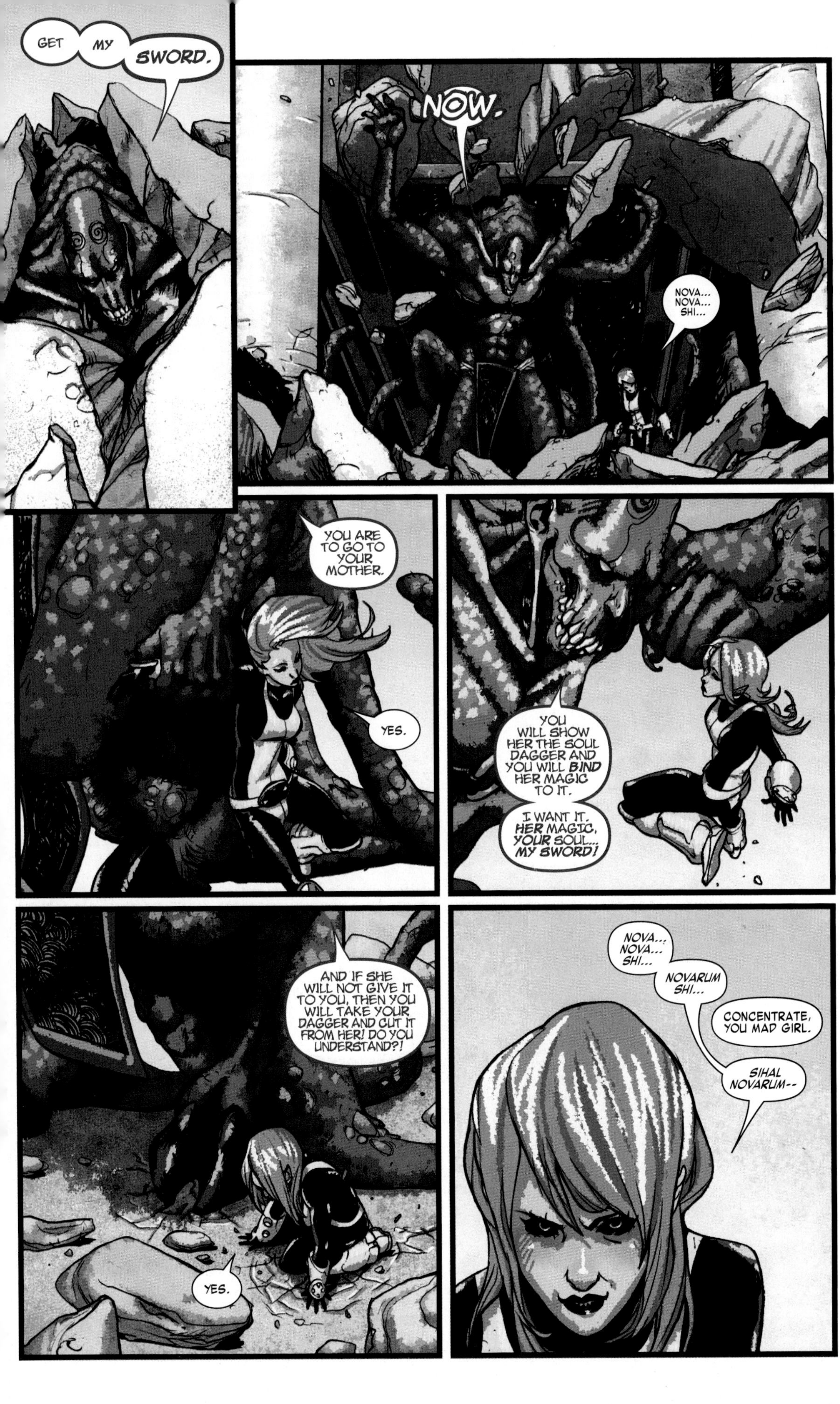
GET MY SWORD.
NOW.
NOVA... NOVA... SHI...
YOU ARE TO GO TO YOUR MOTHER.
YES.
YOU WILL SHOW HER THE SOUL DAGGER AND YOU WILL BIND HER MAGIC TO IT.
I WANT IT. HER MAGIC, YOUR SOUL... MY SWORD!
AND IF SHE WILL NOT GIVE IT TO YOU, THEN YOU WILL TAKE YOUR DAGGER AND CUT IT FROM HER! DO YOU UNDERSTAND?!
YES.
NOVA... NOVA... SHI...
NOVARUM SHI...
CONCENTRATE, YOU MAD GIRL.
SIHAL NOVARUM--

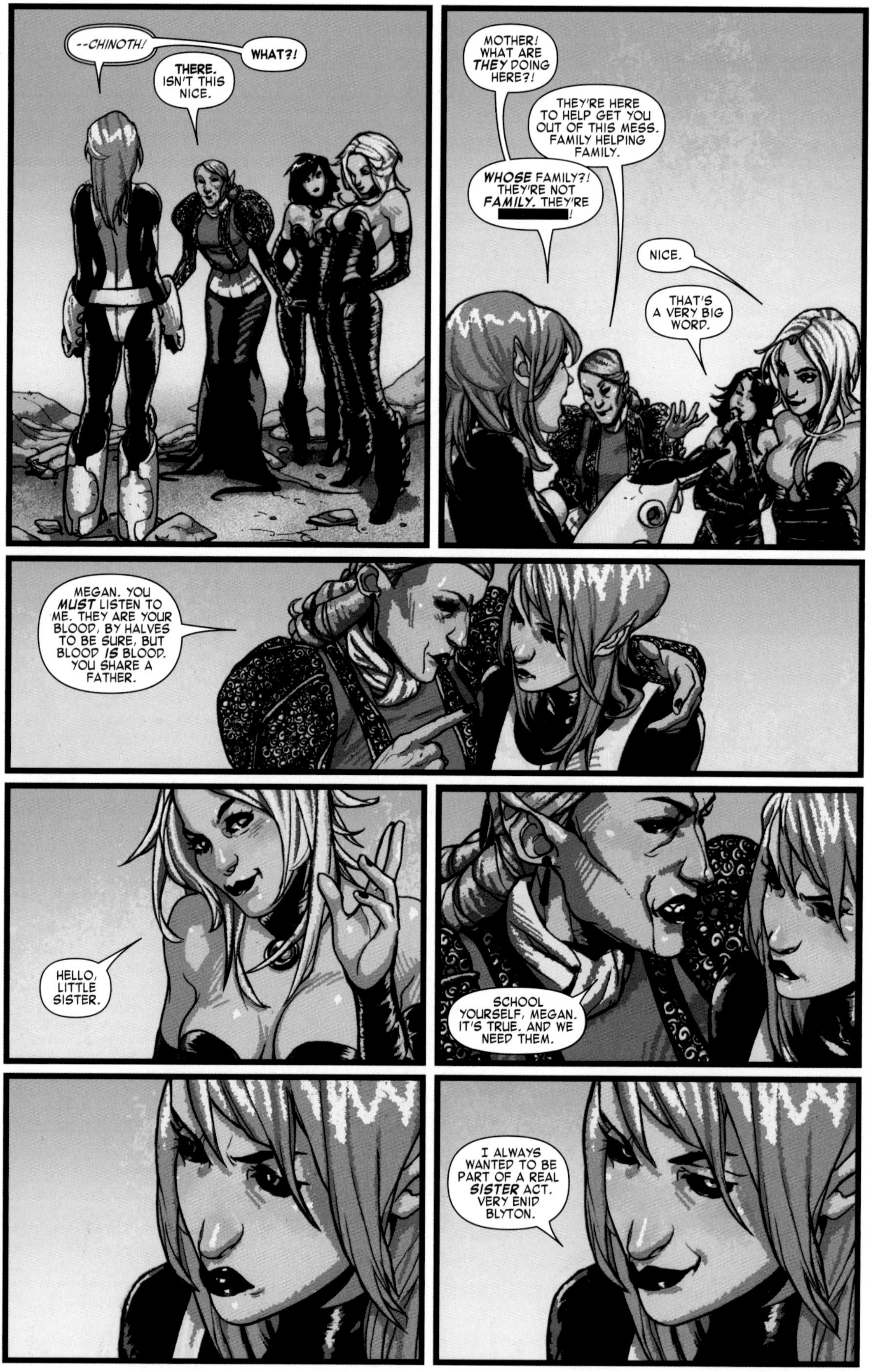
--CHINOTH!
WHAT?!
THERE. ISN'T THIS NICE.
MOTHER! WHAT ARE THEY DOING HERE?!
THEY'RE HERE TO HELP GET YOU OUT OF THIS MESS. FAMILY HELPING FAMILY.
WHOSE FAMILY?! THEY'RE NOT FAMILY. THEY'RE [redacted]!
NICE.
THAT'S A VERY BIG WORD.
MEGAN. YOU MUST LISTEN TO ME. THEY ARE YOUR BLOOD, BY HALVES TO BE SURE, BUT BLOOD IS BLOOD. YOU SHARE A FATHER.
HELLO, LITTLE SISTER.
SCHOOL YOURSELF, MEGAN. IT'S TRUE. AND WE NEED THEM.
I ALWAYS WANTED TO BE PART OF A REAL SISTER ACT. VERY ENID BLYTON.

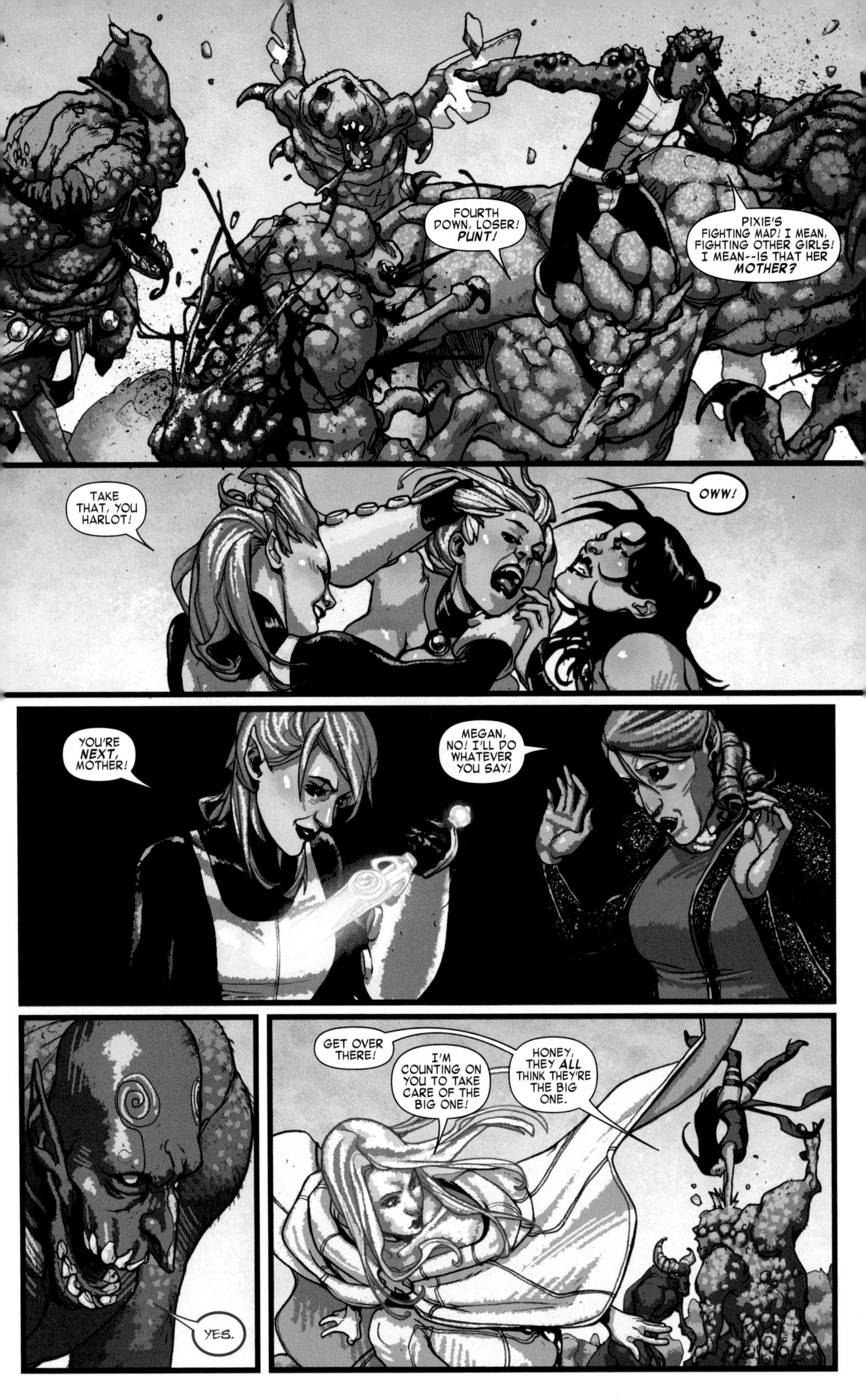
FOURTH DOWN, LOSER! PUNT!
PIXIE'S FIGHTING MAD! I MEAN, FIGHTING OTHER GIRLS! I MEAN--IS THAT HER MOTHER?
TAKE THAT, YOU HARLOT!
OWW!
YOU'RE NEXT, MOTHER!
MEGAN, NO! I'LL DO WHATEVER YOU SAY!
YES.
GET OVER THERE!
I'M COUNTING ON YOU TO TAKE CARE OF THE BIG ONE!
HONEY, THEY ALL THINK THEY'RE THE BIG ONE.

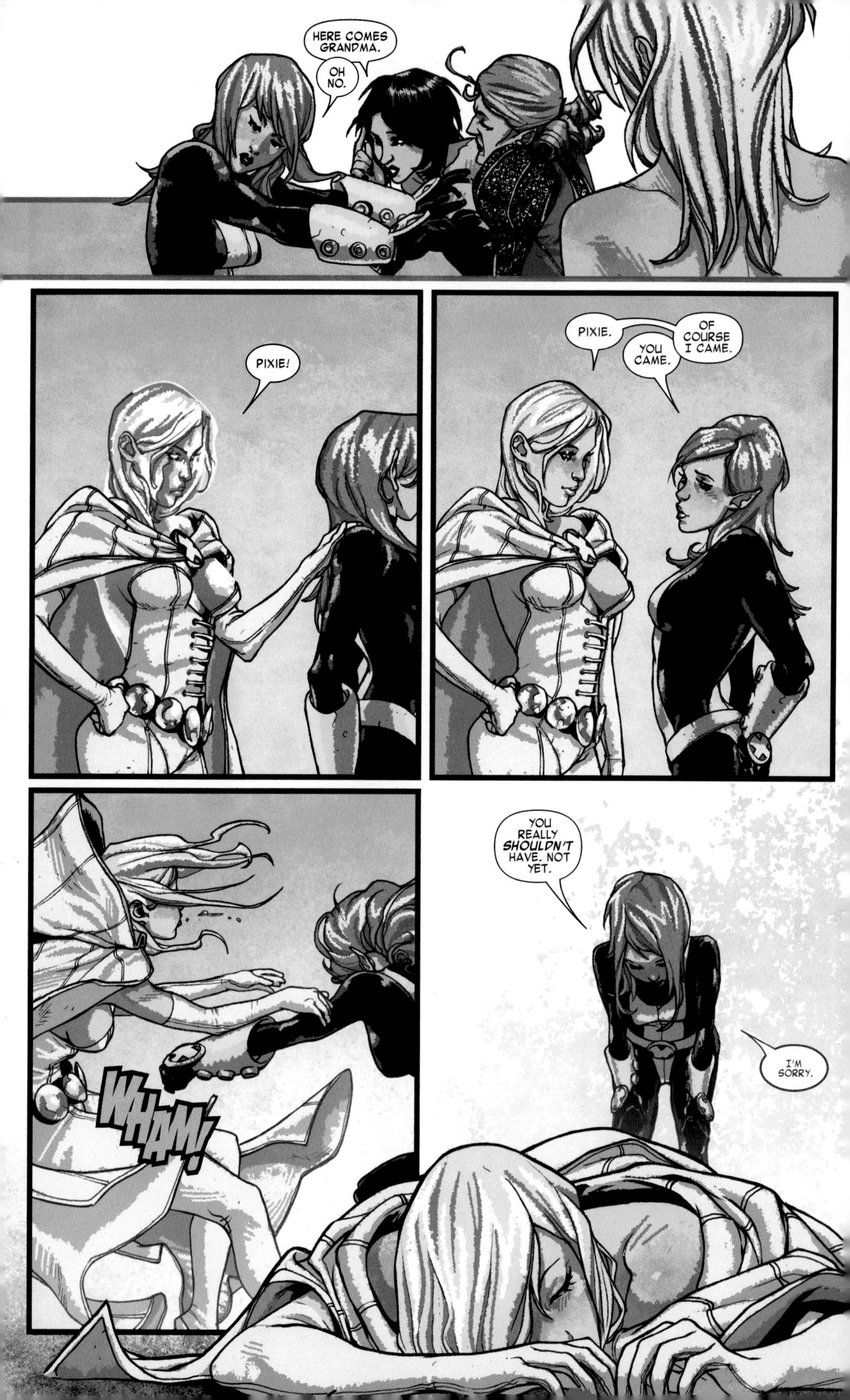
HERE COMES GRANDMA.
OH NO.
PIXIE!
PIXIE.
YOU CAME.
OF COURSE I CAME.
WHAM!
YOU REALLY SHOULDN'T HAVE. NOT YET.
I'M SORRY.

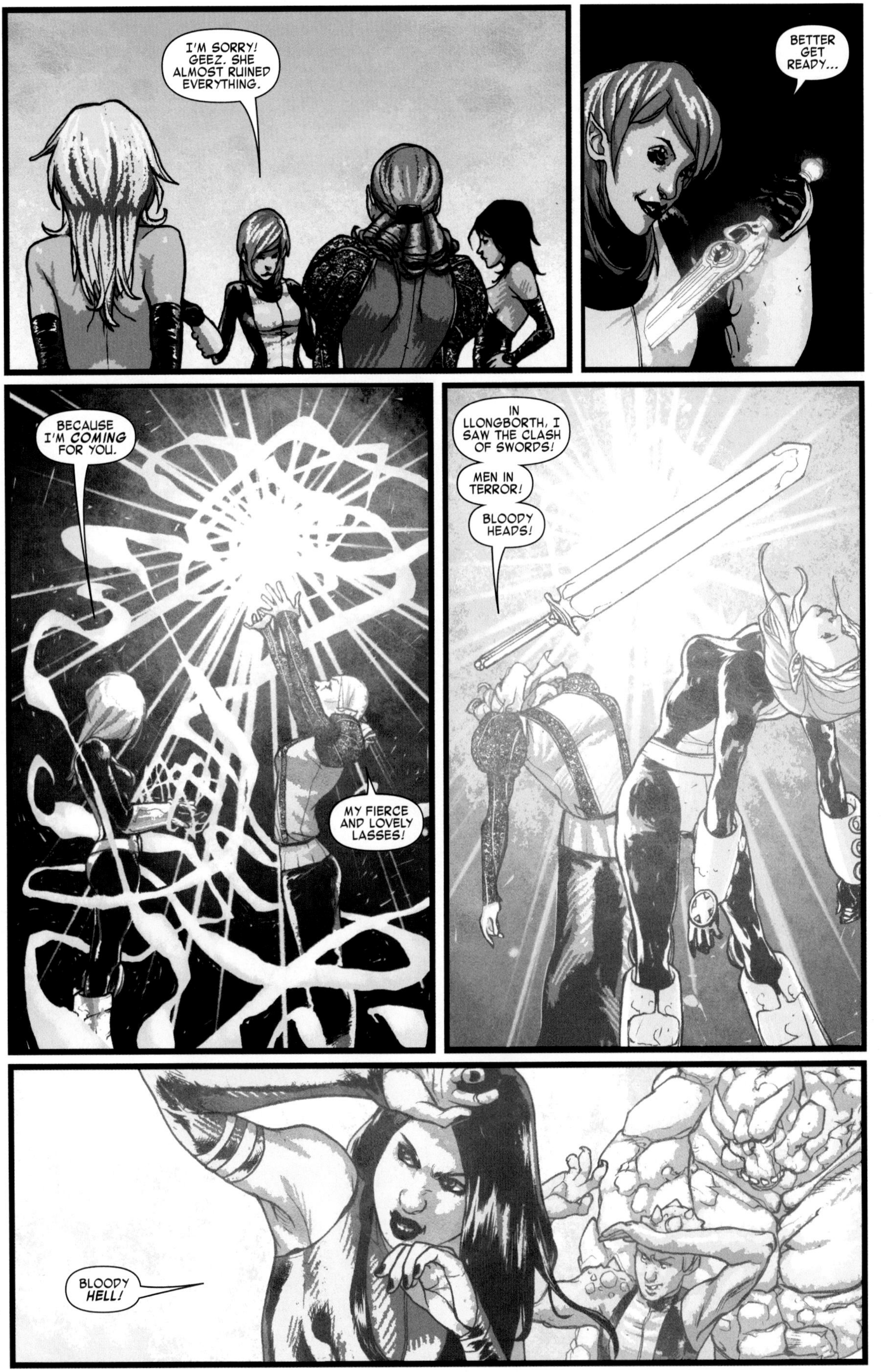
I'M SORRY! GEEZ. SHE ALMOST RUINED EVERYTHING.
BETTER GET READY...
BECAUSE I'M **COMING** FOR YOU.
MY FIERCE AND LOVELY LASSES!
IN LLONGBORTH, I SAW THE CLASH OF SWORDS!
MEN IN TERROR!
BLOODY HEADS!
BLOODY **HELL!**

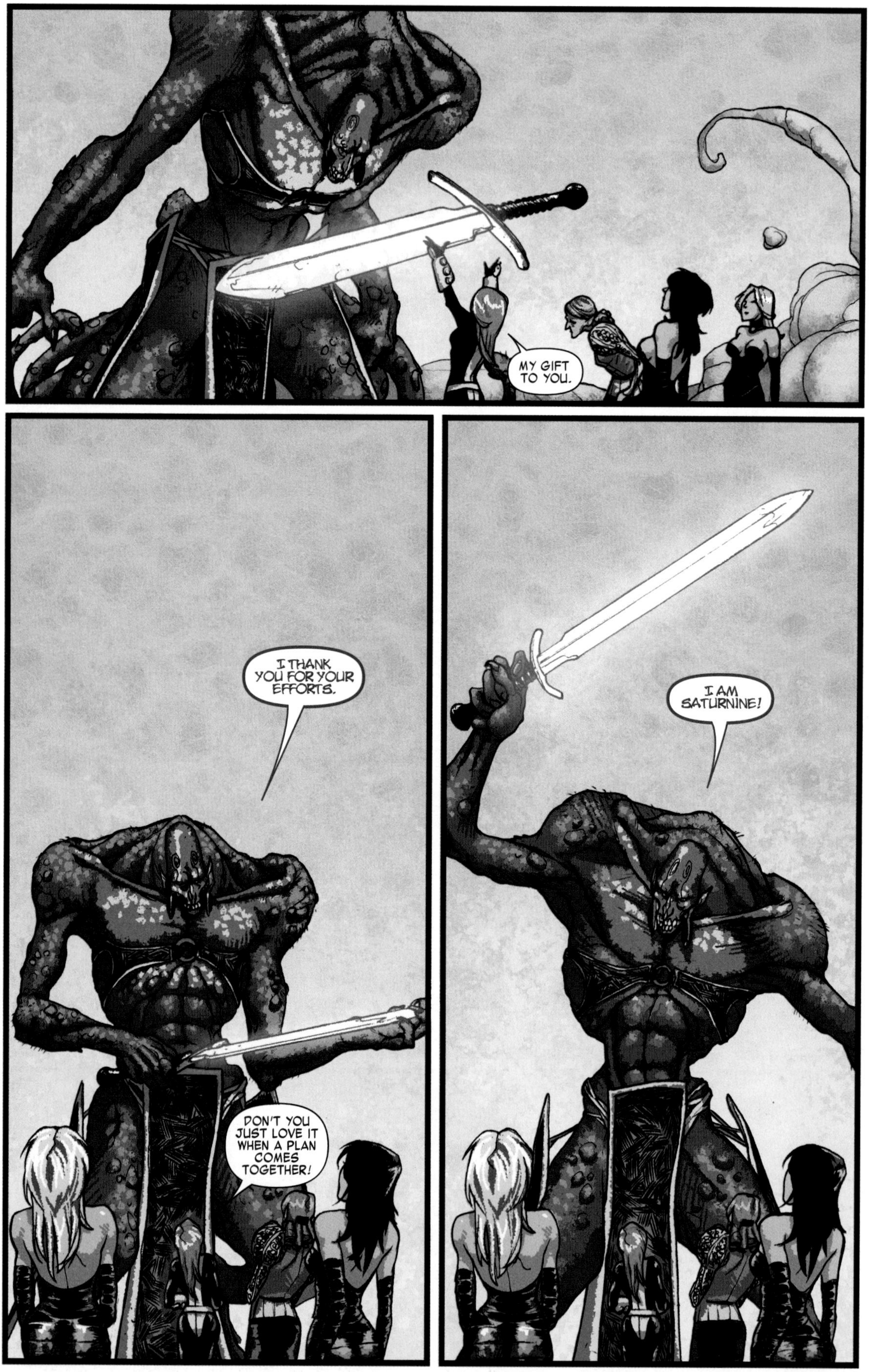
MY GIFT TO YOU.
I THANK YOU FOR YOUR EFFORTS.
DON'T YOU JUST LOVE IT WHEN A PLAN COMES TOGETHER!
I AM SATURNINE!

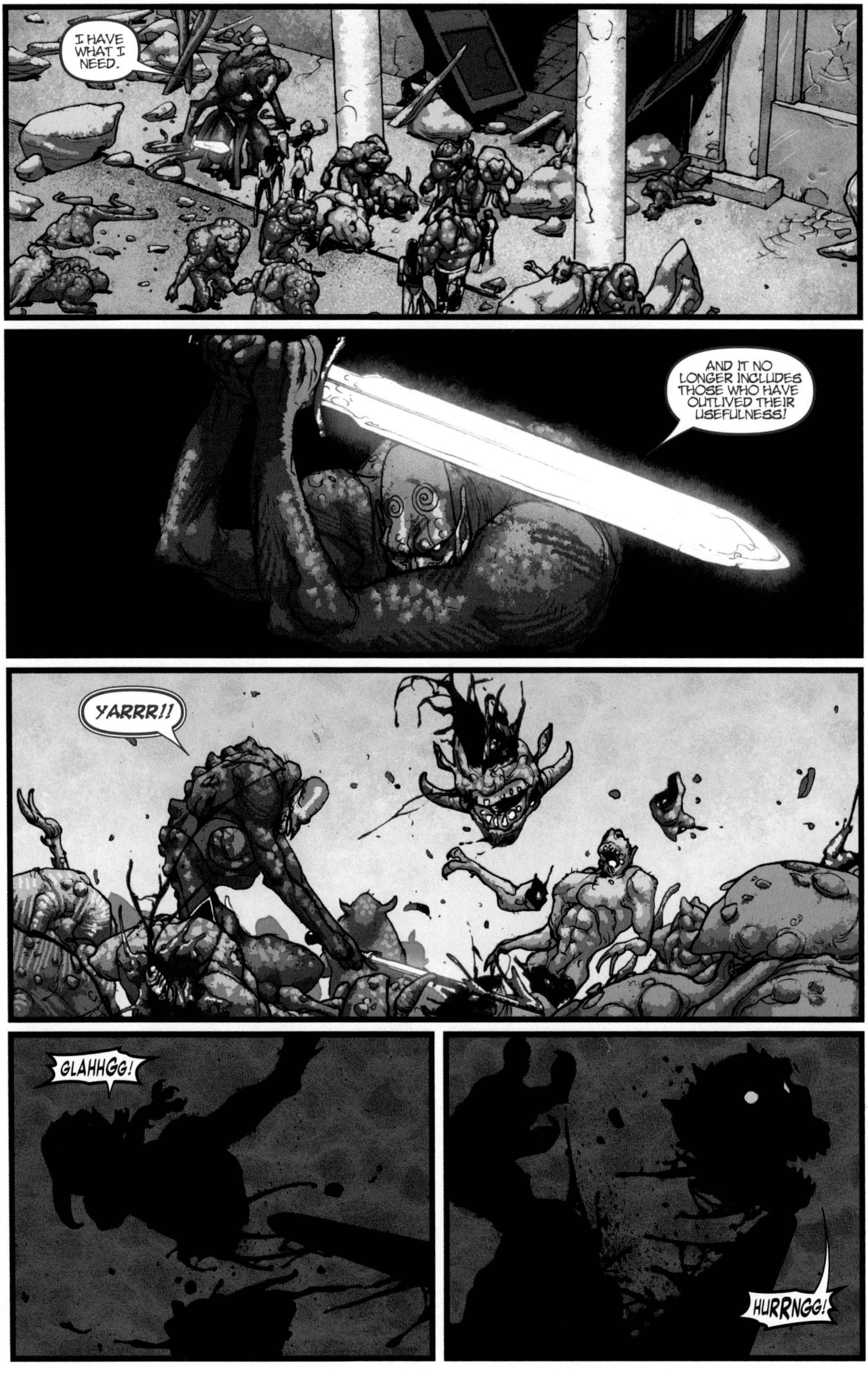
I HAVE WHAT I NEED.
AND IT NO LONGER INCLUDES THOSE WHO HAVE OUTLIVED THEIR USEFULNESS!
YARRR!!
GLAHHGG!
HURRNGG!

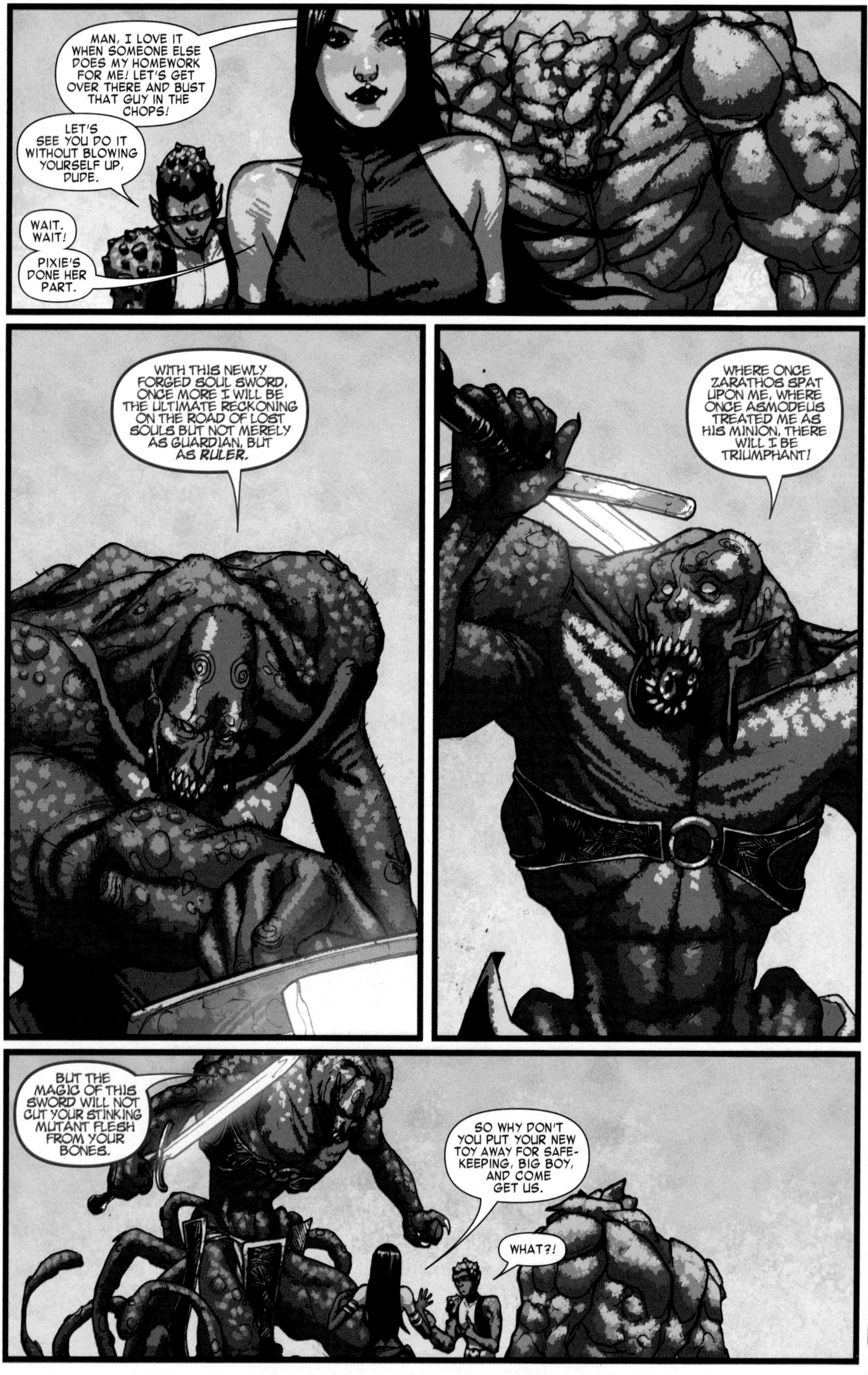
MAN, I LOVE IT WHEN SOMEONE ELSE DOES MY HOMEWORK FOR ME! LET'S GET OVER THERE AND BUST THAT GUY IN THE CHOPS!
LET'S SEE YOU DO IT WITHOUT BLOWING YOURSELF UP, DUDE.
WAIT. WAIT!
PIXIE'S DONE HER PART.
WITH THIS NEWLY FORGED SOUL SWORD, ONCE MORE I WILL BE THE ULTIMATE RECKONING ON THE ROAD OF LOST SOULS BUT NOT MERELY AS GUARDIAN, BUT AS RULER.
WHERE ONCE ZARATHOS SPAT UPON ME, WHERE ONCE ASMODEUS TREATED ME AS HIS MINION, THERE WILL I BE TRIUMPHANT!
BUT THE MAGIC OF THIS SWORD WILL NOT CUT YOUR STINKING MUTANT FLESH FROM YOUR BONES.
SO WHY DON'T YOU PUT YOUR NEW TOY AWAY FOR SAFE-KEEPING, BIG BOY, AND COME GET US.
WHAT?!

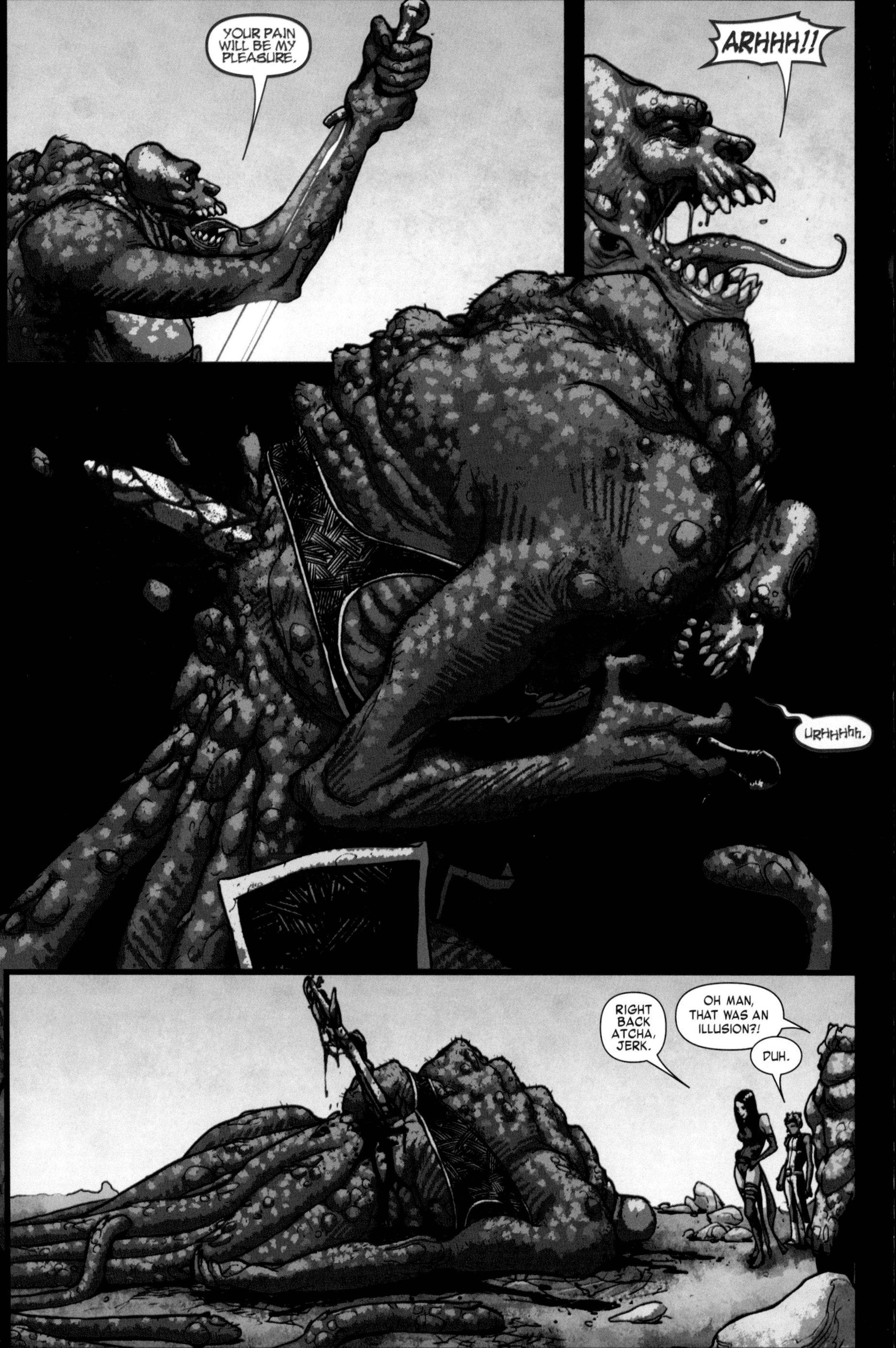
YOUR PAIN WILL BE MY PLEASURE.
ARHHH!!
URHHHhh.
RIGHT BACK ATCHA, JERK.
OH MAN, THAT WAS AN ILLUSION?!
DUH.

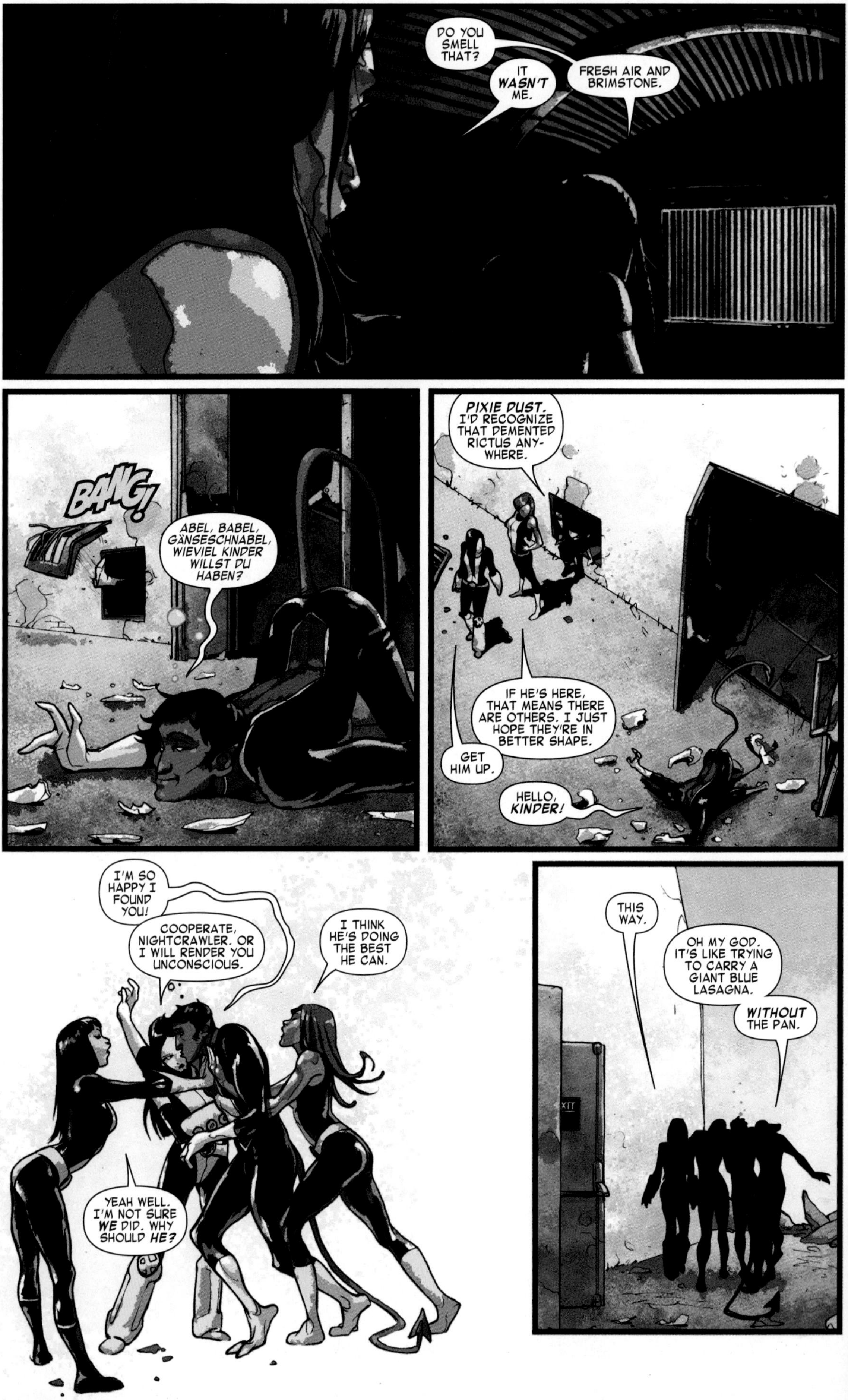

DO YOU SMELL THAT?
IT WASN'T ME.
FRESH AIR AND BRIMSTONE.
BANG!
ABEL, BABEL, GÄNSESCHNABEL, WIEVIEL KINDER WILLST DU HABEN?
PIXIE DUST. I'D RECOGNIZE THAT DEMENTED RICTUS ANY-WHERE.
IF HE'S HERE, THAT MEANS THERE ARE OTHERS. I JUST HOPE THEY'RE IN BETTER SHAPE.
GET HIM UP.
HELLO, KINDER!
I'M SO HAPPY I FOUND YOU!
COOPERATE, NIGHTCRAWLER. OR I WILL RENDER YOU UNCONSCIOUS.
I THINK HE'S DOING THE BEST HE CAN.
YEAH WELL. I'M NOT SURE WE DID. WHY SHOULD HE?
THIS WAY.
OH MY GOD. IT'S LIKE TRYING TO CARRY A GIANT BLUE LASAGNA.
WITHOUT THE PAN.
EXIT

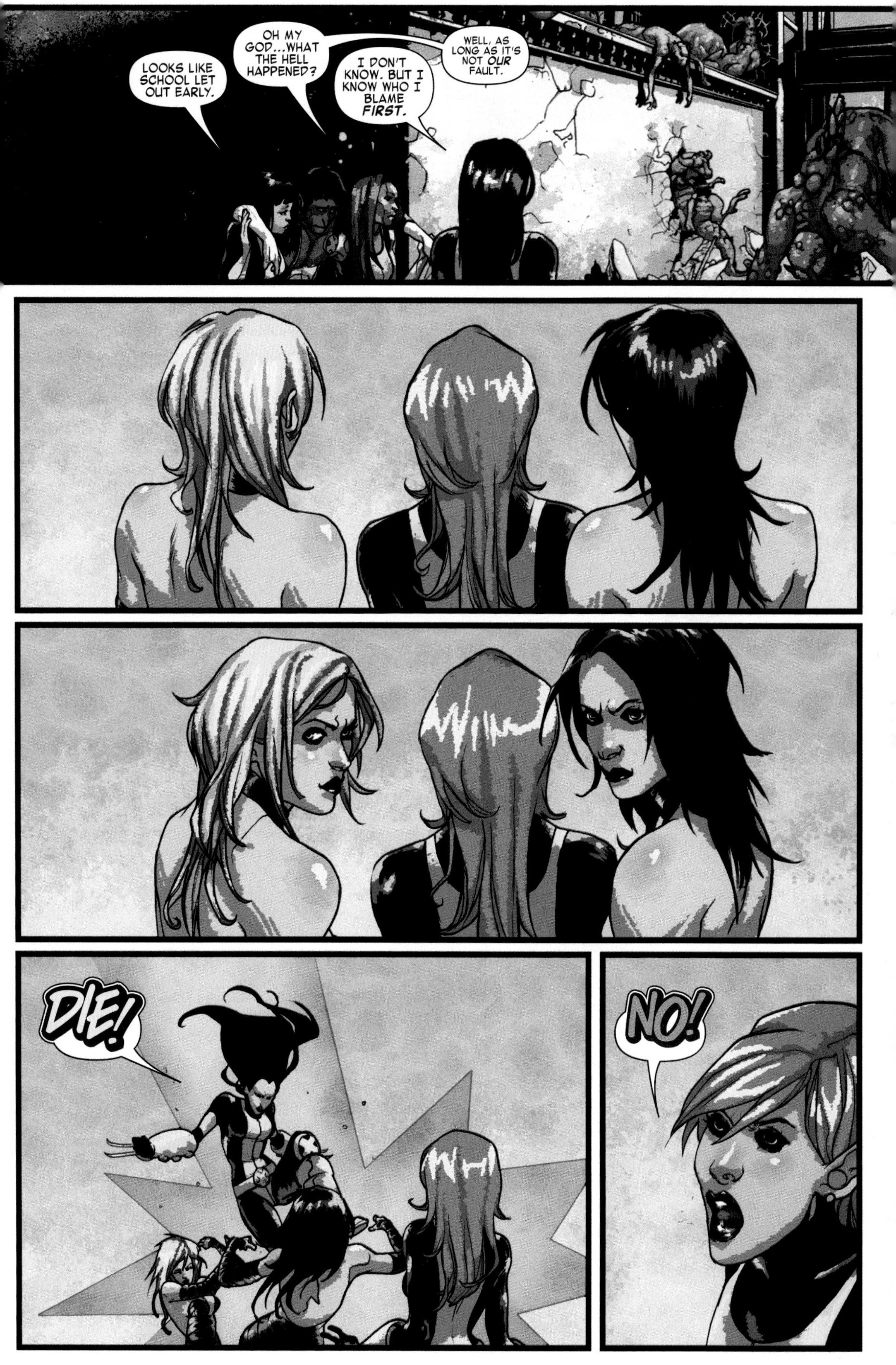
LOOKS LIKE SCHOOL LET OUT EARLY.
OH MY GOD...WHAT THE HELL HAPPENED?
I DON'T KNOW. BUT I KNOW WHO I BLAME FIRST.
WELL, AS LONG AS IT'S NOT OUR FAULT.
DIE!
NO!

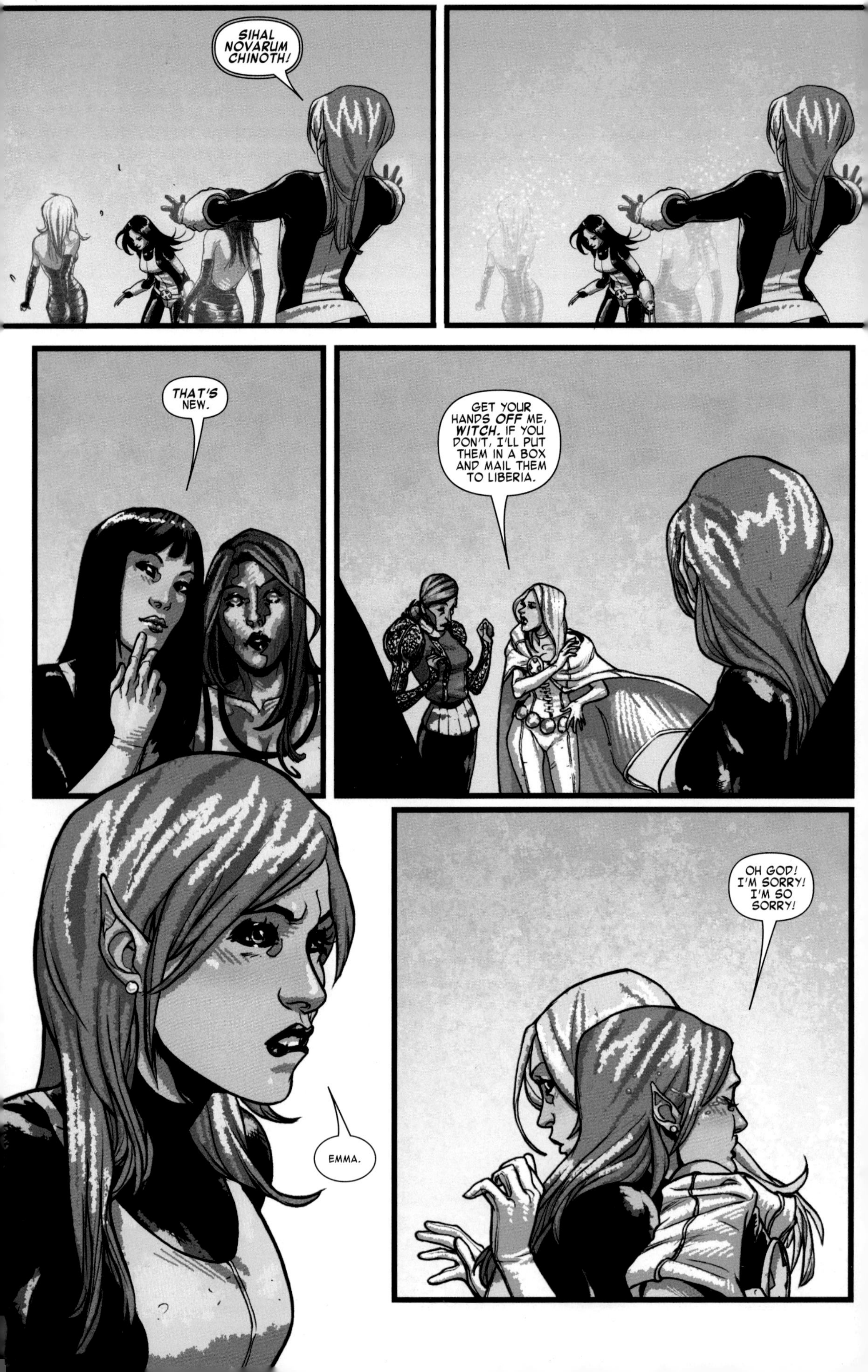
SIHAL NOVARUM CHINOTH!
THAT'S NEW.
GET YOUR HANDS OFF ME, WITCH. IF YOU DON'T, I'LL PUT THEM IN A BOX AND MAIL THEM TO LIBERIA.
EMMA.
OH GOD! I'M SORRY! I'M SO SORRY!

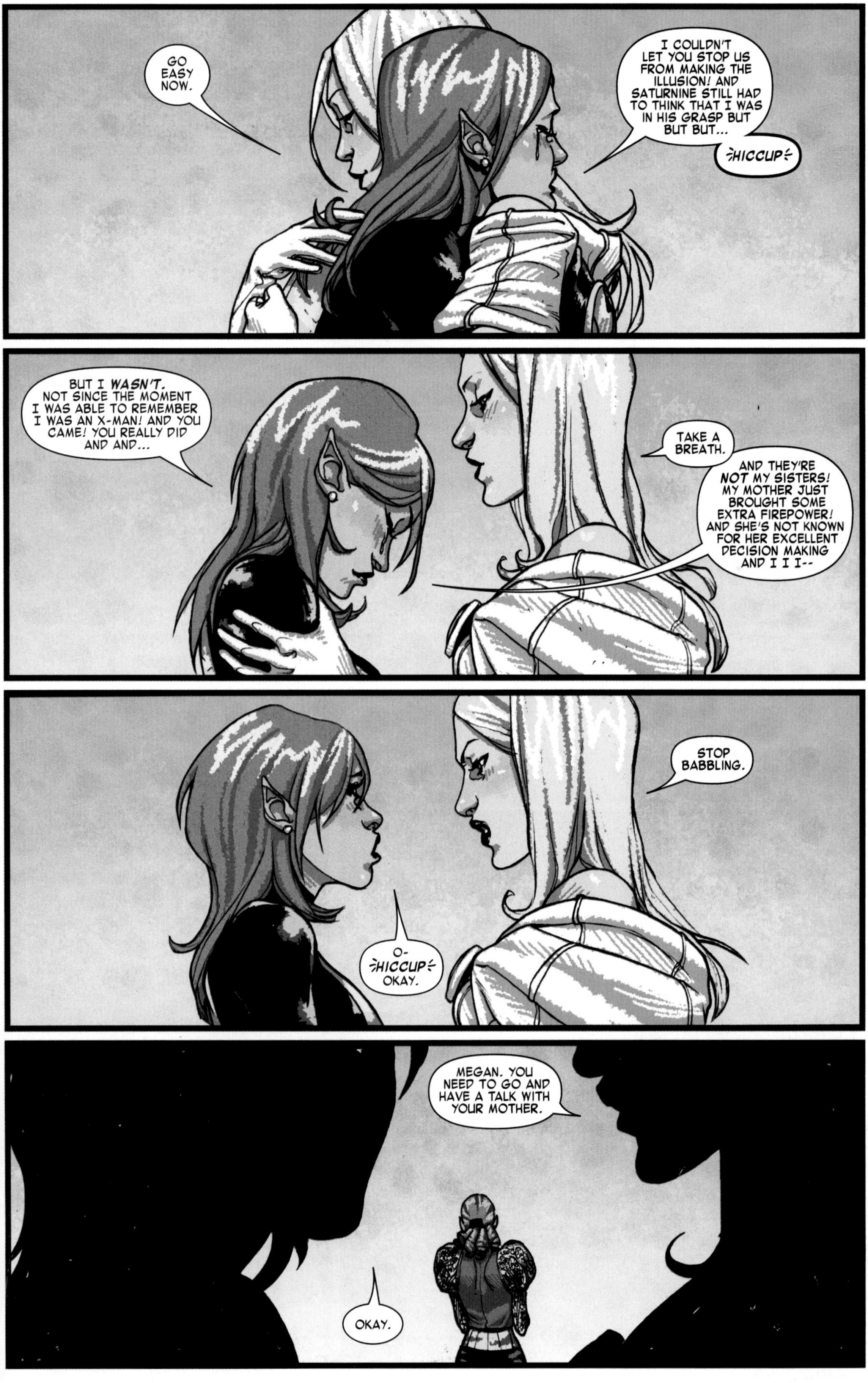
GO EASY NOW.
I COULDN'T LET YOU STOP US FROM MAKING THE ILLUSION! AND SATURNINE STILL HAD TO THINK THAT I WAS IN HIS GRASP BUT BUT BUT...
HICCUP
BUT I WASN'T. NOT SINCE THE MOMENT I WAS ABLE TO REMEMBER I WAS AN X-MAN! AND YOU CAME! YOU REALLY DID AND AND...
TAKE A BREATH.
AND THEY'RE NOT MY SISTERS! MY MOTHER JUST BROUGHT SOME EXTRA FIREPOWER! AND SHE'S NOT KNOWN FOR HER EXCELLENT DECISION MAKING AND I I I--
STOP BABBLING.
O- HICCUP OKAY.
MEGAN. YOU NEED TO GO AND HAVE A TALK WITH YOUR MOTHER.
OKAY.

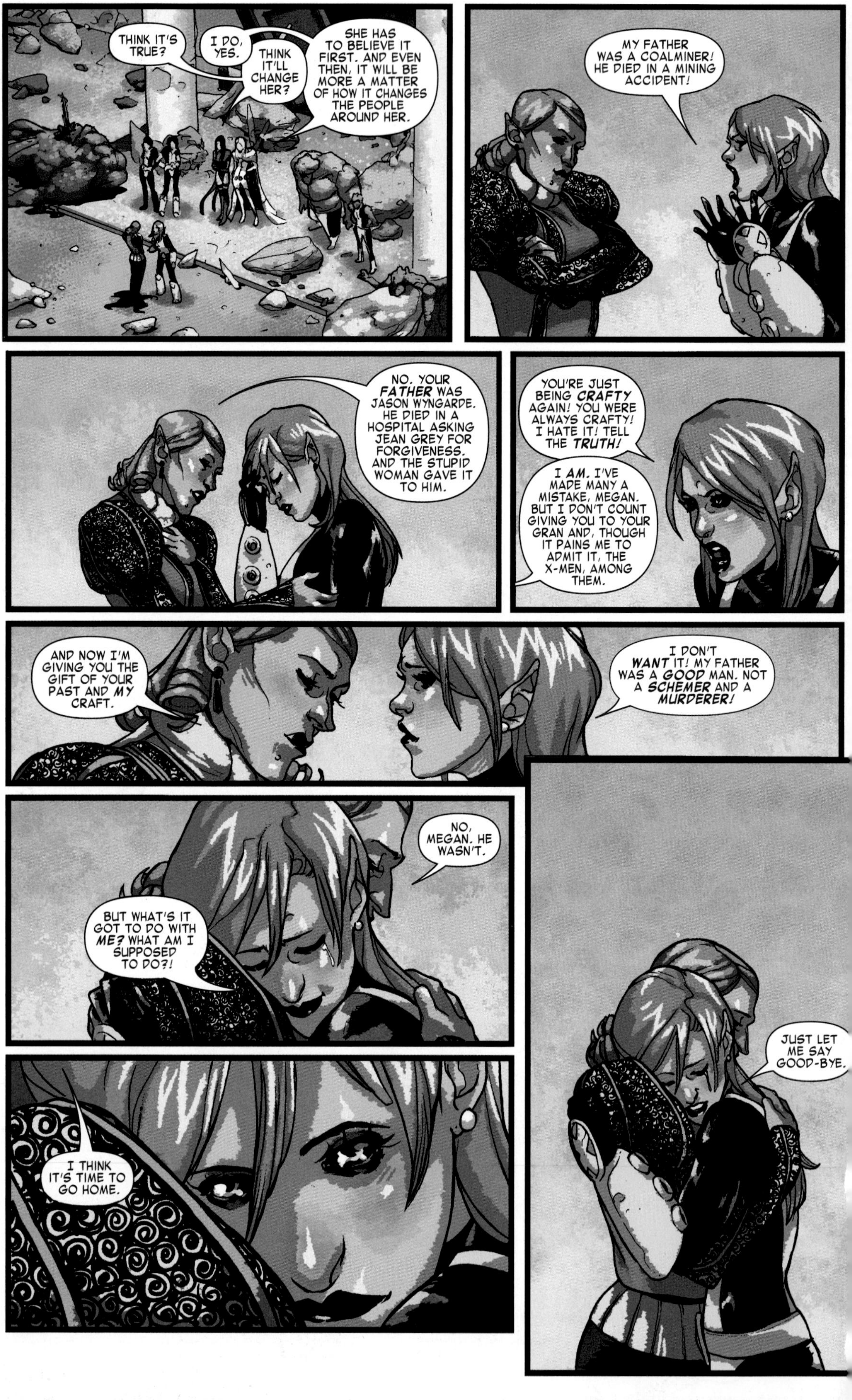
THINK IT'S TRUE?
I DO, YES.
THINK IT'LL CHANGE HER?
SHE HAS TO BELIEVE IT FIRST. AND EVEN THEN, IT WILL BE MORE A MATTER OF HOW IT CHANGES THE PEOPLE AROUND HER.
MY FATHER WAS A COALMINER! HE DIED IN A MINING ACCIDENT!
NO. YOUR FATHER WAS JASON WYNGARDE. HE DIED IN A HOSPITAL ASKING JEAN GREY FOR FORGIVENESS. AND THE STUPID WOMAN GAVE IT TO HIM.
YOU'RE JUST BEING CRAFTY AGAIN! YOU WERE ALWAYS CRAFTY! I HATE IT! TELL THE TRUTH!
I AM. I'VE MADE MANY A MISTAKE, MEGAN. BUT I DON'T COUNT GIVING YOU TO YOUR GRAN AND, THOUGH IT PAINS ME TO ADMIT IT, THE X-MEN, AMONG THEM.
AND NOW I'M GIVING YOU THE GIFT OF YOUR PAST AND MY CRAFT.
I DON'T WANT IT! MY FATHER WAS A GOOD MAN. NOT A SCHEMER AND A MURDERER!
NO, MEGAN. HE WASN'T.
BUT WHAT'S IT GOT TO DO WITH ME? WHAT AM I SUPPOSED TO DO?!
I THINK IT'S TIME TO GO HOME.
JUST LET ME SAY GOOD-BYE.

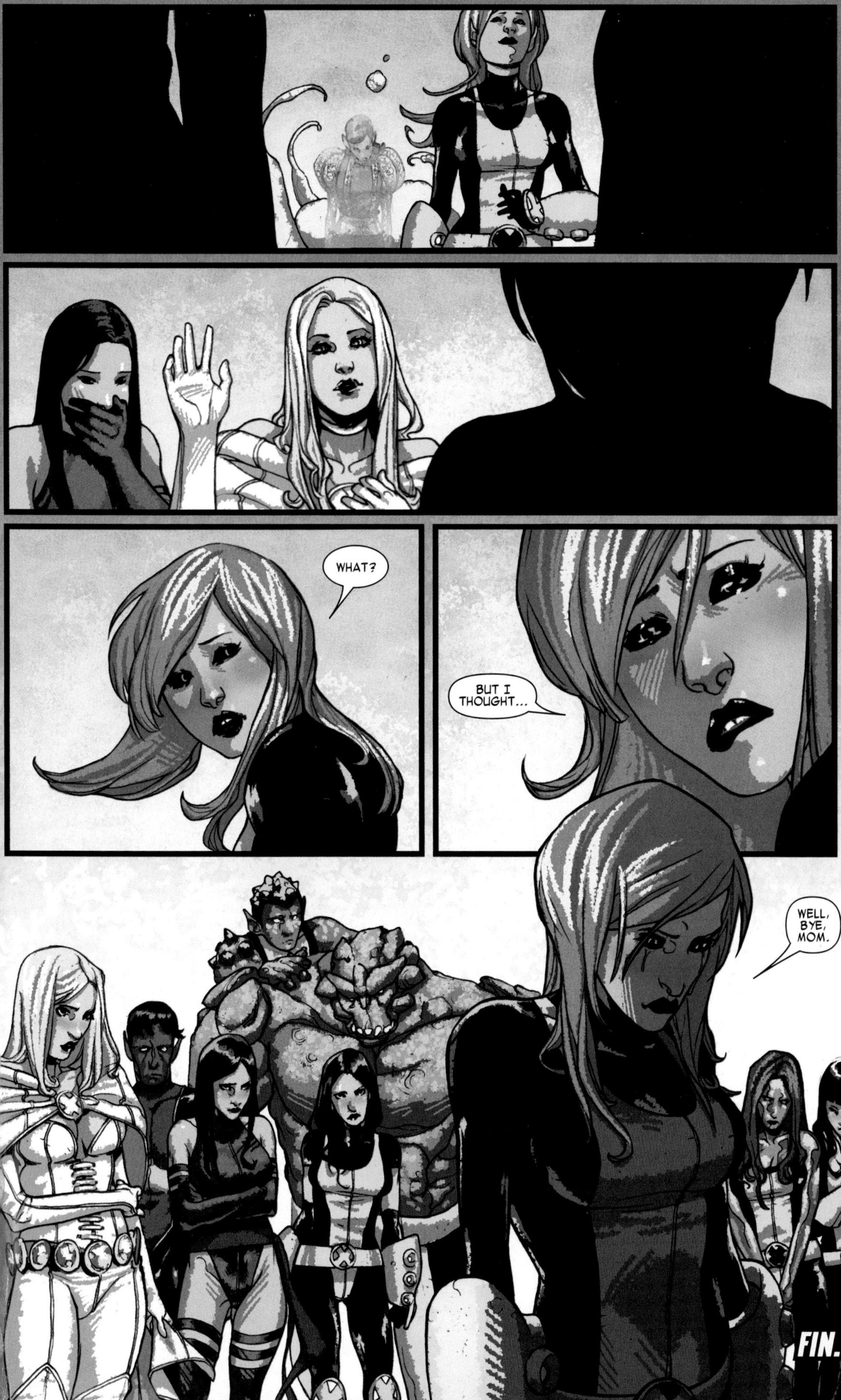
WHAT?
BUT I THOUGHT...
WELL, BYE, MOM.
FIN.

# COVER SKETCHES
## BY STUART IMMONEN

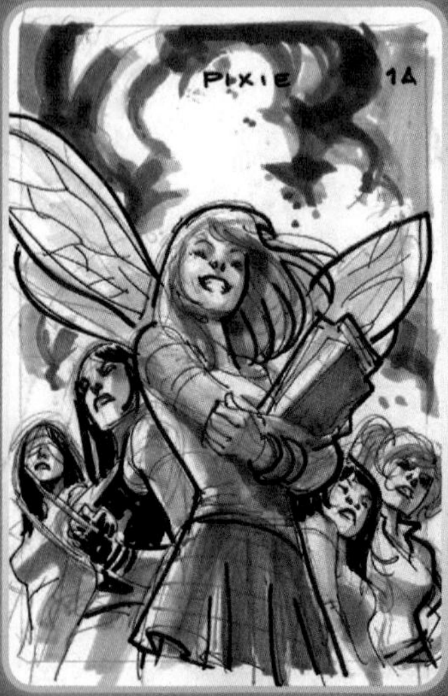
PIXIE 1A
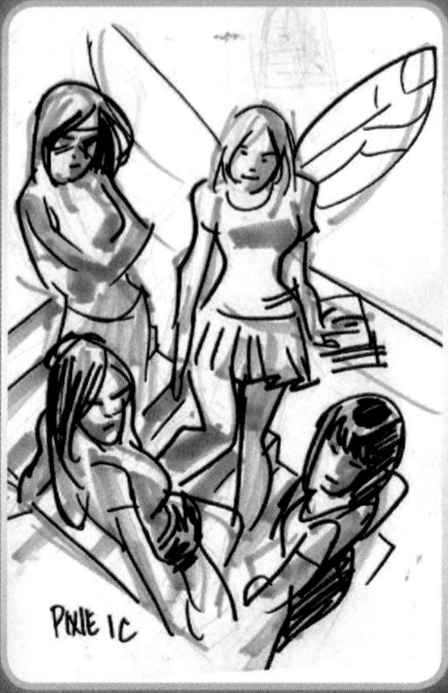
PIXIE 1C
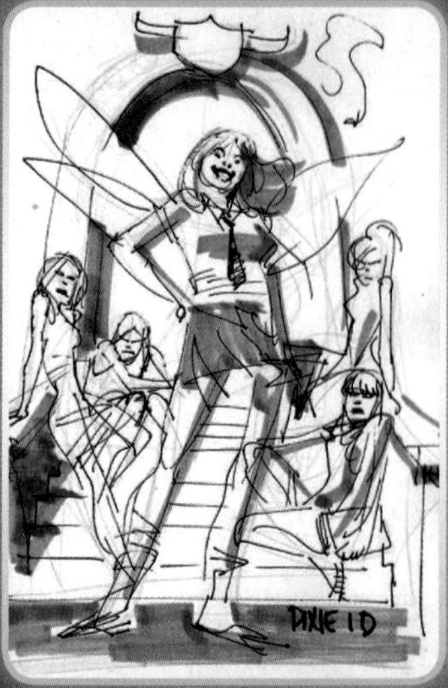
PIXIE 1D
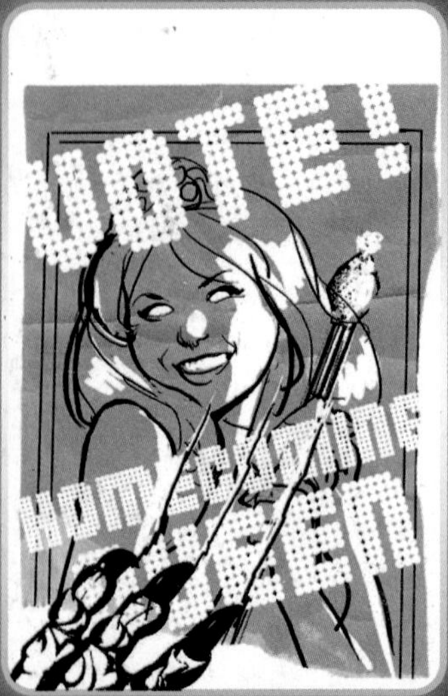
VOTE!
HOMECOMING
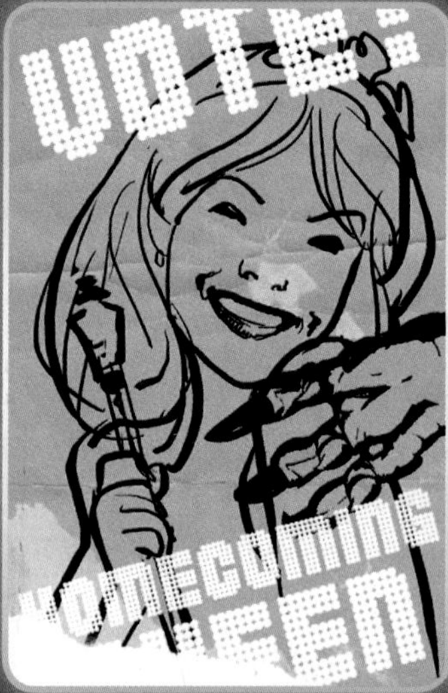
VOTE!
HOMECOMING
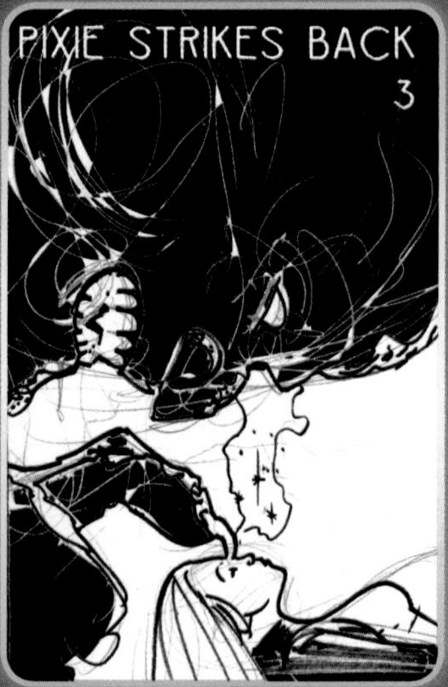
PIXIE STRIKES BACK
3
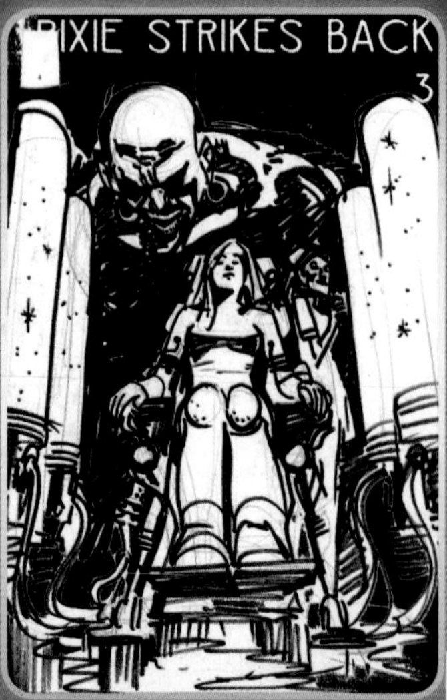
PIXIE STRIKES BACK
3
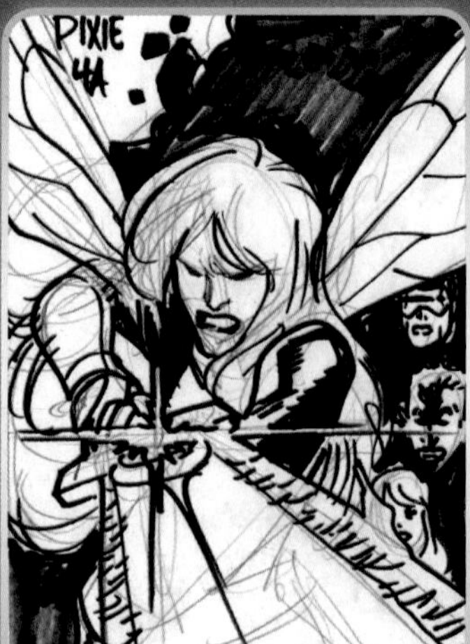
PIXIE
4A
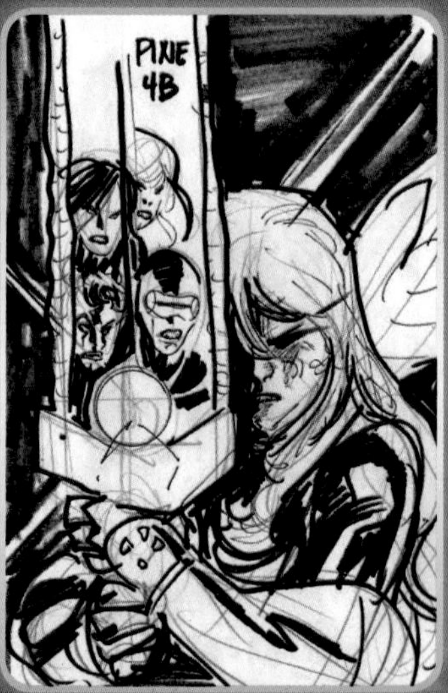
PIXIE
4B